THE PARABLES OF JESUS

THE
PARABLES OF JESUS

GEORGE A. BUTTRICK

BAKER BOOK HOUSE
Grand Rapids, Michigan

Seventh printing, June 1985

Copyright 1928 by Harper & Brothers

Reprinted 1973 by Baker Book House
under arrangement with
Harper & Row, Publishers, Inc.

ISBN: 0-8010-0597-3

Printed in the United States of America

To my

FATHER AND MOTHER,
WHO BY WORD AND LIFE
TAUGHT THEIR CHILDREN TO CHERISH
THE PARABLES OF JESUS,
THIS BOOK
IS DEDICATED
IN
GRATITUDE AND LOVE

PREFACE

This little book began in a series of lectures given during the summer of 1926 on "The Parables of the Passion Week." Publishers suggested that they be printed. It seemed, however, that the Parables assigned by the Synoptists to the last week of the earthly ministry of Jesus, though they show a certain urgency and a valedictory mood, are not sufficiently distinct from the other Parables to justify their separate study. This fact and the inadequacy of the lectures forbade their publication in book form. The proposal was then made of this book of wider scope.

The task at first appeared overwhelming. It has assumed no smaller magnitude now that the book is written. The Parables are inexhaustible in meaning; they would make even the best discussion appear weak. The writing did reveal, however, that the field of this topic is surprisingly clear. Recent books on the Parables are not numerous. It may be said, without disparagement to modern authors, that for a satisfactory general introduction to this subject it is necessary to return to Archbishop Trench ("Notes on the Parables," 1841). Dr. A. B. Bruce's "The Parabolic Teaching of Christ," though first published nearly fifty years ago, still holds its place as a standard work. But in the course of these fifty years Biblical research has crystallized in certain accepted attitudes and certain verified results, which materially affect the interpretation of the Parables. It has become clear, for instance, that the allegorical method of exposition, with its search for finespun analogies, must definitely be abandoned in favor of a more "human" and vital account. The Parables of Jesus stand alone; they defy comparison; but they are far closer in mood and manner to the Fables of Æsop, the Canterbury Tales of Chaucer, or the stories of Abraham Lincoln than to the careful allegories of the Rabbis or the elaborations of the Schoolmen.

The main purpose of this book is to suggest an unfettered

interpretation of these incomparable stories, to trace them back to Jesus' daily life in Galilee; and so to rediscover in them the tang of the human and the glow of the Divine. A new Introduction to the Parables seemed timely, and has been attempted. In the interpretation of the separate stories use has been made, in untechnical language, of the approved findings of reverent and competent critics of the Scriptures; but details of exegesis have been relegated to the Notes where they will not unduly molest the reader.

Scripture quotations are from the American Standard Version except as otherwise specified. The Bible uses "lower case" for pronouns which denote Jesus. The text of this book, however, employs the customary "upper case" in such instances; not in any desire to beg a theological question (for these chapters are not theological), but because the capital letter is the only tribute type can pay Him.

No brief is held for the particular list of Parables here chosen. Some have been included which may seem to be metaphors or similes rather than parables; and other "germ-parables" have been omitted which may seem to have good claim to inclusion. Many of the sayings of Jesus live on the border line of parable, and any list will appear arbitrary. Examination will reveal, I think, that the Parables here selected represent with approximate completeness Christ's parabolic teaching.

It is a pleasant duty to offer hearty thanks to many who have given help and encouragement. The indebtedness of this book to several recent or remoter books on the Parables is abundantly evidenced in the succeeding pages. Grateful confession is made that "others have labored," and that I have "entered into their labor." Acknowledgement is also made of the courtesy which has permitted the use of sundry quotations. Authors and publishers who have granted this favor have been instanced in the Notes. Care has been taken to indicate each indebtedness. Any omissions must be charged to inadvertence or to the failure which besets even the most painstaking investigation. If there are such lapses, they are hereby regretted and apology offered.

There are others who have given invaluable aid. Dr. Finis

King Farr, a true friend, was good enough to discuss with me the plan of the book and the interpretation of several "difficult" parables; and he offered many illuminating suggestions. The Rev. William Raymond Jelliffe and Dr. George Stewart, my comrades in daily work, have left me deeply in debt; the former for a careful reading of several chapters and for helpful corrections and comments, and the latter for generous assistance in the preparation of the manuscript. Thanks are due also to Miss Elizabeth M. Eliot who has been assiduous in typing the copy and in items of research. Finally, my wife has been a constant helpmeet and "heart of grace." Without her furtherance the book would scarcely have been possible. In particular, the Scriptural and General Indexes are her work.

The substance of the last six chapters has already appeared in *The Record of Christian Work*. They are here reproduced (though, in some instances, in radically different form) by the kind permission of the editor.

G. A. B.

New York City,
March, 1928.

CONTENTS

Chapter   *Page*
PREFACE vii

AN INTRODUCTION TO THE PARABLES OF JESUS . . xiii

I. *Parables of the Early Ministry*

THE GOOD NEWS OF THE KINGDOM OF GOD

I THE CONFLICT OF NEW AND OLD 2
    (a) The Parable of THE CHILDREN OF THE BRIDECHAMBER
    (b) The Parable of THE NEW PATCH AND THE OLD GARMENT
    (c) The Parable of NEW WINE AND OLD WINESKINS
    (d) The Parable of TREASURES NEW AND OLD

II SIMILITUDES OF THE KINGDOM (I) 14
    (a) The Parable of SPONTANEOUS GROWTH
    (b) The Parable of THE MUSTARD SEED
    (c) The Parable of THE LEAVEN

III SIMILITUDES OF THE KINGDOM (II) 26
    (a) The Parable of THE HIDDEN TREASURE
    (b) The Parable of THE PEARL OF GREAT PRICE
    (c) The Parable of THE DRAGNET

IV THE RESPONSIBILITY OF HEARING 40
    The Parable of THE SOILS

V EARNESTNESS TO TRANSLATE HEARING INTO DOING . 50
    (a) The Parable of THE CHILDREN AT PLAY
    (b) The Parable of THE WISE AND FOOLISH BUILDERS

VI THE KINGDOM AND THE PERPLEXING PRESENCE OF EVIL 60
    The Parable of THE TARES

II. *Parables of the Later Ministry*

THE CHILDREN OF THE KINGDOM OF GOD

A. *THE CONDITIONS OF DISCIPLESHIP*

VII THE CONDITIONS OF DISCIPLESHIP 72
    (a) The Parable of THE EMPTY HOUSE
    (b) The Parable of THE UNCOMPLETED TOWER
    (c) The Parable of THE RASH KING'S WARFARE

B. *THE MARKS OF DISCIPLESHIP*

VIII HUMILITY 82
    (a) The Parable of THE CHIEF SEATS
    (b) The Parable of THE PHARISEE AND THE PUBLICAN

IX FORGIVEN AND FORGIVING 92
    (a) The Parable of THE TWO DEBTORS
    (b) The Parable of THE UNMERCIFUL SERVANT

Chapter   *Page*

   X   PRIVILEGE AND DUTY 104
      (a) The Parable of THE BARREN FIGTREE
      (b) The Parable of THE BONDSERVANT

  XI   RESOURCEFULNESS AND FORESIGHT 116
      The Parable of THE UNJUST STEWARD

 XII   LIFE—AND "MUCH GOODS" 126
      The Parable of THE RICH FOOL

XIII   THE SPRINGS OF SYMPATHY 136
      The Parable of THE RICH MAN AND THE BEGGAR

XIV   TRUE NEIGHBORLINESS 148
      The Parable of THE GOOD SAMARITAN

C. *THE LOVE OF GOD*

XV   GOD'S APPRAISALS AND REWARDS 158
      The Parable of THE LABORERS AND THE HOURS

XVI   THE GOD WHO ANSWERS PRAYER 166
      (a) The Parable of THE FRIEND AT MIDNIGHT
      (b) The Parable of THE IMPORTUNATE WIDOW

XVII   THE GOD OF THE LOST (I) 176
      (a) The Parable of THE LOST SHEEP
      (b) The Parable of THE LOST COIN

XVIII   THE GOD OF THE LOST (II) 188
      (a) The Parable of THE PRODIGAL SON
      (b) The Parable of THE ELDER BROTHER

III. *Parables of the Passion Week*

THE KINGDOM OF GOD AS A JUDGMENT

XIX   THE TEST OF DEEDS 204
      The Parable of THE TWO SONS

XX   THE REJECTED OVERTURES OF GOD 212
      (a) The Parable of THE CRUEL VINE-DRESSERS
      (b) The Parable of THE REJECTED CORNER-STONE

XXI   MAKING LIGHT OF THE KINGDOM 222
      (a) The Parable of THE GREAT FEAST
      (b) The Parable of THE WEDDING BANQUET OF THE KING'S SON
      (c) The Parable of THE WEDDING ROBE

XXII   PREPAREDNESS AND EMERGENCY 232
      The Parable of THE WISE AND FOOLISH BRIDESMAIDS

XXIII   OPPORTUNITY, FIDELITY, AND REWARD 240
      (a) The Parable of THE TALENTS
      (b) The Parable of THE POUNDS

XXIV   THE JUDGMENT OF THE KINGDOM 252
      The Parable of THE LAST JUDGMENT

      INDEX OF SCRIPTURE REFERENCES 263

      INDEX OF SUBJECTS 268

INTRODUCTION

Let the word "parable" be spoken, and certain well-loved pictures crowd in upon the mind. We see a rocky pass where a man fell among thieves, a shepherd searching through mountains and night, a bend in the road where a prodigal boy caught sight of home. The pictures which instinctively appear are Jesus' art; the kingdom of parable pays willing fee to Him. To refer this sovereignty to His insight, His vibrant mind, His human courage and compassion, His intimate dwelling in God, is but to grant the issue. Jesus is Master of parable because He is Master of Life.

The parables are the characteristic message of Jesus—"Without a parable spake he not unto them." [1] They are His most rememberable message; for pictures are still etched in recollection when a homily has become a blur. They are His most persuasive message; a prosier teaching might not break our stubborn will, but the sight of the father running to welcome his wayward son leaves us "defenceless utterly":

> "Naked I wait thy love's uplifted stroke.
> My harness, piece by piece, thou hast hewn from me." [2]

To know these incomparable stories is to know the teaching of Jesus, and the heart of the Teacher.

Other Parables

There were many parables before the day of Jesus. They can be found in the Old Testament, in the extra-canonical writings of the Jews and in the literature of other ancient peoples. [3]

---

1 Mark 4: 34.
2 Francis Thompson, "The Hound of Heaven" (Burns and Oates).
3 Among recent books is "The Parables and Similes of the Rabbis," Rabbi Asher Feldman. See also Chapter IV, Trench's "Notes on the Parables." There are at least five full-fledged parables in the Old Testament. See, for instance, II Samuel 12: 1-6.

Strangely enough, there were few parables after His day; the Epistles are almost bereft of them. Jesus did not invent this form of story, but under His transforming touch its water became wine. The sonata existed before Beethoven. For two hundred years prior to his time the progress of music had consisted mainly in the development of the sonata and other harmonic forms. But Beethoven, without surrendering the old design, "infused into it a new element of meaning and expression." [4] Such and immeasurably more was the genius of Jesus. He did not cast aside the old pattern. Even His "new commandment" was not new in the sense of being unknown until He spoke it. The Levitical law had decreed, "Thou shalt love thy neighbor as thyself." [5] But in Leviticus the command is lost among a ruck of other rules, many of which now seem trivial. Jesus made it new by giving it new emphasis, by making it a central jewel in the crown of character; and, especially, by lighting it with the radiance of His own life. The conquering sanction of the "new commandment" is in its last phrase: "This is my commandment, that ye love one another, even *as I have loved you.*" [6]

A favorite formula of the rabbinical teaching had been "whereunto shall I liken it?" [7] Jesus would have failed of contact with His hearers had He been unwilling to speak to them in their own tongue and, to some extent, within the range of prevalent ideas. [8] Was not this willingness also, in degree, a necessity in One who "in all things" was "made like unto his brethren"? Nor need we shrink, as some have felt they must, [9] from the admission that Jesus sometimes adopted a well-known parable, and retold it in His own way for His own purpose. Clearly the Parable of the Vineyard is a bold seizure and retelling of an Old Testament parable [10]—but with what significant changes and with what a tremendous issue! It does not

4 See "A History of Music," "Standard Musical Encyclopedia," Vol. I, p. 47.
5 Leviticus 19: 18.
6 John 15: 12.
7 Cf. Matthew 11: 16.
8 There is room for a careful consideration of the meaning of the word "unique," especially as applied (and rightly applied, so I believe) to Jesus. "Unique" does not mean completely strange and new, for, if such were the meaning, the unique could not enter our cognizance let alone our comprehension. The unique always has strong bonds with the familiar.
9 Trench, *op. cit.*, p. 55.
10 Isaiah 5: 1-7 and compare with Mark 12: 1-12.

INTRODUCTION   xv

belittle "The Merchant of Venice" to concede that Shakespeare
was indebted in the writing of the play to certain early Italian
stories. Likewise, Dvorák's "New World Symphony" is enhanced in our regard, rather than dimmed, by the supposition
that it is based on negro folk-songs. Genius is not a fiat-crea-
tion of the new, but a truth-revealing rearticulation of the old.
At least once, and perhaps many times, Jesus made a new world
symphony from an old world song. The difference between the
rabbinical parables and those of Jesus is precisely the difference
between their mind and His. Their parables are mostly arid
and artificial, a strongly exegetical bent having stretched analogies beyond the limits of ordinary human interest. In some
few instances they are at once lovely and compassionate. But
even at their best (as the history of human response well
proves) the rabbinical stories lack the "inevitability" of the
parables of Jesus. Wherein is the elusive mark of distinction?
The question might be asked in another form: Wherein lies the
peculiar authority of His "golden rule," in contrast with the
golden rule which was taught in negative statement before His
day? Only one answer can be given: The authority is in Him
who gave the golden rule and lived it. In Him also is found
the distinction of His parables.

What Is a Parable?

The word means literally "a throwing alongside." The old
definition, "an earthly story with a heavenly meaning," can
hardly be improved. The lines of differentiation have frequently been drawn,[11] insofar as it is possible to draw them,
between parable and the several literary forms which resemble
it; but the fact has not always been made clear that the parable,
among all these forms, is the one singularly fitted to the hand
of Jesus.[12]

11 See Dr. Plummer's illuminating article in Hasting's "Dictionary of the Bible."
12 There is no need to dwell at length upon the difference between parable and
myth. The latter is the "natural product of a primitive imagination" in its endeavor
to explain the wonder-compelling world. As such, it inevitably mixes truth and
error, fact and fiction. Parables employ fiction, but they do it knowingly, holding
it apart, in order to teach fact. The "Myths of Plato" are not myths in the strict
sense of the word, but are rather the parables and allegories of an acute and extraordinarily developed intellect.

Fable has endearing qualities as any reader of Æsop's Fables will testify.[13] Why did Jesus not tell fables? First, because a fable is "fabulous." It breaks the bounds of the natural, endows trees and animals with human powers, and surrenders at its weakest to the repellently grotesque. The mind of Jesus was too divinely natural, too responsive to the world of human joys and tears, to be fond of the fabulous. Again, the fable teaches a merely prudential virtue. It recommends caution, thrift, foresight; and recommends them from the standpoint of human consequence. Its movement is on a horizontal line; its "merit is from man to man." But the movement of a parable is always on a vertical line; it has a "heavenly meaning." Of course a parable may urge that we love our neighbor as ourselves; but that injunction is always pendant to another, "Thou shalt love the Lord thy God." Jesus' intense "feeling with" humanity was but one aspect of His indivisible consciousness; another aspect is revealed in the words, "knowing . . . that he came forth from God, and goeth unto God." [14] For One who had "authentic tidings of the Eternal," parable, not fable, was the proper medium. The Old Testament has its fable of the Thistle and the Cedar.[15] When the thistle presumed to ask that his son might have the daughter of the cedar for wife, a wild beast passing by trod on the thistle with summary destruction. We are thus warned against vaunting ambition; but the warning carries a sting. It casts a sidelong glance of ridicule at human foibles. A parable may speak trenchant condemnation (as the parables of Jesus frequently show), but it has no sarcasm.

> "For mockery is the fume of little hearts." [16]

Parable, like fable, walks the streets of life; but it regards the hurrying crowd with "larger, other eyes." Its vision, though piercing, is ever kind. For it gains access to the streets by means of a Jacob's ladder set up between heaven and earth.

[13] A metaphor (and sometimes a proverb) is a parable in germ—as in the rabbinical "saying," "The ass has kicked over the lamp." This is a contraction of the story of the man who tried to bribe an unjust judge with a lamp and found himself outbid by a rival who offered an ass. Correspondingly, a simile is often an abbreviated allegory.
[14] John 13: 3.
[15] II Kings 14: 9.
[16] Tennyson's "Guinevere" ("The Idylls of the King").

Allegory might have been chosen as the vehicle for the teaching of Jesus; for an allegory, like a parable, is "an earthly story with a heavenly meaning." But in a well-constructed allegory each detail of the story has its counterpart in the meaning; whereas, in a parable, story and meaning meet, not at every point, but at one central vantage ground of abiding truth. Jesus spoke certain allegories, such as the Story of the Soils; but the measure of detail in them, far from being pedantic, is so small that they live on the border line of parable. An allegory is constructed, like a house; but a parable lives, like a night-blooming cereus. An allegory is constrained; a parable is spontaneous. An allegory tends to deteriorate into a pattern; a parable is a flash of light. Need we ask why Jesus chose parable rather than allegory? His mind was not mechanical; it was as fluid, as colorful, as spontaneous and real as life itself. "Therefore speak I to them in parables."

The Parable as a Story

Any careful appraisal of the parables of Jesus must recognize in Him an unrivalled Teller of stories. The modern zest for romances, as seen in the dominance of fiction in our public libraries over that dull assortment called "general literature," is no new trait in human character. The romancer with a genuine gift has a Pied Piper's flute. Little children and children of a larger growth run clutching at his coat with eager clamor, "Tell us a story." Let the story be inherently true, and, though its setting be remote from the semblance of our common life, it casts on each new generation its ancient spell. The modern novelist has a wealth of prompting which, both in range and variety, is past compute. Roads girdling the earth beckon his feet. Scientific prowess has filled his age "full of a number of things," with a fullness which Robert Louis Stevenson never imagined. Even so, it is doubtful if modern stories can compare in simple vigor or poignant plea, in picturesque flavor or dramatic turn, with those told round Arab campfires by the sons of Abraham on their long trek from Ur of the Chaldees. Who worthier than they of high imaginings? Had they not fared forth across sandy wastes "not knowing whither they went," [17] seeking on the desert's rim the minarets of a "city that hath foundations"?

But what teller of stories in east or west can vie with Jesus? Was ever a perception so instant, an imagination so rich, a discrimination so true? The life of His day poured through golden gateways into the city of His soul, there to be changed by a divine alchemy into matchless parables. This gift must have found early use. If only we could have heard the stories He told in the Syrian dusk to the younger children in Mary's cottage! Were those stories parables? If so, they were the more fascinating. "With what comparison shall we compare it?" is an instinctive question. Our delight in comparisons has left its mark on the language: We "like" what is "like." [18] We must have parables. Whether the early stories of Jesus took that form or another the little children who ran to hear them were blessed indeed.

The claim is sometimes made in praise of a novelist that his books have mirrored for all time a well-loved countryside, or crystallized the customs and outlook of an age. Thus Wessex scenery is faithfully portrayed in the romances of Thomas Hardy, while John Galsworthy has caught and reproduced the mood of the later Victorian era. Similar claims can be made with firm assurance for the parables of Jesus. A slender volume would hold them; but from that volume, without access to any other source, we would know the aspect and attitudes of His Palestine. We read the parables, and the poor homes of that little land are before our eyes. We see the baking of bread and the patching of garments; we see even the emergency of a friend borrowing a loaf at midnight for his sudden guests. Rich homes are drawn with a pencil equally shrewd—barns bursting with fatness, laborers not daring to eat until their master has broken his fast, and the unseemly scramble for the chief seats at the feasts of the mighty. The glaring contrasts of our earth are drawn in dramatic line—"chosen" Jews and despised Samaritans, sumptuous Dives and abject Lazarus, householders and thieves, compassionate parenthood and the rascally steward who feathered his nest against the well-merited retri-

17 Hebrews 11: 8.
18 See Trench, *op. cit.*, p. 25.

bution. The whole gamut of human life is sounded—farmers at the plough, fishermen at their nets, a wedding procession moving through the dark with dancing torches, builders rearing towers, kings marching to their wars, and a widow pleading her cause in the persistence of despair before a heartless judge.

Over all there is the mystic glamor of Palestine. Behold a sower tramping weary furrows. Soon the fields will be "white unto harvest." On the high hillside flocks are grazing beneath a watchful shepherd's eye. In the distance there is a vineyard on a favored slope, or a deep defile where brigands lurk. That dry watercourse is a raging torrent when a storm breaks in the mountains, and on its golden summer sand a foolish man once built his house.

This motley array of characters and this vivid scenery are wrought into unforgettable stories. Each parable has lines as sharp as an etching. Sometimes the unfolding comes with a stab of surprise. Occasionally an ending is so abrupt that the mind of the listener is left quivering under the challenge. Surely Jesus must have told these stories eagerly for their own sake. Surely He must have loved folk the more because, ever hungry for a story, they pressed about Him as He said "whereunto shall I liken it?"

"That Seeing They May—Not Perceive"—?

The reasons why Jesus adopted a story method for His customary use have already been hinted. A word-picture, rather than a homily or a syllogism, has always been the ideal teaching medium:

> "Where truth in closest words shall fail,
> When truth embodied in a tale
> May enter in at lowly doors." [19]

It is no accident that the Fables of Æsop, the Odyssey of Homer, the Canterbury Tales of Chaucer, the early stories of Genesis, and preeminently the Parables of Jesus possess the secret of eternal youth. For the imaginative mind, a story is a joy forever; and for the unimaginative, it has power to "enter

[19] Tennyson, "In Memoriam."

in at lowly doors." Lodged in the mind it is not inert like a nugget of gold; it is vital, like a seed-plot continually bringing new flowers to bloom.

Then how shall we come to terms with the assertion of Jesus as recorded in St. Mark's Gospel: "But unto them that are without, all things are done in parables: that seeing they may see, and not perceive; and hearing they may hear, and not understand; lest haply they should turn again, and it should be forgiven them"? [20] We cannot take these words at their face value for the sufficient reason that, so taken, no words could more flatly deny the "mind that was in Christ Jesus." He came to illumine lives and not to darken them; and because lives were self-darkened He spoke in parables, well knowing that the rays of a parable will penetrate "where truth in closest words shall fail." Therein, beyond any peradventure of a doubt, is the dominant motive of Jesus' deliberate choice of the parable as the customary vehicle of His teaching. "And with many such parables spake he the word unto them, as they were able to hear it." [21]

But Jesus recognized, as the Parable of the Soils clearly implies, that some were hostile or indifferent to His teaching.

20 This passage (Matthew 13: 10-15; Mark 4: 10-12; Luke 8: 9, 10) is a quotation from that *locus classicus*, Isaiah 6: 9, 10. Does the prophet there assert that it is God's purpose to harden His people's hearts and to avoid their conversion? If so, we must assign the assertion to that unworthy view of God which exalts His sovereignty at the expense of His moral responsibility to His creatures; or which, at least, represents as designed whatever may be confidently predicted. Where we to-day would point to an analogy or a result, the Jewish scriptures would frequently assume a purpose. Mark and Luke appear to accept the sternest meaning of Isaiah's words, and leave us to infer that Jesus adopted the parable-method in order to render His hearers insensible to divine truth; even as God in earlier days purposed the blinding of the eyes of a stubborn people. (See also John 12: 39, 40; Romans 11: 8.) But a more gracious view, one more loyal to the whole scriptures and more in keeping with the "soul's invincible surmise," is that the Isaiah passage may have been spoken in the irony of sorrow and in warning plea. The blindness was due, not to the Divine will and wish, but to the self-will of a stiff-necked generation.

Accepting Isaiah's words at face value, it is still doubtful if Jesus used them in more than a general sense, namely, to compare a situation existent in Isaiah's day with the situation of His day. Matthew 13: 34, 35 is significant especially as quoted from the Psalms. (Psalm 78: 2.)

21 It is interesting to note that Matthew's version of Isaiah 6: 9, 10 on the one hand, and the versions of Mark and Luke on the other correspond respectively to the *spirit* of the LXX rendering and to the *spirit* of the Targum. Mark, while evidently quoting from LXX, seems to modify it in favor of some earlier form. But Matthew changes Mark's repellent *hina* to *hoti*, Mark's subjunctives becoming indicatives in the change. Matthew's version is surely nearer to the intention of Jesus. He spoke in parables not "in order that they may be blind," but "because they are blind" and in order that they may see. See "I.C.C.," *ad loc.*, Matthew, Mark, Luke. ("I.C.C." hereafter is abbreviation for "International Critical Commentary.")

He knew that human soil, stubbornly refusing a harvest, falls under heavier indictment with each fresh sowing; that privileges abused confirm the abusers in their disobedience. He knew also that no good purpose is served by heedlessly exposing truth to mockery: "Give not that which is holy unto the dogs, neither cast your pearls before the swine, lest haply they trample them under their feet . . ." [22] Thus, in respect to the obdurate, the parabolic method was twice blessed: By veiling truth, it guarded it from raillery; and the hostile received, despite themselves, a story that might germinate in secret, but which did not confirm hostility and deepen guilt, as plainer statement might have done, by provoking enmity to wrath. The parables have but to be read for us to realize how swiftly they arouse the imagination, smite the conscience, and quicken the will.

"Two Worlds Are Ours"

There was more than a natural human delight in a story, more than the fact that it is the oldest human language, and more than the unreceptiveness of His hearers to justify Jesus in the use of parables. This natural delight is itself rooted in a deeper reason:

> "What if earth
> Be but the shadow of heaven, and things therein
> Each to the other like, more than on earth is thought?" [23]

The real world to Jesus was not the seen world; the real world was the unseen of which the seen is but the form. Heaven to us may be a dream of earth; but to Him earth was a broken and shadowy reflection of heaven. The material was ordained as a sign-language of the spiritual: "For the invisible things of him since the creation of the world are clearly seen, being perceived through the things that are made, even his everlasting power and divinity." [24] Jesus saw always a divine congruity between earth and heaven.

Despite the mystic, we cannot escape, except for occasional moments, from the images of sense. In the appraisals of God,

22 Matthew 7: 6.
23 Milton, "Paradise Lost," V., 575.
24 Romans 1: 20.

our brief seasons of ecstasy when we behold with unveiled face,
may have no higher grace than quieter hours when we discern
the essence through the form. "No man shall see God and
live." It is a kindly providence that

> "Life, like a dome of many-colored glass
> Stains the white radiance of Eternity." [25]

Moreover, form reveals, even while it cloaks, the reality.
Would love, that master-motive, be known among us except
through its outward tokens—the surrender of the eyes, the
word tense with feeling, the clasp of the hand? When Jesus
said, "God is a Spirit," He did not therein counsel blindness
to God's embodiment in the round ocean, the living air, and
the mind of man. We also are spirits. Undeniably our means
of communication one with another are poor and fallible—
clumsy Morse codes, at best—but they are not useless. We
remain forever hidden and barricaded behind walls of flesh;
and, despite words (our finest code) we are still pathetically
inarticulate, with

> "Thoughts hardly to be packed
> Into a narrow act
> Fancies which break through language and escape." [26]

Nevertheless, spirit with spirit can meet through the form.
Words, glances, deeds, printing on a page are all parables
shadowing forth the hidden realm of human spirit. In like
manner, all the human was, to Jesus, a parable to reveal the
unseen life of God.

There can be no logic to prove the spiritual; there can be
only the prophet's opening of a window in the hope that clay-
shuttered eyes may find it a "magic casement" looking out upon
the mountains of God. The parable as spoken by Jesus was
such a window. He knew the heaven of a perfectly obedient
and loving life. Heaven, for Him, subjugated this mortal
scene until all creation became heaven's impress and sign. Was
there a forgiving father?—another Father was more forgiving,
though unseen! Did a shepherd brave the darkening storm to

---

25 Shelley's "Adonais."
26 Browning, "Rabbi Ben Ezra."

rescue his sheep that was lost?—another Shepherd was out on
a more hazardous quest for His human flock! Nor was it by
happy accident that the comparisons instanced by Jesus are so
inevitable in their fitness. The human image, rather, was
chosen and ordained by God to be the vehicle of His mystery;
even as Jesus was chosen and ordained to be the Soul of insight
Who should discover the Divine Reality behind the human or
natural form.

So the Son of Fact spoke until worn-out eyes saw a worn-
out world become new. Under His spell men beheld the gleaming robe of the Eternal filling all the courts of earth and
heaven.

> "The angels keep their ancient places:—
>   Turn but a stone, and start a wing!
> 'Tis ye, 'tis your estranged faces,
>   That miss the many-splendoured thing." [27]

To Him all things were a parable. The tenderness on the
world's edge when daylight fades, the green fire of the grass,
and the manifold life of wistful humanity were the handwriting
of the Most High. Ever patient with our filmy sight, He
brought forth from His treasure things new and old; and, to
show us that other world, "He opened his mouth and spake
unto them another parable, saying . . ."

The Interpretation of the Parables

The old adage, "When doctors disagree . . . ," is apropos of
the various prescriptions offered for the interpretation of the
parables. There are those who maintain that the central teaching of the parable must be sought; and who, in regard to the
details of the story, would take Chrysostom's warning as motto:
"Be not overbusy about the rest." On the other hand, there are
those who run out analogies with finespun subtlety, and believe
that no item of action or circumstance is without its intended
significance. Between these extremes of counsel there are
almost innumerable grades and shades of opinion.

Even Trench's eminently sane rules have not been exempt

---

[27] Francis Thompson, "In no strange place." ("Poems," edited by Wilfred Meynell, published by John Lane Co.)

from criticism.[28] Strong exception has been taken to his suggestion that the scriptural introductions to the respective parables, and the scriptural comments upon them, furnish indispensable clues to their meaning. A recent commentator
maintains [29] (and there is sound and reverent scholarship to
support the plea) that the parables themselves are more trustworthy guides than their scriptural settings. He quotes Wernle
with approval: "Our delight in the parables rises regularly in
the exact degree in which we succeed in liberating ourselves
from the interpretations of the Evangelist, and yielding ourselves up to the original force of the parables themselves."

With this strife of tongues echoing in our ears, and the sad
fate of earlier counsels before our eyes, to venture on any
rule for the interpretation of the parables is to give hostages to
fortune. Nevertheless, we make bold to assert:

First, a wise interpretation of a parable will seek its *salient
truth.* A parable is not an allegory. It is a flash of light, not
an ingeniously devised mosaic. It may have divergent rays,
but these derive their virtue from the light itself. It may be
held within a lovely lamp, but "we are to be children of the
light and not slaves of the lamp." [30] Yet even this counsel must
be applied with that "good sense" which Trench wisely enjoins.
For some parables are obviously more allegorical than others.
In the Parable of the Soils every detail seems to have pith and
purpose; while in the Parable of the Unjust Steward the allegorical element is at its minimum, and the teaching is vividly
focussed. Reverent investigation must also determine how
far the scriptural setting of a parable provides a clue to its
meaning. That there are "strata" in the Gospels is more and
more generally admitted. In the last resort, the parable itself,
viewed through such childlike receptiveness and such eager
sincerity as our life and prayers can summon, is its own best
evidence.

Second, the parables are not armories for forging theological
weapons. They were spoken mostly to the common people who

28 Trench, *op. cit.*, p. 31. Trench interpretations of the individual parables have
been partly outgrown; but his "Introduction" to the whole subject of the parables
(pp. 1-62) is invaluable.
29 George Murray, "Jesus and His Parables," Introductory Chapter, p. 8.
30 Hubert L. Simpson writing of the Genesis stories in his "Altars of Earth."

INTRODUCTION

heard them gladly. Their purpose was not for dogma but for
life. The violence done to the parables by those who have
constrained them into the narrow mold of some theological
predilection is past credence, and beyond moderation of language to describe. The "pearl of great price" has become, in
the hands of such theological sacrilege, the Church at Geneva!
The man owing ten thousand talents has been made to typify
a line of Popes! The Unjust Steward has been held to per-
sonify the Devil![31] Even Trench, after warning us that the
parables must not be made the stalking-horse either of dogmatic
controversy or ingenious allegorizing, dallies with the suggestion
that the leaven which the woman hid in the three measures of
meal may represent the sanctification of body, mind, and spirit;
or the salvation of the human race descended from Shem,
Japheth, and Ham, the three sons of Noah! It would have
been more to the point, and a worthier tribute to the mind of
Jesus, had he surmised that Jesus instanced "three measures
of meal" because He had often seen Mary use that much on
baking days in the white cottage on the Nazareth hills.[32]

Truth lives on many levels. The truth of literal fact is on a
lower level than the truth of idea, even as the truth of idea is on
a lower level than the truth of life.[33] A story enshrines the
truth of idea, and so will yield perennial fragrance when our
logics have been forgotten. Dostoievsky's "The Brothers
Karamzov," though it is not literal fact, has truth to abide and
truth to inspire which a census table, however accurate, can
never yield. The Genesis stories will endure longer than our
careful sciences of the origin of matter. Truth of idea is
stronger than truth of fact. The parables have truth of idea
—and more! For in Him Who spoke them their divinest word
became flesh. In Him they gained the highest truth, the truth
of life. He said (with what ultimate wisdom!) not, "I *teach*
the truth," but, "I *am* the truth." In its finality truth is not an
argument, a theology, a metaphysic, or even a story; it is spirit

[31] Hosea Ballou's "Notes on the Parables" is interesting as having been written from an avowedly "universalist" standpoint. As such, it has no more value than any attempt to read something *into* the parables can have—the attempt of a Calvinist, for instance, to read Calvinism into them.
[32] We shall have occasion to note how often Jesus was indebted for the scenery and action of His parables to his home life at Nazareth.
[33] See Canon B. H. Streeter's "Reality," Chapter II on "Science, Art, and Religion."

and life. Through the parable the truth of His life comes to quicken our life.

There is no need to decry theology. So long as God gives us intelligence we shall be under a necessity of nature to order our convictions concerning God and man within a system as self-consistent as we can build it. Nevertheless religion has depths which theology cannot sound. Religion is a hidden spring; theology is the ever changing channel that directs its flow. The parables are in the province of religion; only secondarily are they in the province of theology. So long as we read our prejudices into them, so long shall we live in a pre-Copernican universe; all our suns and stars will revolve in narrow orbits about our narrow house. But if we will bring our prejudices to the judgment of the parables, we shall emerge upon a universe of boundless horizons, lovely with sphere-music.

> "And Tycho told him, there is but one way
> To know the truth, and that's to sweep aside
> All the dark cobwebs of old sophistry,
> And watch and learn that moving alphabet,
> Each smallest silver character inscribed
> Upon the skies themselves, noting them down,
> Till on a day we find them taking shape
> In phrases, with a meaning; and, at last,
> The hard-won beauty of that celestial book
> With all its epic harmonies unfold
> Like some great poet's universal song." [34]

The Arrangement of the Parables

"De gustibus non est disputandum." It is largely individual taste that must determine the arrangement of the parables. Any division will be open to attack, for a parable may have so many aspects of truth that it will leap over any fence of classification by which we may endeavor to confine it. We do not know the chronological order in which the parables were spoken; for the gospelists, especially Matthew and Luke, themselves arrange the parables, each gospelist to subserve a purpose of his own.[35]

Arnot indicates the "insurmountable difficulties" which at-

---

[34] Alfred Noyes, "Watchers of the Sky. (Frederick A. Stokes Co.)
[35] The "Kingdom" parables of Matthew 13, and the three parables in Luke 15 with the words "lost and found" as their motif, will readily occur to mind.

tend any attempt at rigid classification, and instances Bauer's failure to divide the parables into the three groups of dogmatic, moral, and historic. Arnot himself assumes [36] that the sequence in which the parables occur in the Gospels is the "natural order," and that this sequence preserves "in all cases the historical circumstances whence the parables spring." Few scholars to-day would deem such an assumption tenable.

Bruce [37] maintains that the parables are of an "incidental character," and as such are to be treated as "parts of a larger whole in connection with the particular occasions which called them forth." Rather arbitrarily he divides the ministry of Jesus into His ministry as Teacher, as Evangelist, and as Prophet; and groups the parables correspondingly as theoretic, evangelic, and prophetic. But when was Jesus the Teacher without being also the Evangelist and the Prophet? When did He assume any one of these rôles to the exclusion of the other two? With lowly gratitude for a painstaking and eminently valuable work, we still must feel that the parables are too vital to be held within these artificial limits.

Other expositors—among whom George Murray in Scotland and George Henry Hubbard of our United States are recently notable [38]—have made illuminating divisions of the parables on the basis of their subject matter. A comparison of the contents pages of these two writers proves interestingly that topical classifications of the parables may be sharply different while each remains fully legitimate. Dr. Marcus Dods has not raised the question of the arrangement of the parables, but has expounded them in the order in which they occur, first in Matthew and then in Luke.[39]

The chronological order, if it could be determined, would perhaps be the best. It would show the unfolding of the spirit of Jesus; for Jesus was within our human category of growth, since only within that category could He have been genuinely

36 Arnot, "The Parables of Our Lord," pp. 28 and 29.
37 See Bruce's "The Parabolic Teaching of Jesus" which no student of the parables can ignore. The Parable of the Unrighteous Steward is classed as "Evangelic," and that of the Importunate Widow as "theoretic." But why? And is not the Parable of the Leaven in real sense "prophetic," and not merely didactic?
38 George Henry Hubbard, "The Teachings of Jesus in Parables," a most stimulating study; and George Murray, "Jesus and His Parables," an interpretator who has brought "compassion and new eyes" to the exposition of these greatest of all stories.
39 Marcus Dods, "The Parables of Our Lord."

human. "He *learned* obedience by the things which He suffered." [40] If the Hebrews conceived the universe as catastrophic, looking ever for the "great and terrible day of the Lord," and if the Greeks conceived it as static, it is characteristic of our age to regard it as emergent and vitalistic.[41] This conception in our time has been an open sesame to vast stores of new knowledge. Applied to the life of Jesus it would be similarly fruitful, could we but know the order of His dicta and the events which befell Him.[42] Then we would understand how the days that made Him happy unsealed the fountains of His wisdom, and how the tragic forces which beset Him made fertile His spirit as with a ploughshare's cruel mercy. We would see how He "advanced in wisdom and stature, and in favor with God and men." [43]

The arrangement suggested in this book is an attempt, undoubtedly vulnerable, to arrange the parables in approximate natural sequence. The endeavor is foredoomed to failure, because our knowledge is insufficient to give any promise of full success. But a study of the gospels (especially such a study as has produced the best "Harmonies"), the context of the parables, and the intrinsic message of the parables ought to make possible an arrangement which, if not chronological, will at least suggest how His mind unfolded under the impact of events and the beckoning of God. Such an arrangement is here intended. That the attempt is very fallible no one is more clearly aware than the author, who would be well content if his work should prove only one of those hidden stones which make the foundation of a bridge.

"Each in His Own Tongue"

It has been wisely remarked that "the value of a parable does not depend upon the new and varied truth that we are able to extort from it, but upon our progressive and practical applica-

---

40 Hebrews 5: 8.
41 See H. E. Fosdick's "Christianity and Progress," Chapter I.
42 Many studies have been made of the development of Jesus. Recently J. A. Robertson's "The Spiritual Pilgrimage of Jesus" is a study of singular insight and helpfulness.
43 Luke 2: 52.

tion of its single truth to our daily life." [44] A commentator of an earlier day has written similarly: (each) "century must produce its own literature, as it raises its own corn, and fabricates its own garments." He adds a warning that the interpretations of other days are not to be regarded as fixed deposits of truth, but rather as time-vestures of truth. The truth abides within the changing form:—"The intellectual and spiritual treasures of the past should indeed be reverently preserved and used; but they should be used as seed . . . we should cast them into the ground, and get the product fresh every season —old, yet ever new." [45] It is this necessity which justifies another book on the Parables of Jesus. In these unforgettable stories He has given us the enduring truth of idea. Our meticulous sciences and elaborate theologies will dissolve and fade "like an insubstantial pageant"; but those who can "pray, and sing, and tell old tales" have found the secret of perpetual youth.

In every age the parables prove their startling modernity. They are more recent than to-day's newspaper; for a newspaper follows the fashions, and a fashion because it has become a fashion has begun to die. The parables utter the eternal verities by which all fashions, the shifting moods of an indifferent society, are judged. They are as recent as present breathing, as vivid in their tang as the "now" of immediate experience. "The words that I have spoken unto you are spirit, and are life." [46]

Another necessity is laid upon the expositor of the parables— a necessity deeper than that of applying them in their unchanging truth to the changing customs of the world. It is the necessity which Luke acknowledged when he wrote in the prologue of his Gospel, "It seemed good to me also." [47] Earlier writers of the story of Jesus had been "eyewitnesses and ministers of the word." They could boast an intimacy of knowledge which he could never claim. He was not an apostle. His eyes had not seen, nor his ears heard, nor his hands handled.

44 G. H. Hubbard, *op. cit.*, p. xix, Introductory chapter.
45 Arnot, *op. cit.*, Introduction, pp. 11 and 12.
46 John 6: 63.
47 Luke 1: 1-4.

He was not even of Galilee or Judea. He was a physician of Antioch or Ephesus; yet—"it seemed good to me also." He could not forbear to write of the Great Physician who was able to "minister to a mind diseased." That one Face, though never seen in the flesh, reigned in his imagination so benignly, with so winsome a kingship, that he needs must tell of Him!

"It seemed good to me also . . ." How can any expositor of the parables speak a new word? How can he speak an old word more clearly or penetratingly than his predecessors far nobler and abler than he? Yet, perchance, he may speak with a new accent. He may, without doubt, speak to a new generation, since "time makes ancient good uncouth." In any event, and despite the oblivion into which his words may soon pass, he *needs must* speak: "For the love of Christ constraineth us."

PARABLES OF THE EARLY MINISTRY

THE GOOD NEWS OF THE KINGDOM OF GOD

CHAPTER I

THE CONFLICT OF NEW AND OLD

THE PARABLE OF THE CHILDREN OF THE BRIDECHAMBER

"And they said unto him, The disciples of John fast often, and make supplications; likewise also the disciples of the Pharisees; but thine eat and drink. And Jesus said unto them, Can ye make the sons of the bridechamber fast, while the bridegroom is with them? But the days will come; and when the bridegroom shall be taken away from them, then will they fast in those days." *(Luke 5:33-35)*

(Parallel passages: Matthew 9:14, 15; Mark 2:18-20)

THE PARABLE OF THE NEW PATCH AND THE OLD GARMENT

"And he spake also a parable unto them: No man rendeth a piece from a new garment and putteth it upon an old garment; else he will rend the new, and also the piece from the new will not agree with the old." *(Luke 5:36)*

(Parallel passages: Matthew 9:16; Mark 2:21)

THE PARABLE OF NEW WINE AND OLD WINESKINS

"And no man putteth new wine into old wineskins; else the new wine will burst the skins, and itself will be spilled, and the skins will perish. But new wine must be put into fresh wineskins. And no man having drunk old wine desireth new; for he saith, The old is good." *(Luke 5:37-39)*

(Parallel passages: Matthew 9:17; Mark 2:22)

THE PARABLE OF TREASURES NEW AND OLD

"Have ye understood all these things? They say unto him, Yea. And he said unto them, Therefore every scribe who hath been made a disciple to the kingdom of heaven is like unto a man that is a householder, who bringeth forth out of his treasure things new and old." *(Matthew 13:51, 52)*

THE CONFLICT OF NEW AND OLD

The Parable of the Children of the Bridechamber
The Parable of the New Patch and the Old Garment
The Parable of New Wine and Old Wineskins
The Parable of Treasures New and Old

"Why do thy disciples fast not?"—the perennial question which the old flings hotly or perplexedly at the new! In every generation precedent challenges the prophet: "By what right do you defy the established order?" Always custom complains bitterly against the innovator: "These men do exceedingly trouble our city." [1]

Matthew tells us that the disciples of John the Baptist raised the question. Mark says the Pharisees shared it. Luke places responsibility at the door of Christ's own disciples or of interrogators unnamed. Probably all three groups provoked the issue not once but many times. For our most stubborn quarrel is with the sentinel of God who disturbs our slumber amid familiar things, and sounds reveille at the dawn, bidding us strike tents and trek towards the unknown. There is a law of change which compels us to break the systems which we make and love. We must rend what we create so that we may create anew and more worthily. But this lesson of life finds us obtuse and unwilling pupils.

The Parable of the Children of the Bridechamber

The Mosaic law demanded only the annual fast associated with the ancient Day of Atonement.[2] But pious Jews, trusting to purchase salvation by ceremonies, had added to the number of the fasts until they could boast as did the Pharisee, "I fast

1 Acts 16: 20.
2 Leviticus 23: 27.

3

twice in the week." [3]   By the tacit consent of Jesus, His
disciples must have honored these fasts more in the breach
than in the observance.[4]   When their neglect was challenged, He
justified them by the startling assertion that His gospel is an
influx of sheer joy.   It is like a wedding; and for them, the
friends of the Bridegroom, to fast at a wedding would be an
unpardonable gaucherie.

"Like a wedding" is a description of the Christian life which
in our persistent glumness we have refused to allow.   Yet
Jesus used it frequently.[5]   Old Testament prophets had said
with daring, "For thy Maker is thy husband"; [6] and John the
Baptist had claimed as his sufficient honor that he was the
friend of the Bridegroom, his joy being to hear the Bridegroom's voice.[7]   The dominant note of the new religion was
deep joy.

The scribes and Pharisees might fast.   Religion to them was
not joyous; it bound on them burdens grievous to be borne.
By its dreary routine of rules and shibboleths men might gain
merit, but not a song.   Jesus came to lead them from that
slavery into a new land of promise.   They would still be under
the law—God's decrees welling up within the enfranchised
soul—but it was a law whose service was perfect freedom.
"The water that I shall give him shall become in him a well
of water springing up into everlasting life." [8]

The disciples of John the Baptist might fast.   Religion to
them was not joyous.   It was a warning of impending doom, a
fleeing from the wrath to come.   To feel the holiness of God
as a fan winnowing the grain from the chaff, or as an axe of
retribution laid at the root of the tree, was life compared with
the mechanical righteousness of the Pharisees; but it was not
jubilant life.   Jesus drove the Arch-Fear from the sky and
revealed instead a Face of infinite pity, a Holiness inseparable

3 Luke 18: 12.   It was believed that Moses ascended Mt. Sinai on Monday, and
descended on Thursday.   These were the days of fasting.
4 Mark 9: 29 and Matthew 17: 21, in which Jesus recommends fasting, are absent
from the best MSS.; but Matthew 6: 16 seems to imply that He did recognize the
place of fasting in a well-ordered life.
5 See the chapters in this book on the parable of the Wise and Foolish Virgins,
and the Parable of the Great Supper.
6 Isaiah 54: 4-10, Hosea 2: 19.
7 John 3: 29.
8 John 4: 14.

from Compassion. The rainbow was set against the storm. The abounding sin was swallowed up in more abounding grace.

His joy was thus the gladness of an inner law exchanged for the sadness of the rabbinical yoke. It was the song of God's tender-heartedness for the fear of God's anger. But it was more!—for the fullness of joy is love. Jesus replaced the weariness which hangs upon the soul's quest for its own righteousness with the "large delight" of serving another's need. Joy is not in defiance of pain, or in pain's respite. It is *through* pain,—that pain borne for others by which the world is saved. He, "Who for the joy that was set before him endured the Cross," [9] had entered into joy's deep secret. Therefore He could say with utter truth, "These things have I spoken unto you, that my joy might remain in you, and that your joy might be full." [10] It was joy like a wedding—the marriage of earth and heaven!

With such joy as their heritage how could the disciples fast? If the appropriate mood and circumstance are lacking, fasting is a pious mummery. The acts of religion must be the natural issue of the soul, and congruous with the event, or they are a pretense. The day would come, said Jesus, when His followers would fast without compulsion. Already He could hear the first rumblings of the storm. Soon the "old order" would pass, "yielding place to new"; but in its death-struggle it would slay the Bearer of new tidings. "Then will they fast in that day." Then food would have no flavor. Sorrow, weeping for a Bridegroom taken away and for the sin that slew Him, would flee to abstinences then as to a refuge. Fasting then would be the soul's inevitable language.

The Parable of the New Patch and the Old Garment

"Why do thy disciples fast not?" Soon they would ask Him why His disciples ate with unwashen hands,[11] and why they flouted the rigorous law of the Jewish sabbath.[12] All these were but variants of the deeper question: "By what right do you

9 Hebrews 12: 2.
10 John 15: 11.
11 Mark 7: 2-5.
12 Mark 2: 24-28.

break tradition?" Jesus, well aware of the agelong conflict between the old and the new, made answer gently, but keenly: "Nobody sews new cloth on a threadbare garment."

Where had Jesus seen robes so worn that they fell apart under the attempt to patch them? Is this a hint of the poverty of His boyhood home? Did the robe of the oldest descend in turn to each younger brother, fortified against the years by Mary's ingenious needle? Had Jesus watched His mother's anxiety when the robe could be patched no more, when mending only aggravated the holes? Perhaps Mary wondered how new clothes could be bought—but somehow the money was found, and they were bought. Was it that anxiety which scored the incident deeply upon His mind, so that years later it was spoken as a parable?

Creedal-robes and ritual garments become threadbare. The clothes of international polity and industrial systems grow shabby and can no longer give decent covering to the flesh. We ought to be ashamed to be seen on the street in them. We should let them go; God in His mercy will see that new clothes are bought when they must be bought. The way of Jesus came to supersede a worn-out Judaism, but His age had ceased to believe in anything new. There could be no fresh creation invading the established world. There was nothing new under the sun. Rivers flowed to the sea only to return to their source. Events ran in meaningless cycles. War and peace were only the ebb and flow of the tides. Existence was a squirrel-cage. The best the Jew could hope for was the destruction of the old world and the wholesale transfer of good people to another realm. In this despair, as in other recreancies, he was unfaithful to the flaming vision of his prophets. *They* had promised a "new song" and a "new name" and a "new heart." *They* had been ever expectant, looking for "a new heaven and a new earth" fresh from the springs of Divine birth.[13] Afterwards the hope died—until Jesus came claiming to be in Himself the realization of the prophets' dream. "This day is this scripture fulfilled in your ears" . . . "And he closed the book."[14] The

13 For instance, Psalm 40: 3, Isaiah 62: 2. Ezekiel 18: 31.
14 Luke 4: 17-21.

book was superseded by a Life! His way was an original creation, a new thing under the sun!

How could it be a patch on an old Judaism, either on the recreant Judaism of the scribes or even on the more vital Judaism of John the Baptist? To try to patch the old faith would only rend it. In its threadbare state it was at least venerable, and when the demands of life were not too stern it might still be comfortable; but to attempt to repair it would tear it into unsightliness. Jesus had due regard for the old.

Meanwhile new cloth must be fashioned into a new garment. Its strength is pristine. To use it merely for repair debases it and does despite to the renewals of God. The Christ spirit is new. It cannot be a patch on the old ritual—it may retain the Sabbath, but only as it transforms it from bondage to blessing. It cannot be a patch on an old industrialism—how can Jesus who said, "No longer do I call you servants; for the servant knoweth not what his lord doeth: but I have called you friends," [15] ever be regarded as merely tinkering at an economic order still largely feudal? It cannot be a patch on national imperialisms—for when Jesus said to His disciples concerning the Gentile rulers who loved to "lord it" over lesser breeds, "Ye shall not be so," [16] He was pointing them not to the repair of an outworn imperialism but to a new adventure in constructive goodwill. It cannot be a patch on an old life—there can be no hankering after old loyalties, no compromise with old attitudes, no botching up of old selfishness. "A new faith," said Jesus, "demanding new forms of complete allegiance. . . ."

"Wherefore if any man is in Christ, he is a new creature: the old things are past away; behold they are become new." [17]

The Parable of New Wine and Old Wineskins

The truth was re-expressed in a parable not less apt than the last, nor less intimately linked by its imagery with Jewish life. Jesus frequently used twin parables. The parables of the Lost Coin and the Lost Sheep, and the parables of the Hidden

15 John 15: 15.
16 Luke 22: 25, 26.
17 II Corinthians 5: 17.

Treasure and the Long-sought Pearl are instances. Nor do these double comparisons merely repeat a truth; rather they reveal it in different aspects. They are complementary as well as reiterative. In the last parable there was some concern lest the old ritual should be torn asunder; in this the emphasis is upon the preservation of the new.

Jesus was not remote from the familiar life of men. He was a child of "the daily round, the common task." His citizenship in that heaven with which our earth is interfused, did not make Him a stranger in the rough-and-tumble world. He was at home in both realms; so common things were to Him the symbol of things unseen.

How often He had watched the wineskins hanging in His Galilean home! One of the singers of Israel had said of his sorrows: "I am become like a bottle in the smoke." [18] Jesus had noticed how a wineskin would crack and become hard with age. Foolish then to pour new wine into it! Soon the new wine would begin to ferment—with disaster both for the wine and the wineskin!

The heady tumult of the new gospel! It would burst the Judaistic wineskin—the New Testament Epistles shake under that agitation! Later it would stretch the old bottle of slavery beyond limits, and spill over the world in a new wine of freedom. Man's ancient concept of womanhood was unable to hold the ferment, and was thrown to the debris of broken systems. The red tide running from the winepress of Calvary is not easily restrained!

Then why try to save old wineskins? They exist for the wine, and only the wine is precious. In each new generation it must be poured from one perishable vessel to another without the spilling of a drop. The discarded vessel need not be mourned so long as the spontaneous energy of the new life is preserved. But in tragic blindness we invest the wineskins with peculiar sanctity. Religion becomes a creed or a polity, instead of a spirit. Heresy in doctrine falls under the ban, while heresy in spirit goes unnoticed. Furthermore, in our

18 Psalm 119: 83.

concern for the system, we denounce as lawless the man in whom new life pulses and who finds the system too small. We forget that lawlessness is of two kinds. Some lawbreakers, who are unworthy of the system, break it in anger or rebellious greed. Other lawbreakers, of whom the system is not worthy, break it because of the soul's imperious decree. Such say with Luther: "I dare not retract. Here stand I. I can do no other." But we have not learned to distinguish the lower lawlessness from the higher. We hang Jesus and the two thieves on the same hill. . . .

These bottles of our dogmatism—can they ever hold the wine of the grapes of God? These denominational wineskins —how hard and unelastic!—can they ever stretch enough to permit the redeeming fermentation of the spirit of Jesus? New modes of expression, new channels of action—would we ever rebel against them if we had really learned the first lesson in history or psychology? The rebellion will not avail us. We may fortify our poor creeds, our dried-up formularies, with precedents, stern penalties, and acts of legislature; but the Divine ferment will not be held until the wineskin is vast enough to hold it—as vast as the soul of Jesus! Meanwhile the pity is that by our obdurate clinging to old forms the wine of new truth is spilled.

The Parable of Treasures New and Old

Must we conclude, then, that the advent of Jesus was mainly a sign of revolution?—attended, as revolutions always are, by wreck and destruction? Are the ways of heaven iconoclastic? Is the road of human advance to be littered with fragments of shrines long held dear and wantonly destroyed? No; for though Jesus came to bring not peace but a sword [19] (since His coming always precipitates the conflict between old and new), He came, nevertheless, "not to destroy but to fulfill." [20]

The Gospel of Luke adds a significant sentence to the Parable of the New Wine and the Old Wineskins: "And no man having

19 Matthew 10: 34.
20 Matthew 5: 17.

drunk old wine desireth new; for he saith, The old is good."
Therein is the recognition that a new spirit must not only make
its own forms, but must live within them for a time in order
to mature and realize its own nature.   The form gives character
to the spirit.   Furthermore, there is the recognition that an old
system which has won man's affection and given him shelter
should be allowed to live out its honorable day.   The old wineskins may still be used for wine whose fermentation is done.
No one can read the words of Jesus with understanding without reading His debt to the truth of other days.   His mind
kindled to the dreams of holy men of old.   He was not insensible to that mellow half-sadness which hangs about ancient
altars like a remembered fragrance.   "No man having drunk
old wine desireth new"—that is, of course, a warning against
the false conservatism that so easily besets us.   But it is also,
surely, the Master's tribute to the "honest lovers of old ways";
and His admission that upstart theories and the fiery zeal of
new discipleship can taste very harsh and sour, and be raw
almost to the measure of sacrilege!   "The old is good"—it is a
word, not merely of warning against reaction, not merely of
indulgent concession to the old, but of rare insight and
wisdom.[21]

For we cannot escape the old.   In individual and social experience past sins crouch like wild beasts at our door, and past
victories are ministering angels.   "To-day" in the very word
implies a "yesterday."   Every time we date a letter to a friend
we acknowledge the centuries which are beating in our blood.
The language we use has been hammered, shaped, and polished
by successive generations until it rings like steel and shines like
a cloth of gold.   The "clean slate" demanded by the revo-

21 G. H. Hubbard, *op. cit.*, p. 229, seems to me to be too harsh in his interpretation of Luke 5: 39; though one is loth to take issue with so stimulating a book.
The verse surely seems to be not simply a condemnation of blind conservatism—
though such condemnation is implied.   That word "noone," and the whole range
of Christ's teaching bear out the exegesis which A. B. Bruce has suggested *op. cit.*,
pp. 307 and 308.   The interpretation here suggested may be compared with the saying of Rabbi Jose, b. Judah of Chephar Babli (second century): "He who learns
from the young, unto what may he be likened?   Unto one who . . . drinks wine
from the vat.   And he who learns from the old, to what may he be likened?   Unto
one who drinks old wine." (See A. Feldman, "The Parables and Similes of the
Rabbis," p. 141.)   Almost certainly the saying of Jesus in Luke 5: 39 echoed a current phrase.

lutionary has history in its very texture; it cannot be wiped clean. The iconoclast ever waits,

> "till some new world-emotion rise,
> And with the shattering might of a simoon
> Sweep clear this dying Past that never dies" [22]

only to find that the inconsiderate thing about the past is just that "it never dies." It is wiser to "accept the universe"!

Neither can we hope to escape the new. Change is the law of life. Matter is an unending dance of electric energies; and our very flesh constantly decays and is constantly renewed. Old thought-forms must be used as milestones—a man who does not guide himself by them wanders in darkness; but they must not be used as millstones, or we shall find them round our necks and we ourselves drowning in the depths of the sea. Our mental and spiritual constitution impels us onward. Only for a night may we tarry, then we must strike our tents. A conservatism which, for the sake of the future, safeguards the treasure of the past wins its crown. A conservatism which denies the future, counting its little systems as full and final truth, has blood upon its hands—the skyline of the ages is black with the cruel crosses it has raised!

We must journey; but the journey is still one journey. It is from the heart of the old that we gain access to the new. Change is only in the form; the essence abides eternal. The morning may be new, but time is old. The vintage may be of to-day's garnering, and the wine from to-morrow's winepress, but the seed is from the foundation of the earth. If the new has no root in the old, it withers. If the old grows no new leaves, it dies. "Therefore every scribe who hath been made a disciple to the kingdom of heaven is like unto a man that is a householder who bringeth forth out of his treasure things new and old." Only such a scribe, filled with the spirit of that kingdom which is love and peace, can interpret the old to the new and the new to the old, and clothe the eternal verity in its fresh and appropriate time-vesture.

Mankind still divides into two camps—those who cry "The

---

[22] William Watson, quoted by J. Brierley in "Religion and Experience." (Collected Poems of William Watson are published by The Macmillan Co.)

old things," and those who cry "The new things." Neither camp understands God's wise law of change. Standpattism and garish novelty in religion are equally blasphemous. Standpattism helps to nail Jesus to His Cross; and novelty, with that stark beam before its eyes, discards it as a morbid and meaningless symbol. The reactionary and the radical must always share the guilt of revolution. How the troubled realm of industry needs the "scribe who has been made a disciple to the kingdom of heaven," so that he might "bring forth from his treasure things new and old"—the old basic law of individual leadership with the new friendliness which, because it shares all its leader's mind and heart, is the conquest of slavery! How theology needs that scribe to bring forth eternal truths (such as that of atonement which has been written on sacrificial altars since human life began) along with new science!

> "The old order changeth, yielding place to new,
> And God fulfills Himself in many ways,
> Lest one good custom should corrupt the world." [23]

"If any man is in Christ, he is a new creature. Old things are passed away. Behold they (the old things) are become new."

[23] Alfred Tennyson, "The Passing of Arthur" (from "The Idylls of the King").

CHAPTER II

SIMILITUDES OF THE KINGDOM (I)

THE PARABLE OF SPONTANEOUS GROWTH

"And he said, So is the kingdom of God, as if a man should cast seed upon the earth; and should sleep and rise night and day, and the seed should spring up and grow, he knoweth not how. The earth beareth fruit of herself; first the blade, then the ear, then the full grain in the ear. But when the fruit is ripe, straightway he putteth forth the sickle, because the harvest is come." *(Mark 4:26-29)*

THE PARABLE OF THE MUSTARD SEED

"And he said, How shall we liken the kingdom of God? or in what parable shall we set it forth? It is like a grain of mustard seed, which, when it is sown upon the earth, though it be less than all the seeds that are upon the earth, yet when it is sown, groweth up, and becometh greater than all the herbs, and putteth out great branches; so that the birds of the heaven can lodge under the shadow thereof."

(Mark 4:30-32)

(Parallel passages: Matthew 13:31, 32; Luke 13:18, 19)

THE PARABLE OF THE LEAVEN

"Another parable spake he unto them; The kingdom of heaven is like unto leaven, which a woman took, and hid in three measures of meal, till it was all leavened." *(Matthew 13:33)*

(Parallel passage: Luke 13:20, 21)

SIMILITUDES OF THE KINGDOM (I)

The Parable of Spontaneous Growth
The Parable of the Mustard Seed
The Parable of the Leaven

The new religion was "the good news of the kingdom of God." [1]   The ideal of a "kingdom" is one which the historic creeds of Christendom have virtually ignored, but which Jesus proclaimed as His one purpose and passion.   It dominates His manifold message as a prayer-bell rules the shrines, cloisters, and courtyard of a temple.   He defined that ideal quite clearly: "Thy kingdom come; Thy (Fatherly) will be done on earth as it is in heaven." [2]   It comprised not merely the perfection of the individual, for "if religion ends in the individual, it ends"; [3] nor yet the perfection of a super-community submerging the individual; but, rather, a Divine Commonwealth in which each personality is realized in seeking the welfare of all, and in which each is regarded "not as a means but always as an end." [4]

Jesus described the kingdom in terms of startling paradox. It will one day *arrive* (. . . "until the kingdom of God shall come") [5] yet it is ever *present* ("the kingdom of God is within you"). [6]   It is like that realm of music in which we live, but which did not "come" until the radio caught faint snatches of its song.   The kingdom is *possessed* ("Blessed are the poor in spirit for theirs *is* the kingdom of heaven"), [7] yet it must ever be *sought* ("Seek ye first his kingdom . . .").[8]   Though

---

1 Mark 1: 14.
2 Matthew 6: 10.
3 A. B. Belden, "The Greater Christ," p. 128.
4 See Kant's "Kingdom of Ends" in the "Critique of Pure Reason."
5 Luke 22: 18.
6 Luke 17: 21.
7 Matthew 5: 3.
8 Matthew 6: 33.

it is within all life, it may be *entered* as a man crosses the bounds of one country and enters another, its passport being a childlike spirit—"Whosoever shall not receive the kingdom of God as a little child, he shall in no wise enter therein." [9] Conversion serves to open blind eyes upon the kingdom—"Except one be born anew, he cannot see the kingdom of God." [10] Beyond conversion lies the joy of the once-blind exploring a now-seen universe. . . .

> "O glory of the lighted mind!
> How dead I'd been, how dumb, how blind.
> The station brook, to my new eyes,
> Was babbling out of Paradise,
> The waters rushing from the rain
> Were singing Christ has risen again." [11]

On this ever-recurring theme of the kingdom of God, Jesus played sphere-music.

Early in His ministry He portrayed it in a series of little parables, three of which give likenesses of the kingdom's growth. They were spoken in the mood of unshakable confidence—as though He held the future in the hollow of His hand. The hope probably was needed by the disciples! They must have had their seasons of misgiving about this Galilean who sought without benefit of sword, hierarchy, wealth, or learning, to conquer the world! But surely their hope was kindled by these stories. They must have sensed that His hope was sure—not from any "foreknowledge," which would have killed hope (for "hope that is seen is not hope" [12]); but from His soul's invincible surmise and His faith in God.

The Parable of Spontaneous Growth—(The Vitalism of the Kingdom)

"What is a farm but a mute gospel?" asks Emerson. Never more of a gospel than in the mystery of growth! No one knows what a seed really is, or how it is changed into a flower.

9 Mark 10: 15.
10 John 3: 3.
11 John Masefield, "The Everlasting Mercy." ("Collected Poems," The Macmillan Co., 1921.)
12 Romans 8: 24.

Science may talk in polysyllables; the polysyllables only serve to acknowledge a mystery.

> "Flower in the crannied wall,
> I pluck you out of the crannies;
> Hold you here, root and all, in my hand,
> Little flower;—but if I could understand
> What you are, root and all, and all in all,
> I should know what God and man is." [13]

Jesus faced the enigma of growth in brimming gratitude to God who "made every tree to grow." [14]   He confessed our human ignorance: man "knoweth not how" a seed fructifies. Then He declared that the kingdom of God has the spontaneity of a seed.   It possesses a divine vitality, the inherent forces of a self-fashioning life.

A harvest field demands two seasons of human toil—the times of planting and reaping.   After the planting, the farmer can do little until the harvest, except pursue other tasks in patience and trust.   He must be content to "sleep and rise, night and day."   "It is good that a man should hope and quietly wait for the salvation of Jehovah." [15]   Meanwhile inscrutable energies are loosed beneath the ground.   Soon the tender blade appears, then the ear rich in promise, and finally the grain driven by the wind into the waves of a golden sea. Gladly the farmer "thrusts in the sickle."   How have a few handfuls of seed filled his barns with food?   "He knoweth not how."   He is baffled and blessed by the mystery of life— spontaneous, self-ordering, self-developing.   Such a mystery is the kingdom of God.[16]

The kingdom is a *vital force*.   It thrives not primarily by

13 Tennyson's "Flower in the Crannied Wall."
14 Genesis 2: 9.
15 Lamentations 3: 26.
16 The pith of this beautiful and fundamental parable has been sadly overlooked. Some have deemed it only a shorter version of the parable of the Tares.   Bruce, *op. cit.*, [p. 122, 123, wrongly fastens on the phrase, "first the blade," etc., as crucial; while Greswell dismisses the phrase as parenthetical.   It is neither parenthetical nor crucial.   It indicates that the *development* of the seed is also inherent; the germ quickens into a cycle of life.   But Bruce staunchly insists on the slow development of the kingdom as the central teaching, and makes the parable merely a counsel of human patience.   Arnot, *op. cit.*, p. 313, and Trench, *op. cit.*, p. 289, place this exquisite simile on a rack and torture it with such questions as, "Who is symbolized by the 'man'?" and "What is represented by the 'reaping'?"   This, as G. H. Hubbard has said, is as if a man should scrutinize Da Vinci's "The Last Supper" to inquire, "What is the texture of the table-cloth?"   There is an illuminating discussion of this parable in G. H. Hubbard, *op. cit.*, p. 17.

human aid, but by inherent power. A man may dissect the
roots of a flower, and analyse the soil, but the secret of growth
will still elude him. "God giveth the increase." Here is the
antidote for the stern message of the Parable of the Soils. That
story gives warning that a seed may fail of fruitfulness because
of the stubbornness or shallowness of human earth; whereas
this gives assurance that, despite the unreceptive quality of
the soil, the seed has still strong hope of survival. The kingdom
of God is within human life as vitality is in the seed. Given any
reasonable chance, it will grow!

> "Truth is within ourselves; it takes no rise
> From outward things, whate'er you may believe.
> There is an inmost center in us all,
> Where truth abides in fullness; and around,
> Wall upon wall, the gross flesh hems it in,
> This perfect, clear perception—which is truth.
>   . . . and to know
> Rather consists in opening out a way
> Whence the imprisoned splendor may escape,
> Than in effecting entry for a light
> Supposed to be without." [17]

This intrinsic divinity in life is no encouragement to sloth.
It rebukes a feverish trust in human agency. It shames complacent self-praise. But it is an encouragement to hope: "Work
out your own salvation . . . for it is God which worketh in you
both to will and to do of his good pleasure." [18]

The kingdom is also one of *wondrous adaptations*. "The
seed springeth up"—"the earth bringeth forth fruit," because
soil and seed are in harmony. The soil provides the very elements needed for the seed's nourishment, and the seed gives
the soil its opportunity. So, says Jesus, the kingdom fits
human life. The universe shows many instances of mutual
adaptation. The eye and the seen world are made each for
the other. The ear and the realm of sound are in divine
accord. The mind finds the objective world comprehensible;
intellect and phenomena swim in a common medium. (This
latter assumption is the venture of faith of both philosophy
and science, and except they believe they shall not be saved!)

17 Browning, "Paracelsus."
18 Philippians 2: 13.

But of all adaptations, that which most inspires to awe and confidence is the one that Jesus here teaches, namely, that the kingdom of God and our life are native each to the other:

> "Our wills are ours, we know not how:
> Our wills are ours to make them thine." [19]

When a man "comes to himself," he is at home with God.

Again, the kingdom of God moves through *orderly development* to a resistless harvest. The seed appears to have a precarious existence. Buried in the earth, who knows that it will ever survive? Then is seen the miracle of the first shoot piercing its way through the hindering soil; then the ear; then the full grain! Quietly and without haste the moral and spiritual powers resident in human life unfold. The tender green of spring, the pledge of the summer's ripening wheat, the reapers' song, and the bursting granaries are all stored within the seed. Unhurried but sure, the hidden vitality evolves through its full cycle of development. What a history of Puritan achievement was hidden in the seed of the "Mayflower"! What centuries of Christian growth were folded vitally in the seed of the Apostles' band!

So Jesus cast Himself into the rough furrows of our little earth. The blade even now is visible. The harvest song shall one day be raised in joy!—"Except a grain of wheat fall into the earth and die, it abideth by itself alone; but if it die, it beareth much fruit." [20]

The Parable of the Mustard Seed—(The Expansion of the Kingdom)

In two pregnant sentences Jesus traced the lowly origin and mighty climax of the "realm of heaven" among men. The pedants have protested that the mustard seed is not "the least of all the seeds that be in the earth," and that the grown plant can hardly be dignified as a "tree." [21] It is enough to retort

---

19 Tennyson's "In Memoriam," first canto.
20 John 12: 24.
21 The travellers Irby and Mangles were first to suggest that the mustard "tree" of this parable must be identified with the tree called *"khardal"* (Arabic for mustard). See Bruce, *op. cit.*, p. 99. The conjecture, though plausible, is not proven; nor is it necessary.

that proverbially the mustard seed was smallest. As such it found a place in the similes of the rabbis, and in those of Jesus.[22] Moreover, a tree was a favorite Old Testament symbol for the growth and beauty of the "age of gold," or for the might of a foe.[23] The minuteness of the mustard seed compared with its relatively vast growth, made it an excellent figure for the expansion of the kingdom.

The commonwealth of God, Jesus daringly foretold, would increase from tiniest beginnings until "the height thereof reached to heaven, and the sight thereof to the end of all the earth." In Galilee it seemed a speck, too trivial for reckoning. Men did not heed the birth of Jesus. Bethlehem, amid the bustle of the Roman census, talked not of Him, but of the oppression of the conqueror, the movement of the legionaries, the arrival of caravans from Damascus, and the probable yield of harvest—of all the momentous affairs of the world. He found no room in that hubbub of voices, even as He found no room in the inn. Had they been told that salvation was near to them in a little Child, they would have laughed incredulously, and perchance bitterly. A savant with a new learning, or a priest making patriotism blaze with a new fervor, or a Maccabeus to be a living sword against their foes—such a one might be a savior, but not an obscure Babe!

> "They all were looking for a king
>   To slay their foes and lift them high:
> Thou cam'st, a little baby thing
>   That made a woman cry." [24]

Grown to manhood's estate His witness was still negligible. The Roman State and the Jewish Church both frowned upon Him; He was only a Carpenter from a village in an inconsequential and conquered province. In our times the means of travel, together with the telegraph, telephone, and radio, have changed the world into a neighborhood. The ends of the earth are at the end of every street. If Jesus returned in the flesh and we recognized Him (which is doubtful, since His

22 Matthew 17: 20, Luke 17: 6.
23 Daniel 4: 10; Ezekiel 17: 22, 31: 3-9.
24 George MacDonald, "The Holy Thing." ("Poetical Works," E. P. Dutton & Co.)

own land knew Him not), His every word and gesture would
be flashed around the planet. But in the days of His flesh,
His opportunity as compared with that of almost the obscurest
preacher to-day, was "cribbed, cabined, and confined."

His end was a gallows—with only a handful of friends to
mourn His death. How could His faith endure? In very
truth it was "less than the least of all seeds." Yet Jesus was
sure it would survive and grow. Let it be buried deep in the
earth; it would germinate and find the sun! Let it be cast to
the winds; it would gain lodgment in some obscure rock-crevice
and there blossom! Let it be drowned in a sea of blood; red
tides would carry it to the soil of some strange shore! An
incredible optimism—but history has kept troth with Him.
The microscopic seed is now a plant overtopping all others in
the planet-garden.

We are victimized by bigness. Our banks claim their millions in deposits. Our buildings, like the tower of Babel, must
"reach unto heaven" and "make us a name." Every village
not pathetically passé is eager to disfigure its beauty with factories. Every city not hopelessly moribund is ambitious to
double its population. Meanwhile, in our crass chamber-of-
commerce philosophies, we ignore the leading fact that a bigger
city does not therefore breed better people. Even the Church
brings forth "movements" which flourish for a day like a green
bay tree and then die, having printer's ink for sap and being
stricken by the blight of statistics.

Science has lately shown us "the infinitude of the little."
A drop of water is a Venice with tides of traffic flowing
through its streets. A drop of blood is a battle ground with
marshalled hosts of red and white corpuscles. An atom is not
the ultimate smallest particle, but a universe with worlds weav-
ing amazing patterns in its fields of space. . . .

Significantly Jesus spoke often of "the infinitude of the little"—the grain of mustard seed, the cup of cold water, the
one talent, the widow's mite, the lost coin, and the kindness
done unto "one of these least." Jesus craved the peace of the
whole world as the fruit of His travail; but He knew what we
forget—that spread of branch and towering loveliness depend
on the vitality of the seed. A vital seed, however minute, will

produce its tree, with foliage to give shelter to both man and
bird. Some day we shall learn His mind and rest our hopes on
God's tiny seeds—this man's utter consecration; that mother's
prayer; this girl's joy, "as white as river sand"; that boy's
imagination, glorious with ideals unfurled like banners! For
of such is the tree of the kingdom of heaven.

The Parable of the Leaven—(The Permeating Influence of the Kingdom)

This parable has suffered many offences at the hands of the
allegorizers. Trench,[25] following commentators as early as
Jerome, gives symbolic meaning to the "three measures of
meal." They represent the three parts of the ancient world;
or body, mind, and spirit,—the three elements of human life;
or the race descended from the three sons of Noah. Even
Arnot [26] allows that these analogies "are entitled to a respectful
hearing"; and so discriminating a mind as Dr. Bruce [27] finds it
"hard to reconcile ourselves to such conclusions" as would com-
pel us to forego these "tempting" comparisons. Arnot takes
sharp issue, however, with those who contend that the "woman"
in the parable represents the Holy Spirit or the Church.[28] For
that word of protest we may be thankful! Allegorizing of the
parables dies a stubborn death.

Three measures were an ephah of flour, the amount of a
customary baking. The virtue of the parable is that it is at
once homey and apt—so homey that every peasant woman
listening to Jesus would understand it, and so apt that no one
would miss a truth so fitly pictured. The kingdom of God is
a permeating and transforming influence; it conquers the life
of mankind as leaven subdues dough.[29]

Leaven is a *silent agency*. So is the kingdom of God.

25 *Op. cit.*, p. 119.
26 *Op. cit.*, p. 113.
27 *Op. cit.*, p. 110.
28 He adds the pungent and timely comment: ". . . while I endeavor to keep my
mind open for everything that the Scriptures bring to the Church, I am disposed
to shut the door hard against everything that I suspect the Church is bringing to
the Scriptures." Arnot, *op. cit.*, p. 144. See also Trench, *op. cit.*, p. 119.
29 That leaven is ordinarily used, even by Jesus, as a symbol of evil influence
(Matthew 16: 6, I Corinthians 5: 7, Galatians 5: 9) need not debar us from the
interpretation which is explicit in this parable.

Shrewd ears would be required to detect leaven busy at its task. No one overhears a seed in process of germination. Victimized by bigness, we have succumbed also to the noisy and the obtrusive. Our music is a strident frenzy. Our art is lurid and bizarre. Notoriety feasts in plenty; reputation is a beggar at the gates. News shrieks from the public press, and the din of our cities is like bedlam broken loose. A raucous age has discovered, and bequeathed to posterity as an eternal truth, that "it pays to advertise."

Jesus said His kingdom is like leaven. His followers are the "salt of the earth," "the light of the world." He did not "strive or cry aloud," nor did "any one hear his voice in the streets." [30]   Leaven, salt, light, are silent forces—as are all God's mightiest powers. The stars do not chatter on their orbits. The armies of spring blow no trumpets as they march with leafy banners down the furrowed fields. Human love holds deepest converse when the clumsy tongue is still. The kingdom comes not in the boisterous tumult of our doings, or in the fever of our excitements: "Be still and know that I am God." [31]

Leaven is *invisible and inward*. So is the kingdom of God. It "cometh not with observation." [32]   It has no tariff-laws or trade returns. Its thrones are not propped on bayonets. Its stock is not quoted on Exchange. Its coming is not heralded in the press. Its fortunes are not debated in senates and parliaments. Its advance is not registered in church statistics, nor do denominations mark its bounds. It is invisible and inward, like honor, pity, and courage. These last become articulate in words and splendid in deeds, and without words and deeds they would be of scant worth; nevertheless, words and deeds are but the "meal." Honor, pity, courage, are the invisible leaven which make of words and deeds that living bread by which mankind is truly fed.

Leaven works *by contagion* "until the whole is leavened." So does the kingdom of God. "One loving heart sets another on fire." When Jesus came from His wilderness of temptation

30 Matthew 12: 19.
31 Psalm 46: 10.
32 Luke 17: 20.

to win the world to God, He began that transcendent task by talking to two men on a country road [33]—"and they abode with him that day." Later He chose twelve "that they might be with him"; [34] and lavished on them His full spirit, that they in turn might spread the contagion of the kingdom. So it came to pass. Andrew found Peter, and Philip found Nathanael. Jesus did not meet many people, but "as many as touched him were made whole." [35] That Divine health still spreads. Words which He flung away on sadly blemished people like the woman of Samaria, or on people of fitful courage like Nicodemus, shine with an ever-growing luster; not primarily because of the words themselves, but because *He* was a living radiance. The spirit of the kingdom broadens on the world like light, preserves and adds savor like salt, permeates and transforms like leaven.

How far the leaven has penetrated who can tell? Many who do not name His name implicitly confess His benign mastery. Many who deny or forget Him live under freedoms and ameliorations that He has given. Hospitals are but one visible token of His spreading influence. The process will continue until the whole is leavened—our business, churches, politics, and pleasures. There is a pathetic mustering of excuses evident in such phrases as "business is business," "competition is the rule of life," "self-preservation is the first law" (as though it were therefore the last law or the best law!). There are specious pleas against the cooperative venture of the nations into goodwill,—an adventure which must be made, and at risk, if history is to be better than a recurrent slaughter-house. But these excuses and unworthy pleas are but the acknowledgment that the leaven is at work! The presence of Jesus is proving awkward. His counsels are too difficult, we say; but their loveliness haunts us. His way is too hard; but we cannot forget its austere glory. Soon or late we must come to terms with Him—or suffer torment. "For the kingdom of God is like leaven"—"until the whole is leavened."

33 John 1: 39.
34 Mark 3: 14.
35 Mark 6: 56.

CHAPTER III

SIMILITUDES OF THE KINGDOM (II)

THE PARABLE OF THE HIDDEN TREASURE

"The kingdom of heaven is like unto a treasure hidden in the field; which a man found, and hid; and in his joy he goeth and selleth all that he hath, and buyeth that field." *(Matthew* 13:44)

THE PARABLE OF THE PEARL OF GREAT PRICE

"Again, the kingdom of heaven is like unto a man that is a merchant-man seeking goodly pearls: and having found one pearl of great price, he went and sold all that he had, and bought it."

(Matthew 13:45, 46)

THE PARABLE OF THE DRAGNET

"Again, the kingdom of heaven is like unto a net, that was cast into the sea, and gathered of every kind: which, when it was filled, they drew up on the beach; and they sat down, and gathered the good into vessels, but the bad they cast away. So shall it be in the end of the world: the angels shall come forth, and sever the wicked from among the righteous, and shall cast them into the furnace of fire: there shall be the weeping and the gnashing of teeth." *(Matthew* 13:47-50)

SIMILITUDES OF THE KINGDOM (II)
THE KINGDOM—A TREASURE
AND A TESTING

The Parable of the Hidden Treasure
The Parable of the Pearl of Great Price
The Parable of the Dragnet

The stories of the treasure and the pearl are twin parables with likenesses so evident that they cannot deny the blood bond. Yet, as with twin children, each is markedly individual. The resemblances and the differences can best be shown as they are considered in company. The little known parable of the dragnet forms their rather natural sequel.

The Parables of the Hidden Treasure and the Pearl of Great Price

The kingdom of God is to rule both man and mankind. It is both a personal good and a social order. The parables discussed in the last chapter seem to emphasize the wider reference. These two stress the worth of the kingdom to the individual. If the leaven influences the "whole lump" and the tree gives shade to the world, the treasure is primarily a personal possession. Though latterly the "social Gospel" has been proclaimed as the sorely needed corrective of a rampant individualism in religion, it remains inevitably true that the determinative unit of human life is a person. *"A man* shall be as a hiding place from the wind. . . ."[1]

The purpose of both stories is to depict the surpassing worth of the kingdom of God. Every detail converges on this focal truth.[2] The joy of the man finding hidden wealth, his tremu-

1 Isaiah 32: 2.
2 G. H. Hubbard, *op. cit.*, p. 86, maintains that the two parables are sharply distinct in their teaching, that of the Treasure depicting the *value* of character, and

lous fear lest his secret cannot be kept, his eagerness to purchase "that field" reckless of the cost—each item quickens our
sense of the value of the treasure. The morality of the purchase has been called in question, because the original owner
of the field was left in ignorance as to its real value.[3] The
question is irrelevant. Jesus is not here discussing a business
ethic, or He would not have instanced a transaction tinged with
unscrupulous dealing, except to condemn it. He is approving,
rather, the man's instant appreciation of supreme worth when
it is found.

So with the Parable of the Pearl, every circumstance—the
persistent search of the pearl-collector, his passion for the
"one pearl," his willingness to part with everything for the
sake of it—serves to throw the preciousness of the pearl into
bold relief. The kingdom of God is the ultimate blessing whose
glory makes all other riches "of nothing worth."

There is tingling excitement, as Jesus well knew, in a story
of treasure-trove. Who has read of Long John Silver and
Treasure Island without a romantic thrill? In Palestine the
discovery of concealed riches was not unlikely. For centuries
life and property had been insecure in a land which was the
battlefield of the ancient world. Under a threatened inroad
of some foe, it was natural that a man should bury his wealth
in the ground. That was his safest bank. Through death, or
some other untoward happening, buried treasure was not always
reclaimed. Men were known in the time of Jesus to forsake
their learning or trade to become treasure-hunters,[4] and to this

that of the Pearl the *cost* of character. He bases the contention on the fact that
the one parable says, "The kingdom of heaven is like unto a treasure . . ." and
the other, "The kingdom of heaven is like unto a man. . . ." But sound exegesis
cannot be built merely on arrangement of words or on accidents of grammar. This
author does not always adhere to the rule he here observes. Of the parable which
begins: "The kingdom of heaven is like unto a net . . ." he says: "It is rather the
picture as a whole, the casting, the gathering, the separating, as a continuous action,
that is designed to represent something with regard to the kingdom of heaven."
(*Op. cit.*, p. 103.) This comment suggests a much sounder canon of interpretation.
A friend once wisely remarked to me that it would help to the understanding of
the parables, and especially of those in Matthew 13, if there could be a colon
printed after the word "unto"—"The kingdom of heaven is like unto:", for then
the reader would be led in search of the central impact of the parable. Arnot has
convincingly argued (*op. cit.*, p. 169, 170) that this central impact "must be determined otherwise than by the mere juxtaposition of the clauses."

3 The question of the morality of some of the characters in the parables comes
to its sharpest point in the Parable of the Unjust Steward, and is there discussed.
See p. 116.

4 See the lovely phrase in Proverbs 2: 4, and the poignant phrase in Job 3: 21.

day excavators in Palestine report the hostility of villagers who suspect that they have knowledge of hidden wealth. Jesus pictures a man finding concealed treasure. The supposition is that he came upon it by accident. Perhaps he was a ploughman. Faithfully trudging the weary furrows, he one day—a never-to-be-forgotten day—drove his ploughshare into the lid of a sunken chest. With quivering hand he uncovered his "find"—gold and gems beyond his wildest dream! Then he glanced around furtively: what if some one had seen? There was nobody in sight! With nervous fingers he hid his treasure again, and hurried home to buy the field!

The Parable of the Pearl is equally dramatic. A diamond is our stone of greatest value, but in Christ's day it was so rare and costly that it had little place in popular thought. The pearl, however, was well known and everywhere admired.[5] Possibly Jesus as a boy had seen traders, in the caravans that passed through Galilee, proudly exhibiting their precious stones. The ancients were willing to pay fabulous prices for "goodly pearls." Cleopatra had two valued each at $400,000. The "merchantman" of the parable was a pearl collector, a connoisseur, rather than a mere tradesman. His interest was not mercenary; the lovely jewel had become his passion. The name also suggests one who travelled far, perhaps around the Persian Gulf and to fabled India. There was always the exhilarating chance that some day a diver or a jeweller might confront him with the pearl of pearls. Nay, the chance befell! What now should he do? Return home; sell every pearl he possessed, and house, and lands! Not that his pearls were poor—he had never dealt in paste; but they seemed poor indeed beside the sheen, the purity, the opalescent glory of this surpassing jewel. So he bought the pearl of great price and was satisfied.

Thus far the stories offer an identical teaching. There is in life a *summum bonum*—a joy awaiting discovery! Jesus calls it the kingdom of God—one man's utter consecration to God, a commonwealth of men animated through and through by the

5 See Bruce, *op. cit.*, pp. 72, 73. Those who saw the crowd which constantly thronged the case in the Wembley Exhibition, London, England, to see replicas of famous diamonds found in South Africa, can testify to the lure of celebrated jewels.

Christ-spirit. This is the ultimate and ineffable blessing; it is like sudden treasure, like the pearl of pearls!

Having exalted that *summum bonum,* the stories then diverge to show "the varieties of religious experience." One man stumbled upon his joy; the other discovered the pearl by an unremitting quest.

There are those of whom God says: "I was found of them that sought me not." [6] There are those whom life has used so harshly that they have surrendered the quest, though hungry in soul. The days have been "a fury slinging flame"; or the struggle for bread has been so hard, that they have had neither hope nor heart for the struggle to reach a heaven on earth. . . . There are other people who have made shipwreck of conscience. Once they were adventurers in the quest for God. Then came the dark, irreparable lapse. They have learned their lesson: the folly is outgrown; but splendid dedication is no longer possible. There must be instead a quiet trudging through the years until the light fades. . . . Others, again, are disillusioned. In their youth the ideal beckoned; but stars (they found) have small chance in the light of common day. A selfish world mocks the stars. Youth's ideals are well enough in youth, but stern facts gainsay them. All that a man can do is to make truce with the soul's discontent, and face the routine of "to-morrow and to-morrow" with conscience and courage.

God finds these faithful ones who cannot find Him. Therefore the ploughman in that humdrum field, of which he knew every clod, stumbled on hidden treasure! Therefore faithful shepherds heard the angels' song, and the very stars that had been the steadfast sentinels of their weary vigil became heralds blowing trumpets of goodwill "from the hid battlements of eternity." Therefore the kingdom surprised Nathanael—a good man and true, in whom there was "no guile," but who was quite sure that nothing divine could come from Nazareth! —with the promise that he should "see angels ascending and descending upon the Son of man." [7]

The "merchantman," on the contrary, never surrendered the

6 Romans 10: 20, quoting Isaiah 65: 1.
7 John 1: 43-50.

quest. Many "goodly pearls" were his, but he sought persistently the best pearl. On what voyages of sense and thought such seeking souls embark! The adventure is well told in that old story of the Holy Grail. One knight, riding on the quest, came to a singing brook, deep meadows, and laden fruit trees. But even as he ate the fruit it turned to dust . . . for no feeding of the flesh could still his deepest hunger. Riding on, he saw a home, its open door a promised welcome, and in the door a woman standing, her eyes innocent and kind, "and all her bearing gracious." Surely the love of woman and the sweet shelter of home are his heart's desire!

> ". . . But when I touched her, lo! she too,
> Fell into dust and nothing, and the house
> Became no better than a broken shed. . . ." [8]

His soul's craving all unsatisfied, he rode on again, and found a warrior clad in golden armor. But he also turned to dust . . . for pride of battle never answers to man's profoundest cry. At last, in the long quest, he saw a city on a hill, its spires piercing heaven, and at its gates a great throng shouting acclaim as he climbed the slope. Surely civic honor, the esteem and affection of fellowmen, is his journey's end. But when he reached the crest there was neither city, man, "nor any voice," so that he cried in grief,

> "Lo, if I find the Holy Grail itself
> And touch it, it will crumble into dust." [8]

"Goodly pearls" of home, food, friendship, and rightful fame leave the soul still restless and ill-content. Ever and anon comes a stinging realization that life is incomplete. Then the "merchantman" goes seeking, seeking a power, an enrichment, a forgiveness, a pearl of final joy. If, for some, the kingdom is flashed like a treasure on unexpectant eyes, others find it as the rich reward of an unwearied quest.

Now the lines of the two parables again unite. Though there are various ways of finding, there is only one way of entering

[8] Tennyson's "The Holy Grail" ("The Idylls of the King").

into full possession. The finder of treasure sold everything
and bought the field; the merchantman bartered his whole collection of "goodly pearls," together with his house and lands,
for the pearl of great price. In both cases the transaction (so
we are told or left directly to infer) was made in abandon of
joy.

The question, "How can the kingdom of God be at once a
gift of heaven's grace and a purchase by man?", which has
been raised by many commentators, betrays a failure to appre-
ciate the purpose of the parables. The index finger of both
stories points to the exceeding worth of the kingdom. Its
value is so far beyond all reckoning that at any cost of purchase it is still a gift. The "buying" is indescribable good fortune, the "sacrifice" is joy, the "duty" is sheer exhilaration; for
the kingdom has driven irksomeness from the world. The
disciples "left all and followed" eagerly. Paul yielded up without regret his pride of Pharisaic birth and learning: "But what
things were gain to me these I counted loss for Christ." [9]
Augustine parted gladly with his darling sins: . . . "what I
feared to be parted from was now a joy to surrender. For
Thou didst cast them forth from me, Thou true and high
sweetness. Thou didst cast them forth, and in their place didst
enter in Thyself, sweeter than all pleasure." [10] These men
found the kingdom. It rolled away the intolerable load of
their sins; it quickened and fulfilled their soul's aspiring; it
was a life eternal in the midst of time. For such a treasure
who would not impetuously abandon every lower good?—

> "Thou hope of every contrite heart,
>   Thou joy of all the meek,
> To those who fall how kind Thou art,
>   How good to those who seek.

> "But what to those who find? Ah, this
>   Nor tongue nor pen can show!
> The love of Jesus, what it is
>   None but His loved ones know." [11]

Those who saw the kingdom in His face became reckless of

9 Philippians 3: 7.
10 Augustine, "Confessions," ix: 1.
11 The hymn "Jesus, the Very Thought of Thee," by Bernard of Clairvaux, translated by Edward Caswall.

SIMILITUDES OF THE KINGDOM

loss, that they might "know him, and the power of his resurrection, and the fellowship of his sufferings. . . ." [12]

But if the literal mind, still pestering, asks: "Then the 'living water' is not the 'gift of God,' but must be bought by human energy?"; if these lovely stories cannot be saved from that musty and singularly fictitious controversy of "faith" and "works," the answer must be made as patiently as possible: "Salvation, however you may like the fact, is both a gift and a purchase—and trying to resolve a paradox is as futile as trying to catch the light." For we live in a paradox. An opportunity is a gift, as the very word implies; but it must be "improved," and Paul wisely counsels us to buy it. [13] The fertility of a field is a gift, but it must be purchased by man's labor. A noble book is a gift—the distillate of wisdom from experience; but before we can make it ours we must expend far more than time for its reading. We must "sell" other books, for instance; for, as Ruskin said, "If I read this book I cannot read that book." A worthless treasure is a contradiction in terms; and if character is not to be a topsy-turvydom more insane (and far less happy) than any Alice found in Wonderland, the rule must hold that when one ideal is supreme other ideals shall serve it, and find their life in its life.

The surpassing worth of the kingdom of God—have we ourselves not known it? One day we stumbled on our treasure. It surprised us in the splendor of duty, or in the radiance of a child. One day we saw the Face of Jesus, and knew in Him the "Holy Grail" of our long quest. We knew that other wealth is not to be compared with the unsearchable riches of His kingdom. But those who had not seen praised our "goodly pearls" of comfort, pleasure, learning; so we tarried on the very threshold of a passionate devotion. Why will we not trust our soul's conviction? The unspeakable gift is ours; why will we not sell all in scorn of trivial consequence?

> "It was my duty to have loved the highest;
> It surely was my pleasure had I seen:
> It would have been my profit had I known:
> We needs must love the highest when we see it." [14]

12 Philippians 3: 10.
13 Ephesians 5: 16.
14 Tennyson, "Guinevere" ("The Idylls of the King").

"Where your treasure is, there will your heart be also." [15]   The
kingdom of God flashes on weary eyes like treasure unsur-
passed; or is given, a priceless pearl of reward, to all who
truly seek.

The Parable of the Dragnet

The similitudes considered in this and the preceding chapter
show the kingdom under aspects of favor—its spontaneous
growth from vital resource, its expansion from a small seed to
a sheltering tree, its leavening health, and its exceeding worth.
The sequence of little parables attains completion (and not
by accident, we think, but by the intention of the redactor) in
this story which represents the kingdom as a standard and
testing.   The last parables hinted that the *summum bonum* is,
in one aspect, divisive.   It lays the sword of an alternative
across a man's life, compelling him to choose between lesser
riches and the highest wealth.   That truth now becomes explicit; the realm of heaven is like a net whereby the good and
bad are unerringly brought to judgment, and parted, "the one
on the right hand and the other on the left." [16]   Thus the spec-
trum of His teaching has colors dark and bright.   He brings
both rigor and hope.

The people who lived in the villages around the lake of
Galilee had often seen the drama of the dragnet.   At a little
distance from the shore the fishing-boats would "cast" the net.
Its lower edge was weighted so as to trail on the bed of the
lake, and its upper edge fastened to floats.   As it was dragged,
it became an advancing wall more and more circular in shape
(the ends being hauled towards the shore and ever closer together), until at length it rested a prison-mesh upon the beach.
See the squirming, leaping mass of fishes!   See the flash of sunlight on their iridescent scales!   Soon the fisher-folk, sitting
on the sand, gather the good fishes into vessels and fling away
those that are worthless for food.   Then the net is once more
cast into the sea.

Jesus had observant eyes, a wholesome admiration for honest
human toil, and a mind quick to detect the truth of heaven

15 Luke 12: 34.
16 Matthew 25: 33.

through the forms of earth. There is no need to seek the special significance of "net," "sea," "beach"; [17] or to belabor the parable into precise analogies. Its teaching is this: the kingdom of God gathers men irresistibly to a judgment and sifts them by its own high ethic. The story thus becomes an antidote to the Parable of the Tares which counsels patience in the presence of badness. Here we are assured that the blemish of badness is not allowed to persist, and that goodness is not cheated of its bright perfection.

The figure is startling in its fitness. Unless a net is cast, some criterion launched, character is not brought to judgment: "Sin is not imputed when there is no law." [18] The Pharisees once asked Jesus: "Are we also blind?" The reply was incisive: "If ye were blind, ye would have no sin: but now ye say, We see: your sin remaineth." [19] A tiger may slay a child and do no wrong, but a man committing such a deed is not innocent; for the man has within him a court which never adjourns, whereas a tiger's only "right" is that he must eat. In the absence of a moral standard and power to recognize it, right and wrong have no meaning. The story of the Garden of Eden and the Forbidden Tree is a searchingly true account (as any one can testify who has consulted the memory of his own transition from the un-moral to the knowledge of good and evil) of the way in which the "net," a new norm of right, was cast into the undifferentiated "sea" of Adam's innocence to gather him to a judgment.

Jesus tells us that the realm of heaven is such a net. In His time good character had lost its bold distinction. The lines of right and wrong were blurred. "Right" in respect of the Sabbath was the meticulous observance, as "wrong" was the ignoring, of certain multiplied, petty prescriptions of the rabbinical law. "Right" in regard to filial duty could be achieved and "wrong" avoided (however grossly the ancient law "Honor thy father and mother" might be transgressed) by the parroting of a shibboleth: "It is Korban." [20] Religious virtue was concerned with prayers ostentatiously spoken in the streets,

17 See Trench, *op. cit.*, p. 138.
18 Romans 5: 13.
19 John 9: 40, 41.
20 Mark 7: 11.

with the payment of tithes and the keeping of fasts—with the whitening of the outside of the sepulcher, though the inside might be "full of dead men's bones and all uncleanness." [21] Thus men went groping "through the feeble twilight" of the world, "forging a life-long trouble" for themselves by taking false for true and true for false. They lacked the loadstone to determine enduring values. Their need was for some new Mt. Sinai of inescapable authority.

Then Jesus came, the "divinest symbol" of that kingdom which He preached. He was a living conscience. Men awoke to a new knowledge of right and wrong. The ancient Law, forgotten in its enfeebled descendant of scribal interpretations, was revived and transcended. Never spoke Mt. Sinai with more Divine finality: "Ye have heard that it was said by them of old time . . . but I say unto you." [22] His words carried the sanction of a universal law, and the world found itself obliged to adjust itself to His decrees or perish. "Whence hath this man this wisdom?" [23] His authority abides. The only possibility of a man remaining neutral in regard to Jesus is that he shall dismiss Him completely from thought. It is not an easy dismissal, for as of old He enters "the door being shut." He makes wrong apparent (how the coarse indulgence of a Herod, the shuffling cowardice of a Pilate, the scheming ambition of a Caiaphas are revealed in His light!), and goodness He makes positive and winsome. Life cannot remain unchanged in His presence. Rejection of Him hardens the soul; acceptance bestows new peace. What a squirming within the net of judgment! Existing doctrine did not take kindly to His challenge. Existing institutions recognized in Him a threat to their life. Men and women shrank from His ruthless revealing of their hidden motives. . . .

"There came a man, whence, none could tell,
    Bearing a touchstone in his hand;
And tested all things in the land,
    By its unerring spell.

21 Matthew 23: 27.
22 Matthew 5: 33, 34.
23 Matthew 13: 54.

"And lo, what sudden changes smote
   The fair to foul, the foul to fair!
Purple nor ermine did he spare
   Nor scorn the dusty coat.

"Of heirloom jewels prized so much
   Many were changed to chips and clods,
And even statues of the gods
   Crumbled beneath its touch.

"Then angrily the people cried,
   'The loss outweighs the profit far,
Our goods suffice us as they are,
   We will not have them tried.'

"But though they slew him with a sword
   And in a fire his touchstone burned,
Its doings could not be o'erturned,
   Its undoings restored." [24]

The net is flung on a wide sea without regard to creed, caste or clime: "God is no respecter of persons: but in every nation he that feareth him, and worketh righteousness, is accepted with him." [25]   None can escape those meshes, and the line of separation drawn across the "catch" over-passes all other lines. It is not now a question of a man's creed, either of smug orthodoxy or dazzling heterodoxy; or of his punctilious obedience to the letter of a law.   It is not now a question of a man's birth, even though he be a child of Abraham; or of his outward act, save as that is the reflection of his motives.   "They gathered the *good* into vessels, but cast the *bad* away!"   Such is the testing which proceeds deliberately, inexorably: "Does this life reveal a living and compassionate ethic?   Is it humane after the high manner of Jesus?"   This was the criterion applied by prophets of old,[26] but in Jesus it became inescapable.   He was its embodiment, "Inasmuch as ye have done it unto one of the least of these my brethren, ye have done it unto me." [27]

"And the choice goes on forever twixt that darkness and that light," says Russell Lowell.   The parable assigns the testing

24 Quoted in Hastings, "Great Texts of the Bible," St. Luke, p. 71.
25 Acts 10: 34, 35.
26 See, for example, Micah 6: 6-8.
27 Matthew 25: 40.   The separation above described raises certain questions: Is character either black or white, or is it one of innumerable shades of grey?   Can the division be made with such finality?   The standard of judgment here posited is also beset with problems: Is philanthropy a substitute for vital faith?   And what of the "acknowledgment of God in Christ"?   These questions and problems are discussed in connection with the Parable of the Last Judgment.   See p. 255 ff.

and the separation to the shores of another world; but there is strong reason to believe that the verses in question (Matthew 13:49, 50) were not originally part of the story but were transferred to it by the redactor from another setting,[28] possibly from the Parable of the Tares. In any event, some persistent fallibility in us ever refers judgment to the future and ignores the cruciality of the present.[29] John the Baptist had truer insight when he cried: *"Now* is the axe laid at the root of the trees."[30] *Now* we are in the midst of life. Hereafter life may be more intense (and the judgment therefore more searching), but the axioms of character which will hold then hold now. Life in that realm of clearer seeing will not be inconsistent with life in this realm of dimmer sight. *Now* we are in the midst of life. To-day is judgment day. This very hour the scales are set, the books opened and the verdict read. The kingdom of God is about us now, nor can we escape its invisible meshes. So urgent are our swiftly passing moments that our present character is in itself the condemnation or approval of all our past life. Now the net is being drawn. Now selfishness is its own curse and love its own blessing. Now deceit sows its own darkness and honor springs up a harvest of light. Of those whose happy life can stand before the testing of the kingdom, there is none "who shall not receive manifold more in *this present time,* and in the world to come life everlasting."[31]

28 See G. H. Box, "Century Bible," pp. 228, 230 (Matthew), who quotes so sound and careful an exegete as Dr. Denney.
29 Thus Arnot, *op. cit.,* p. 170: "The net . . . drawing them . . . towards the boundary of this life and over it into another" where "ministering spirits, on the lip of eternity that lies nearest time, receive them and separate the good from the evil."
30 Matthew 3: 10.
31 Luke 18: 30.

CHAPTER IV

THE RESPONSIBILITY OF HEARING

THE PARABLE OF THE SOILS

"And he spake to them many things in parables, saying, Behold, the sower went forth to sow; and as he sowed, some seeds fell by the way side, and the birds came and devoured them: and others fell upon the rocky places, where they had not much earth: and straightway they sprang up, because they had no deepness of earth: and when the sun was risen, they were scorched; and because they had no root, they withered away. And others fell upon the thorns; and the thorns grew up and choked them: and others fell upon the ground, and yielded fruit, some a hundredfold, some sixty, some thirty. He that hath ears, let him hear. Hear then ye the parable of the sower. When any one heareth the word of the kingdom, and understandeth it not, then cometh the evil one, and snatcheth away that which hath been sown in his heart. This is he that was sown by the way side. And he that was sown upon the rocky places, this is he that heareth the word, and straightway with joy receiveth it; yet hath he not root in himself, but endureth for a while; and when tribulation or persecution ariseth because of the word, straightway he stumbleth. And he that was sown among the thorns, this is he that heareth the word, and the care of the world, and the deceitfulness of riches, choke the word, and he becometh unfruitful. And he that was sown upon the good ground this is he that heareth the word, and understandeth it; who verily beareth fruit, and bringeth forth, some a hundredfold, some sixty, some thirty."

(Matthew 13 : 3-9, 18-23)

(Parallel passages: Mark 4 : 2-8, 13-20; *Luke* 8 : 4-8, 11-15)

THE RESPONSIBILITY OF HEARING

The Parable of the Soils

The first word of this story challenges attention—"Hearken!" The last word repeats the challenge—"He that hath ears to hear, let him hear." Hearing is an urgent business. We assume that because initiative is with the speaker a message controls the hearer. But the parts may be reversed: the hearer may control the message. An appeal, even the appeal of Jesus, may be frustrated by unreceptiveness. This is the salient truth of the parable and the ground of its terse counsel: "Take heed, therefore, how ye hear."

The story is autobiography, a transcript of the experience of Jesus. Probably He did not expect swift victory to crown His proclamation of the kingdom, but it is certain that He did not expect such checks and reverses as befell Him. Sometimes His disillusion is plain to see, as when "He marvelled because of their unbelief." [1] Baffled hope [2] cries aloud in the doom He pronounced on the Cities of the Lake: "Woe unto thee, Bethsaida! for if the mighty works which were done in you had been done in Tyre and Sidon, they would have repented long ago in sackcloth and ashes." [3] It was clear to Him that, if the kingdom was to reach full harvest, His hearers must be quickened into self-examination. Hence a parable which is strictly not a parable of the Sower, nor of the Seed, but rather a Parable of the Soils. [4]

1 Mark 6: 6.
2 George Murray, *op. cit.*, pp. 219, 220, interprets this parable as a message of hope. The failures indicated are only "incidents—shadings in the picture." The mass of the seed "succeeded—in fact was marvellously multiplied." It is an interesting interpretation, but the parable does not appear to justify it, and the Gospels' frequent references to the (at least temporary) defeat of Jesus' expectations make it still more untenable. The hope of Jesus remained but He did not blink the stern facts of an experience which was not free from disappointment.
3 Matthew 11: 21.
4 It is difficult to hold with Bruce, *op. cit.*, p. 20, and others that this is chronologically first of the parables, and that previously Jesus had spoken in explicit state-

The "sower" is any sower of truth, but primarily Jesus.[5] The title well befits Him. Pioneers such as Abraham and Moses had cut away the tangled growths from Jewish soil, prophets had driven through it the ploughshare of teaching sternly kind, and the alternating storm and shine of national experience had weathered it. Now Jesus came to sow the seed. A lonely Figure, for the sower is always lonely! The reaper has comradeship and the harvest-song, but the sower's task is solitary. Theophile Gautier looked at Millet's famous picture, "The Sower," and said: "With a superb gesture he who has nothing scatters far and wide the bread of the future." So it might be said of Jesus. But the parable does not primarily concern the Sower.

Nor is its main emphasis upon the "word of the kingdom" which, Jesus tells us, is the seed. That symbol likewise is inspired and it is not surprising that Jesus often used it. His simple teaching about God, duty, death and life seemed as precarious as seed; but it was vital, as history has shown. Like seed it has produced more seed from its own growth. Beginning in Galilee it has come to harvest in every land. Yet, though the figure is so apt, the parable is not about the seed.

It is about the soil of human understanding and response into which the teaching falls. "And there were gathered unto him great multitudes"—there was the soil! Why had they come? Some came from curiosity—idle followers of the crowd. Some came from self-seeking motives—it might be profitable to cultivate the company of this seven days' wonder. Some came as revolutionaries—to make Him king, to use Him as a flag of revolt or a party cry. Some came in quick but shallow enthusiasm, others in deep longing, and others they knew not why. How would they receive His words? As variously as the soil of a Galilean hillside receives the seed! Not in vain had He watched the sower tramping his furrows.

ment, resorting to parables only because of the spiritual blindness of His hearers. A teaching method of which Jesus is so divinely a Master cannot have been a patch on a failure and for Jesus to have neglected the accepted medium of instruction (see p. xiv) would have invited misunderstanding. But this parable, as its mood and message indicate, does undoubtedly mark a turning-point in His ministry.
[5] In the words "the sower" the article is generic and means any typical sower. But if the parable is autobiographical the immediate reference would be to Jesus. Wellhausen goes so far as to say, "Jesus is not so much teaching here as reflecting aloud upon the results of His teaching."

He would tell the multitudes a story about themselves. Being under no illusions (brave Son of Fact!) He would tell them just what chance His teaching would have with them, and why in some of them it would find no lodgment. "And he spake many things . . . saying, Behold, a sower went forth to sow. . . ."

By some perversity we are quick to blame the sower or the seed and correspondingly slow to blame the soil. The factors of initiative are cankered, so our hasty accusation runs, while the factors of receptiveness are incorruptible. Thus we condemn our political or social leaders when the fault may be in their followers. "Every man," said Russell Lowell, "is a prisoner of his date"; and every leader, we might add, is a prisoner of the visionless sloth of those whom he would rally to his cause. Not that the light of a great man can be utterly quenched: he comes bearing divine fire. He cannot be explained in mundane terms: the sky of heaven's intention opens to let him through. Yet his message may be maimed, his achievement circumscribed, by a stiff-necked generation. "He did not many mighty works there because of their unbelief." [6] Similarly we blame the institution rather than the man. We have keen eyes to discover grievous faults in old forms of government, but blind eyes for faults within the governed. Establishing with enthusiasm a new city charter, but leaving unimproved the old quality of citizenship, we are pained at our failure to induce forthwith a heaven on earth. We can detect innumerable flaws in the institution of marriage, but few in married people. Therefore, we cry, "Away with marriage," or, if our laws miscarry in justice, "Away with laws." A man suffering from indigestion might as wisely cry, "Away with food."

But our bitterest quarrel is with the prophet and his message, and our imperturbable complacence is with the hearer. If the prophet would only speak vigorously for this "cause" or strike lusty blows at that corruption!—by which we mean that religion must become an economic crusade, and be robbed of its essential mysticism. Or if the prophet would "only stick to

6 Matthew 13: 58.

the gospel"!—by which we mean that he must take an innocuous orthodoxy for an airing every Sunday, that religion must never be *applied* religion, and that in particular, it must never come within telescopic range of modern business or pleasure. If only the prophet were a different man and his message a different message!—on that text, as our magazines (their sensitive finger meanwhile on the pulse of circulation) are well aware, we are always glad to hear a sermon.

Let the sins of the prophets and the impoverishment of the message be frankly admitted. The genuine prophet, conscious of unworthiness, will be first to make confession. But this fact remains: There was once a Messenger who spake "as man never spake" the words of eternal life—and they nailed Him to a cross! The fault then was not in the Factor of initiative, but in the factor of response; not in the Sower or the seed, but in the soil. The hearer was to blame: "Neither will they be persuaded, if one rose from the dead." [7]

Mark, therefore, the interpretation: [8] "Some seed fell by the wayside"—at the edge of the beaten track. There it found no lodgment. It rolled away before the wind. Birds came and gathered it at will. Seed sown on bare stone would have almost as good a chance to fructify. There are lives that are a beaten track!—hardened not by heredity or crushing circumstance (as lives sometimes are), but self-hardened. This parable, because its whole emphasis is on responsibility, so declares; and the indictment is made not in censure but in compassion. Why had such people come to listen to Jesus? To satisfy an idle curiosity perhaps, or to follow the crowd, or to kill time! They were of the same soil as their brethren, but the soil had been trampled. They had made their souls a thoroughfare. Everything had gone over them—weddings, funerals, pleasures, trade; but nothing had stirred them to the depths. Finally they were impervious, a roadway for whatever procession of inter-

---

[7] Luke 16: 31.

[8] The "interpretations" of parables given in the gospels have been called in question as to their genuineness by critics of good standing (see p. 68). This interpretation (Matthew 13: 18-23, Mark 4: 13-20, Luke 8: 11-15) seems by its simplicity, force and convincing "fitness" to be the utterance of Jesus or directly derived from such an utterance. The interpretations appended to the parables respectively of the Tares and the Dragnet do not seem to stand these tests, but to be rather the conventional apocalyptic of the early church.

ests and happenings might choose to pass that way. Matthew's Gospel describes them in words of singular insight—poignant words on the lips of Jesus: "When any one heareth the word . . . and understandeth it not." They did not understand! There was a man who visited Rome and afterwards could recall nothing of the visit save that he had found a new gambling device: he did not understand the "grandeur that was Rome"! There were people at Niagara Falls who hurried from that marvellous torrent to a cheap and crowded carnival: they did not understand that thunder-majesty! There are people to whom the Fifth Symphony is only a farrago of sounds: they do not understand Beethoven's spirit-rapture. So there were people who listened to Jesus and had no comprehension of His message. He spoke one tongue and they another. He lived in one world and they in another. He was always below the surface and they were always on the surface: they had made their lives a common pathway!

What could Jesus do? At the moment, nothing! Soon the birds would come and gather the seed. Some twittering interest, some new excitement, some trivial item of gossip would eat up all He had said. He could do nothing until God should drive a ploughshare of pain or loss in cruel mercy through their lives to make new furrows for the seed. Tragedy is indeed gain that compels men to meet life with serious purpose. . . .

"And others fell upon rocky places"—not on soil impoverished by many stones, but on shallow earth with a ledge of rock two or three inches below the surface. On such ground the harvest follows the rule of "quickly come, quickly go." The thin earth begets a feverish growth which straightway withers from lack of moisture. Applied to human nature this description is startling in its psychological truth. "I will follow thee whithersoever thou goest," [9] vowed one would-be disciple, but Jesus quenched the sudden, thin enthusiasm: "Foxes have holes, and birds of the heaven have nests: but the Son of man hath not where to lay his head." There was no calmness, no insight, no counting the cost in that wild word "whithersoever." "Straightway with joy," says Jesus of our

[9] Luke 9: 57, 58.

shallow loyalties. "Straightway"—no deep pondering, no trem-
bling of reverence! The serf in olden days pledged fealty to
his feudal chief in noble words: "Dear, my lord, I am liege
man of thine for life and limb and earthly regard, and I will
keep faith and loyalty to thee for life and death, so help me
God." Dimly we realize that we owe such a vow to Jesus, that
life without Him is black confusion, but we make our vow with
glib and over-reaching protestations, not with sacramental surrender. "Straightway"—there is no realization that discipleship means a revolutionary change of life, a stern battle against
odds, a forsaking of the world. . . .

"When persecution cometh straightway he stumbleth"—it is
"straightway" both in vow and in the apostasy! The emotion
ruffled only the surface of life, and when contradictions appeared its strength was spent! Our "persecutions" are not
physical. So far as Jesus is concerned they are not even opposition in words, for the world unites to pay Him lip-service,
and editorial columns vie to do Him honor. Our persecution
is by a prevalent cynicism which hints or openly asserts that
the ideal is but a momentary phosphorescence, a day-dream,
or, at best, an impossible counsel of perfection. The cynicism
takes deadliest form in the atheism of conduct—an omnipresent
worldliness with its crass standards of "success." Before such
persecution our precipitate enthusiasms soon wither!

"And others fell among the thorns"—not on ground already
covered with thorns, but on land "fouled" by latent weed-seeds.
Who has not seen a grain field brilliantly but ruinously streaked
with red poppies or defaced by patches of thistles? The weeds
were not visible when the crop was sown; they were in the
uncleansed soil. There is a gradual ascent in quality of the
three types of character thus far described. The first is im-
penetrable, the second shallow, but the third is rich earth with
possibilities of a generous harvest. This hearer is a man of
high imagination, of genuine passion, but he is not whole-
hearted. He is divided between irreconcilable loyalties: "Ye
cannot serve God and mammon." [10]

"The care of the world and the deceitfulness of riches choke

10 Matthew 6: 24.

the word." Sometimes carking anxiety slays the good grain, and sometimes money "deceiving" people with its promise of life. Soon or later we must come to terms in industry, social ethics, and the teaching of religion with the conviction held by Jesus in regard both to the poverty that crushes and the wealth that deceives. . . . In the quest for the Holy Grail the knight Gawain was shallow and his impulse soon withered, but Lancelot was "our mightiest," a man of magnificent parts. Yet Lancelot failed in the quest only less signally than Gawain, nor did he flinch to confess the cause of failure:

> ". . . but in me lived a sin
> So strange, of such a kind, that all of pure,
> Noble and knightly in me twined and clung
> Round that one sin, until the wholesome flower
> And poisonous grew together, each as each,
> Not to be plucked asunder." [11]

He failed because the soil of his life was "thorny ground" in which the weeds "growing up choked the word"!

But there was good soil, and therefore Jesus sowed in hope. Among the multitude there were men and women who were sin-sick and world-weary, who prayed to the ideal within them as to a healing shadow thrown across their path, who cherished every sanctifying motive.

Jesus found in these valiant spirits His great cheer, and they found in Him their dreams come true. Luke's Gospel has described them in three little phrases which glow like torches. They were "such as in honest and good heart"—not faultless people, but sincere. Sinning or striving, they always "consented to receive the knowledge of themselves," and despite all lapses they refused to parley with anything lower than the highest. Again, they were "such as . . . having heard the word, hold it fast." They clung doggedly to every intimation of eternity. They walked in the light while it was day, and when night came they kept faith with the illumined hour, nor allowed the world's glare to make them disobedient. Again, they were "such as . . . bring forth fruit with patience." Mahatma Ghandi is reported as saying, "If a man would know God he must be as patient as one transferring an ocean drop

11 Tennyson, "The Holy Grail" ("Idylls of the King").

by drop at the end of a straw." There is no get-rich-quick blasphemy in the land of heavenly treasure, for the treasure must still be bought by the pains and patience of good character. These translated their hopes into deeds, and "brought forth fruit with patience"; and the Farmer of Human Fields did not rashly plough up the land because the harvest was slow to appear.

No parable can be pressed to a rigorous conclusion. There is a point at which analogy ends. The soil of life is not in every regard like the soil of nature. Some soils in nature are never cultivable: arctic icefields and the sands of the Painted Desert yield no bread; but human soil is never completely bereft of promise. The soil of nature cannot change its climate; but human soil can help to create its own weather: "Take heed therefore how ye hear." Hearing is an urgent business. The factor of receptiveness conditions the factor of appeal. We may make even the toil of Jesus a failure, or we may receive it as good soil receives the seed and cause it to fructify according to the plenitude of our gifts, "some thirty-fold, some sixty, and some an hundred."

CHAPTER V

EARNESTNESS TO TRANSLATE HEARING INTO DOING

THE PARABLE OF THE CHILDREN AT PLAY

"Whereunto then shall I liken the men of this generation, and to what are they like? They are like unto children that sit in the market-place, and call one to another; who say, We piped unto you, and ye did not dance; we wailed, and ye did not weep. For John the Baptist is come eating no bread nor drinking wine; and ye say, He hath a demon. The Son of man is come eating and drinking; and ye say, Behold, a gluttonous man, and a winebibber, a friend of publicans and sinners! And wisdom is justified of all her children."

(Luke 7:31-35)

(Parallel passage: Matthew 11:16-19)

THE PARABLE OF THE WISE AND FOOLISH BUILDERS

"Every one therefore that heareth these words of mine, and doeth them, shall be likened unto a wise man, who built his house upon the rock: and the rain descended, and the floods came, and the winds blew, and beat upon that house; and it fell not: for it was founded upon the rock. And every one that heareth these words of mine, and doeth them not shall be likened unto a foolish man, who built his house upon the sand: and the rain descended, and the floods came, and the winds blew, and smote upon that house; and it fell: and great was the fall thereof."

(Matthew 7:24-27)

(Parallel passage: Luke 6:46-49)

EARNESTNESS TO TRANSLATE HEARING INTO DOING

Parable of the Children at Play
Parable of the Wise and Foolish Builders

"The doings of grown folk," writes Robert Louis Stevenson of children, "are interesting only as the raw material of play . . . and they will parody an execution, a death-bed, or the funeral of the young man of Nain with all the cheerfulness in the world." [1] Similarly Francis Thompson: "Know you what it is to be a child? . . . it is to be so little that elves can whisper in your ear: it is to turn pumpkins into coaches, and mice into horses, lowness into loftiness, and nothing into everything . . . it is to know not as yet that you are under the sentence of life, nor petition that it be commuted into sentence of death." [2]

"Under sentence of life"!—pathetic recognition by one who knew and loved children as few have done that, though they may live by right in a God-given country of make-believe, a man must move in a world of stern realities. We buy knowledge at the price of innocence, and, ill-satisfied with the bargain, we petition that "sentence of life" be "commuted into sentence of death." But we must serve out our sentence. Jesus never lost the key to childhood's enchanted realm. He loved children and was loved by them. He knew and shared their games. But He knew also that though *childlikeness* must never be lost (or if lost, then regained in the pains of a new birth), there are natural limits to *childishness*. Make-believe becomes a child but it is sorry guise for a man: "When I was a child I thought as a child . . . now that I am become a man,

---

[1] In "Children at Play." ("Virginibus Puerisque," published by Chatto & Windus.)
[2] In the Essay on "Shelley." (Prose Works, edited by Wilfrid Meynell; published by John Lane Co.)

I have put away childish things." [3]   A childish man is an anachronism too pathetic to be a joke.

Hence the trenchant satire of the Parable of the Children at Play.   He characterized His generation [4] as children playing in the market-place.   The Pharisees, typical of their time, were as petulant, as fickle in temper, as prone to find fault as a group of children, who despite all appeals by their playmates, were still querulous. [5]   They would play at neither weddings nor funerals.   The distinguishing trait of the age was its lack of moral earnestness.   Refusing to face realities it was playing at religion in a land of make-believe!

Thus Jesus caught and transfixed in a parable the mood of His contemporaries.   At the same time He impaled on a word (surely not without a glint of humor!) first John the Baptist's ministry and then His own.   John's was like a funeral!   It was as sombre, as starkly real, as inescapable.   But His was like a wedding!—as momentous, as joyous, as deeply in tune with the law of life.   John came as a recluse, an uncouth yet piercing spirit.   In the fierce crooning of the desert wind he had heard God's voice and feared not the voice of men.   With a lash of corded words he flayed the prevalent sin, and called on rich and poor, priest and people, to repent.   But an indifferent age could not understand him.   He was an enigma.   He would not fit into any of their thoughtless categories.   "Who art thou?" [6] they asked him.   Then, fretfully resenting his flaming protest, they labelled him "demon-harried" and dismissed him from mind.   Jesus, on the contrary, came "eating and drinking."   He was not ascetic or aloof.   He was genial.   He loved the common life.   He responded eagerly to the hospitality of His friends, [7] and instructed His disciples to be similarly compan-

---

3 I Corinthians 13: 11.

4 A careful study of the sayings of Jesus reveals His keen historical sense, and His accuracy of historical appraisal.

5 Wellhausen makes the interesting suggestion that, "We piped unto you and ye did not dance" and, "We wailed, and ye did not weep" are antiphonal rhymed responses used by two groups of children in a game.   But if we think of Jesus or John making the complaint against their age, or of their age making it reciprocally against John and Jesus, the latter become party to the game and therefore one with their generation.   The view here suggested seems (despite Wellhausen's ingenious suggestion) the most natural, and the most straightforward in its solution of the difficulty instanced.

6 John 1: 19-23.

7 See, for instance, Matthew 8: 15, 9: 10, 26: 6.   Many such references in the gospels serve to emphasize His constant friendliness.

ionable.[8] But the Pharisees stigmatized Jesus as a "wine-bibber and a glutton," just as they had branded John "possessed of a demon." [9]   In every age, and especially in one devoid of earnestness, an epithet has damning power. Catchwords deliver the unthinking into the hands of the unscrupulous. The Pharisees slew John and Jesus with a phrase. Jesus' love they pronounced laxity; and His friends, they hinted, were people of loose life. John's austerity also failed to satisfy; it was too stern. They were like children refusing to play at either weddings or funerals.

The cardinal sin of John and Jesus was that they were real and positive in a generation which, despite all its pretensions, was still trifling at heart. Neither John nor Jesus was tepid. Both were of a consuming zeal. Each in his own way was a strongly etched and independent soul. It was fitting that John should sternly conclude a stern line of prophets. It was fitting that Jesus (whose shoes John felt unworthy to unloose) should come as an influx of joy; for though like John He was burdened by the world's sin, He knew (by fullness of its indwelling) the love "that taketh away the sin of the world." [10]   But their generation received neither John nor Jesus, because it abhorred enthusiasm. Lacking the saving grace of earnestness, it substituted the form for the spirit—and is it not the very essence of child's play to rate the reproduction above the reality?

"And yet," said Jesus (and what a deeply pondered conclusion that "yet" implied!)—"wisdom is justified of all her children." [11]   Such was His quiet reply to the savage taunts hurled at Him. The "wisdom" of God—His immemorial intention lately personified in John and Jesus—would be "pronounced right " [12] by all the inheritors of insight. The shallow and

---

8 Luke 10: 7.
9 The word is "demon," not "devil."   See article on demonology, Hastings Dictionary of the Bible.
10 John 1: 29.
11 Luke's version of the dictum is preferable because closer to the Hebrew idiom. The interpretation: "is justified against her children" (i.e., the wisdom of Jesus and John will be vindicated against a generation which prides itself on being the offspring of Divine wisdom) is not convincing.   See Plummer (ad. loc. I.C.C. Luke).
12 Such is the meaning here of "justified," a noble word all through the New Testament. Spoken of man's act it usually means "to pronounce right" and of God's act "to make right."

capricious estimates of the time would be overturned. The issue would show that the kingdom heralded by John and inaugurated by Jesus had its origin in the will of heaven. Some in that generation but not of it (scattered souls keeping faith with an inner lantern) and multitudes in coming years would acclaim the kingdom as Divine! Thus Jesus, with heartbreaking courage of patience, drew no "circle premature," but looked to the "far gain," being cheered meanwhile by the approval of God and of God's illumined minority.

> "What's time? Leave Now for dogs and apes!
> Man has Forever." [13]

Still the generations face life's high adventure as irresponsibly as children. Still His earnest soul lights each generation on its upward way.

Parable of the Wise and Foolish Builders

"And great was the fall of it!" Thus Jesus ended a sermon.[14] His hearers went away with the crash of doom reverberating in their ears. This was not fictitious thunder. Mock heroics are inconceivable in Him. Moreover, every word of the abrupt story leads on in tense feeling to the dramatic issue. Even through the opaqueness of the printed page we can see Jesus quivering under the urgency of the plea.

This mood of urgency is dominant. Other moods sound their theme but quickly retire. Momentarily there is the mood of pity—"foolish man," not "wicked man." This man in the business of living was guilty of folly which he would have deemed incredible in the business of shop or store. His deed was not premeditated: it came from lack of premeditation. He built his house on the smooth deposit of a flood where the sand shone firm and golden in the summer sun, and took no account of winter's storms. "Foolish man," says the parable. Then its mood of pity subsides to a constant undertone.

13 Robert Browning, "A Grammarian's Funeral."
14 A fact which holds true whether the "Sermon on the Mount" is considered as one sermon delivered at one time, or (as most commentators believe) as a brilliant collation, by the author of the "Logia" of Matthew, of sermonic material delivered on different occasions. The parable has a finality which proclaims its "clinching" function.

The sharp challenge of authority is sounded—only to be overcome by the throbbing urgency. "These sayings of mine, whosoever hears them"—what a regal claim! The words of the Nazareth Carpenter are to be absolute law, a touchstone by which men and nations rise and fall. There are, perhaps, only two facts in human story more amazing than that categorical assumption of authority—first, His life, death, and continuing influence divinely attesting it; and, second, the instinctive reverence by which mankind, though disobedient, admits His right to rule:

> "O Lord and Master of us all,
> Whate'er our name or sign,
> We own Thy sway, we hear Thy call,
> We test our lives by Thine." [15]

But even this challenge of authority is conquered by the recurrent urgency which now and again sounds out in a word like a sudden trumpet note—"Do!" "He that heareth these sayings of mine and *doeth them*"—"he that heareth these sayings of mine and *doeth them not.*" Insistently, compellingly, that note is struck until it vibrates in our minds. It is the culmination of the teaching of the Parable of the Children at Play. The kingdom demands in its hearers not earnestness alone, but earnestness which will translate truth heard and truth pondered into truth lived! Only such earnestness, said Jesus (and He said it in tones of destiny), can establish a man or nation; and without it life crashes in ruin.

Here is also the culmination of the Parable of the Sower. The responsibility of hearing is that the hearer shall obey: "Why call ye me, Lord, Lord, and do not the things which I say?" [16] Hearing is a generic term. It includes reading, for instance, and the impress made by living example. In the strict sense there is no such thing as "reading for diversion." Who can read George Eliot's "Adam Bede," or Carlyle's "Heroes and Hero Worship," or Shakespeare's "King Lear" without feeling as if the true road had been made as clear as a white ribbon of road in moonlight, and as if a voice had spoken saying: "This is the way: walk ye in it?" [17] If a sentence leaps from

15 Whittier in "Our Master." ("Poetical Works," Houghton Mifflin Co.)
16 Luke 6: 46.
17 Isaiah 30: 21.

a page or a deed from a life and proclaims itself true, it there
and then becomes a lamp which we may keep bright and use
for our pilgrimage, or which we may neglect until it pollutes
the air as neglected lamps and neglected duties always do. The
psychology of an inveterate novel-reader or theater-goer is dangerous: it easily substitutes the thing felt for the thing done.
The manna in the wilderness grew rancid if it was not straightway gathered;[18] so does a nourishing emotion if not carried
into deeds. There is in the Russian the story of a lady who
went to the theater on a winter's night and wept copious tears
over fictitious sufferings in the play, while her coachman was
perishing of real cold outside the door.

Under the simile of building Jesus asserts the necessity of
true deeds in enduring character. He employs the simile so
repeatedly in His teaching that it has been surmised that Jesus
Himself may have been by trade a builder.[19] At first blush the
figure seems unjustified. Is our manifold experience like a
house in plan, shape, and close-knit structure? Surely our impressions, thoughts and volitions are more like a tumbled heap
of bricks. But psychology endorses the simile. Consciously or
unconsciously character gathers into a unity with its individual
color and form. Our days are not piled haphazard. They are
built together like cemented stones, riveted together like gird-
ers. We must dwell in the character-home we build. This
real estate cannot be leased or sublet. By imposture we may
live for a time in other homes, but, soon or late, we are driven
back to our own habitation to make there such poor shelter as
we may!

In outer semblance human houses are similar. The factor
of difference is hidden: some houses have a foundation, while
others are built "upon the earth without a foundation."[20] The

18 Exodus 16: 19, 20.
19 Holtzmann suggests that *tekton* ("carpenter") should be translated "builder."
For the references to building, see Matthew 21: 33, 23: 29; Luke 12: 18, 14: 28,
20: 17; and John 2: 19-21.
20 So Luke. The differences in this parable as reported in Matthew and Luke
are an interesting study. Matthew attributes blame because the "foolish man"
chose a poor location, Luke because he built without a foundation. According to
Luke both houses may have been built on the same tract, but the one rested on
the surface and the other deep upon the rock. Matthew is more dramatic in description of the storm, but Luke has telling phrases: "digged and went deep," "it
had been well-builded," "and it *fell in*." If any one wished to draw invidious
comparisons among four indispensable gospels that of Luke the physician could
stand the test.

foundation is not essential in still weather, but in the lashing of the storm the house cannot stand without it. The energies of a will doing His words, Jesus avows, constitute the solid rock by which alone the house of life endures.

There are three prime forces in personality—emotion, intelligence and will—and the history of ethics might be defined as a succession of attempts to represent one or other of the three as supreme and the other two as subsidiary.[21] No such attempt has won success. Emotion is wild until guided by reason and focussed by will. Reason ends in futile theorizing until the emotion kindles it and the will makes it effective. Similarly the will (even though it is the "foundation") can be no better than a frenzied digging until emotion covets the home, and reason plans and supervises the building. The three are inseparable and each is essential. If any is lacking (even though one may temporarily be dominant) the personality is to that measure weak. They are the living triangle, perfectly balanced, around which life revolves.

Yet it is true, and especially of religion, as Jesus discerned, that the balance is more likely to be upset by the absence of will than by the absence of feeling or intelligence.[22] Jesus did not minimize the place of reason in religion. The doors of a church should be high enough to allow the worshippers on entering to retain their heads. That grand word "rationalist" should be recaptured from the sorry camp of the sceptic and given honor in Christian vocabulary, for the life of Jesus is the most rational thing our befuddled planet has ever seen. Reason quickly reaches frontiers of mystery, but as far as those frontiers religion should march with reason. A man's faith must be consistent with (though not necessarily slave to) his whole range of knowledge, or it sinks into black magic. But the reason without the will never arrives. It discusses with utmost care all the swimming-strokes, but it never enters the water or learns to swim. It was characterized once with penetrating truth: "Foolish man."

Similarly there is ample room for emotion in religion. The

21 Thus Schopenhauer ("the world is my will") might be regarded as a typical proponent of the volitional, Lotze of the emotional, and Hegel of the rational.
22 Jesus reverts to His emphasis on the word "do" (a favorite word with Him both in speech and in practice) in the Parable of the Two Sons. See Chapter XIX.

sight of weak faith beating the air in an orgy of emotion should not dictate a cold and expressionless worship. Strong souls are blessed by the supernal vision and lifted at times into a seventh heaven of ecstasy, so that they cry with Paul: "I know a man in Christ—(whether in the body, I know not; or whether out of the body I know not; God knoweth)—how that he was caught up into Paradise and heard unspeakable words.[23] True religion knows its magic hours,—

> "those hours of birth,
> Those moments of the soul in years of earth. . . .
> That curlew-calling time in Irish dusk
> When life became more splendid than its husk,
> When the rent chapel on the brae at Slains
> Shone with a doorway opening beyond brains." [24]

Jesus Himself was transfigured in such unearthly radiance that His very garments seemed luminous. Nevertheless, His warnings against the abortive emotion which fails of practice were frequent and severe. Feeling is shifting sand—a poor foundation for a house!

"Ye are my friends if ye *do* the things which I command you." [25] "If any man will do his will, he shall know of the teaching whether it is of God or whether I speak from myself." [26] So Jesus pleaded fearlessly that His teaching should be brought to the acid test of deeds. But we are slow to obey—a slowness of which Mark Twain spoke whimsically when he declared that the parts of the Bible which gave him trouble were not those he could not understand but rather those he could understand. "Can any man look round," asks Oliver Wendell Holmes, "and see what Christian countries are now doing, and how they are governed, and what is the general condition of society, without seeing that Christianity is the flag under which the world sails, and not the rudder that steers its course?" So Ruskin: "Every duty we omit obscures some truth we might have known." [27] So William James: "Never suffer yourself to have an emotion without expressing it in some active way." But the warning

---

23 II Corinthians 12: 2, 4.
24 John Masefield, "Biography." ("Collected Poems," The Macmillan Co., 1921.)
25 John 15: 14.
26 John 7: 17.
27 Quoted pertinently by Dr. Halford E. Luccock in his valuable little book, "Studies in the Parables of Jesus," p. 31.

was never so forcibly uttered as when Jesus condemned with quivering urgency the house of the man who failed in deeds: "And great was the fall of it."

For the storm comes—since life intends not that we should be superficially happy but that we should be blest in strength and sacrifice. Jesus describes the storm in abrupt and flashing words: "Torrential came the rain! Down swept the floods! Angry roared the winds!" [28] Thunder-clouds gathered ominously in the hills, lightning tore the sky, and then, amid the crash of thunder, the flood came swirling down the river-bed, a livid turbulence, and away went the house that had looked so fair in summer suns!

Who has not seen human houses "fall in"—crumple in sudden ruin—before the onset of business calamity, or the overwhelming storm of sorrow? And who has not seen other lives strong to endure however the pitiless rain of a friend's unfaithfulness might beat, however the cruel winds of pain might lash and tear? Such souls are "builded well" on the impregnable rock of a Christ-instructed will.

> "O living will that shall endure
>   When all that seems shall suffer shock,
>   Rise in the spiritual rock,
> Flow through our *deeds* and make them pure." [29]

[28] The very order of the Greek words heightens the dramatic effect.
[29] Tennyson, "In Memoriam" (CXXXI).

CHAPTER VI

THE KINGDOM, AND THE PERPLEXING PRESENCE OF EVIL

THE PARABLE OF THE TARES

"Another parable set he before them, saying, The kingdom of heaven is likened unto a man that sowed good seed in his field: but while men slept, his enemy came and sowed tares also among the wheat, and went away. But when the blade sprang up and brought forth fruit, then appeared the tares also. And the servants of the householder came and said unto him, Sir, didst thou not sow good seed in thy field? whence then hath it tares? And he said unto them, An enemy hath done this. And the servants say unto him, Wilt thou then that we go and gather them up? But he saith, Nay; lest haply while ye gather up the tares, ye root up the wheat with them. Let both grow together until the harvest: and in the time of the harvest I will say to the reapers, Gather up first the tares, and bind them in bundles to burn them; but gather the wheat into my barn."

"Then he left the multitudes, and went into the house: and his disciples came unto him, saying, Explain unto us the parable of the tares of the field. And he answered and said, He that soweth the good seed is the Son of man; and the field is the world; and the good seed, these are the sons of the kingdom; and the tares are the sons of the evil one; and the enemy that sowed them is the devil: and the harvest is the end of the world; and the reapers are angels. As therefore the tares are gathered up and burned with fire; so shall it be in the end of the world. The Son of man shall send forth his angels, and they shall gather out of his kingdom all things that cause stumbling, and them that do iniquity, and shall cast them into the furnace of fire: there shall be the weeping and the gnashing of teeth. Then shall the righteous shine forth as the sun in the kingdom of their Father. He that hath ears, let him hear."

(*Matthew* 13 : 24-30, 36-43)

CHAPTER VI

THE KINGDOM, AND THE PERPLEXING PRESENCE OF EVIL

The Parable of the Tares

This is a perplexing parable. As we read it the questions bristle. Why, we ask, does God tolerate the sowing of tares?—an old, old question! And this reference to the "enemy"—does Jesus therein lend explicit endorsement to the doctrine of a hoofed and horned being, the satanic author of all mischief? Furthermore, is wrong to be allowed to root and grow, crowding and counterfeiting the right, age after age, until "angels" finally intervene? And the terrible climax to the story, the binding of bundles ready for the fire—did Jesus light this parable with the lurid flames of Hell? Such are the vexing questions which the parable provokes. It is not surprising that competent and conservative critics have doubted its claim to genuineness.[1]

Moreover, the interminable controversies waged around the parable have deepened perplexity. The Donatists (a group of schismatics in Northern Africa in the fourth century) were churchmen who believed in purity before peace. They deemed it a duty to exclude from the church every one guilty of heresy, the Donatists themselves (so one gathers) being the standard and test of orthodoxy. Ranged against them were the Augustinians who pleaded that heresy, however unfortunate, should not be cut off; Christ's own dictate was that tares should be permitted to grow until the harvest. The Donatists retorted that the parable is a description of the world ("the field is the

[1] Even such a critic as James Denney. Loisy is of the view that the parable in its present form is framed to fit the "interpretation" which, he believes, is of a later origin. He suggests, however, that the parable itself may have been spoken by Jesus in some simpler form. But the parable as it now is, if it could be freed from controversial accretions, would, we think, be seen to possess in its insight and compassionate wisdom, the characteristics of a genuine utterance. Regarding the authenticity of the interpretation (Matthew 13: 36-43) there is wider room for doubt. See footnote, p. 68.

world") and not of the church. Tares may be tares with some impunity in the world, but in the church they must be handled without mercy. Books multiplied on the absorbing topic and the battle raged with fury.[2]

> " 'But what they fought each other for,
>   I could not well make out;
> 'But everybody said,' quoth he,
>   'It was a famous victory.' " [3]

The story again became a bone of contention in early Reformation times. Luther taught (by reasoning whose consistency is not now apparent) that the church may *exclude* heretics but not *slay* them, whereas the State may do both since the prohibition against uprooting tares is guidance for Christian ministers and not for the civil authorities! Beza put Luther's timidity to shame; argued that the parable is not relevant in matters of church discipline and that, consequently, both church and state may mete out appropriate punishment to heretic-tares; and ended by justifying the burning of Miguel Serveto!

> "But things like that, you know, must be
> After a famous victory." [3]

The strife was joined again in the Erastian and Arminian controversy, continued through the time of birth of Nonconformity, and its reverberations may be felt in the present day. Often in these tumultuous years the battle has been pitched on the sacred ground of this simple story. Thus Arnot charges (and rightly) that Trench interprets the parable from an Erastian bias, but meanwhile betrays an Arminian bias of his own.[4] We can imagine Jesus regarding these conflicts, ancient or modern, with grieving and incredulous eyes, and wondering why men should forge fratricidal weapons from His words of eternal life.

Let the questions raised by this controversy be answered categorically and then forgotten. Does the parable concern church discipline?[5] Primarily, no!—for the good and sufficient rea-

---

2 Bruce, *op. cit.*, p. 49 ff., has a résumé of the various controversial interpretations of the parable.
3 Robert Southey, "The Battle of Blenheim."
4 See Arnot, *op. cit.*, p. 85.
5 Trench begs the question by ignoring the interpretative phrase, "The field is the world," and by claiming: "It must, however, be evident . . . that the parable

son that the Christian Church did not exist when the parable
was spoken. Has it any bearing on church discipline? It
bears on life and the disconcerting presence of evil; it is applicable to the church only as the church is a province of life
and beset by evil influence. Does it offer a rule of thumb for
practical conduct? No, it offers more than any rule of thumb;
it breathes the spirit from which alone wise action can proceed.

Then how shall we regard the parable? We shall regard it
first as a story graphically told. It is not a picture-puzzle in
which to search for hidden and ingenious meanings. It is not
an allegory in which every detail has definite significance. It
is a story that flames like a torch to guide our pilgrimage.
Perhaps it was based on an actual incident of Jesus' boyhood.

A farmer living, perhaps, near Nazareth had sown his field
with wheat. He had been particular about the good quality of
the seed; the poor seed from the last harvest had been ground
into flour, and the best saved for the new sowing. But under
cover of darkness his enemy scattered darnel over the field.
Darnel is false wheat, hard to distinguish from the real grain,
and poisonous to eat. The cool of the night should have abated
the wrath of his enemy, and the stars should have seemed like
the eyes of God; but nothing could stay the man's vengefulness.
Thus, in cruel deceit, he fouled the crop. The farmer could
detect no fraud while the wheat was in the blade, but when it
formed in the ear his servants hurried to him in dismay: "Didst
thou not sow good seed in thy field? Whence then hath it
tares?" He was a man of few words and of iron self-control.
He did not storm nor curse. "An enemy hath done this," was
his only comment. A man of fine patience also; for when his
servants were all for violent measures, he restrained them:
"Nay; for if you pull up the tares you will pull up the wheat.
Let both grow until the harvest. Then we will burn the tares
and gather the wheat into the barn."

is, as the Lord announces, concerning the 'kingdom of heaven' *or the Church.*"
(Italics mine.) (*Op. cit.,* p. 92.) Bruce offers five ingenious reasons why the tares
are to be taken as a symbol of "counterfeit Christians" and why the parable must
be so interpreted. (*Op. cit.,* p. 45 ff.) He denies the parable has any reference to
bad men in general. His position is thus only slightly different from that of Trench
and untenable for the same reason, namely, the church, as such, did not exist when
the parable was spoken, and "Christian" had not become a defined and determinative discipleship. Though limiting its field of application, Bruce's interpretation of
the parable is nevertheless eminently wise and illuminating.

Can you imagine such a story racing through the village street when Jesus was a boy? Can you imagine the excited whispering that guessed the identity of the culprit? "So-and-so," they said, "has sworn revenge ever since he was 'fired' for his trickery." Years later Jesus looked out over the field of human life with its wheat and its false wheat and pondered the patience of God's dealings. How unlike the impatience of our dealings! "Let me tell you a story about it," He said. "And he put forth another parable unto them saying, The kingdom of heaven is like a man who sowed good seed in his field: but while men slept"—and with dramatic application that old story, scored into His boyhood imagination, was retold!

Well Jesus knew the questions that perplex us. Why is the world so unlike God's world and so tragically like the ill-cultivated patch of an indifferent proprietor? Why are the tares of war among the grains of wheat? Why is the acreage of our national life so choked with weeds? All indiscriminate indignation aside, all wild rumor-mongering forgotten, there is laid bare from time to time an astounding lack of truth in high places. Why is the wheat so often ruinously intermingled with false wheat?

The realm of private character is hardly more reassuring. There is, in very truth, many a high emprise and many an obscure fidelity, which shine like candles "in a naughty world." But there is also the mad scramble for money and notoriety, the lust and the murder, the selfishness which first usurps the throne of love in the home and then wrecks it, the unexamined life of multitudes who appear to be dead on the whole upper register of being. These facts must be reckoned, even while we admit the bright and cheering balance. Who has not raised a cry Godward?—"Didst Thou not sow good seed in Thy field? Whence then hath it tares?"

The fact of failure in the church is even more conspicuous, because there the soil is favored. The church is a garden reclaimed from the outlying wilderness, walled with mercy, and fertilized by the blood of her Lord. When weeds are discovered in that garden perplexity becomes dismay. But the church has had her warfare. The lives cut short and the persecuting torture practised in the name of religion almost put paganism to blush. In bloodless fashion, though not without bitterness, our day continues the strife. While ministers dispute about the name of Jesus, He Himself is forgotten. To sin in doctrine is execrable, while to sin in that spirit which is a denial of the brotherhood passes uncondemned. The world regards professed Christianity and remarks, not without cause: "These, then, are the 'redeemed.' But from what are they redeemed? Not all are redeemed from the money standard. Not all are redeemed from class pride. Not all are redeemed from intolerance and the unbrotherly heart. Pray, why do they call themselves redeemed?" Christ's own garden rank with noxious weeds provokes the sharper cry: "Good Father of mankind, didst Thou not sow good seed in Thy field? Whence then hath it tares?"

Thus the parable confronts us with the stubborn fact and mystery of sin in a God-created world. Does Jesus explain that fact? No; but, as has been pertinently said, He "does not explain it away." He gives no cut-and-dried solution to that ultimate enigma—the problem of the origin of evil. It is no irreverence to suggest that He may not have possessed in knowledge the full data for a solution. He shared our humanity in its limitations of body and mind; otherwise the sharing would have been fictitious. Mystery dictated for Him, we must believe, as for us, the odds of faith. The parable is not to be construed as though Jesus lent either countenance or denial to the doctrine of a personal devil. Whether the "enemy" of the human field is "devil," or ingrained perversity of human choice, or some other antagonism, is a question to be met on different terrain from this parable; for the parable was spoken, not to establish dogma, but to establish life.

But if evil is not explained, it is not explained away. The tares are tares. They are not immature grain. They are not imaginary. They are weeds and poisonous. They positively war against a good harvest. Whether we call the power that sows them "devil" or the wrong choice of human freewill, that power is the foe of our souls: "An *enemy* hath done this." Tares have entered the field—whether sown by Satan or by our perversion of a God-given liberty; and life will be clarified if we fixedly regard them as a hostile growth, and resolve to be rid of them. To regard evil as illusory solves no problems. A God who, eager to create children of His love, confronts them with a good and evil choice and so fills His universe with danger, is a God who by that act fills our minds with dismaying questions. But a God who suffers His children to live under illusions is not a winsome substitute! A world of real good and real evil does at least provide the setting for heroic character, but a world in which every one is victimized by false impressions is a mad world in very truth. Jesus says of the choking weeds of life: "I do not account for them, but they are the work of an 'enemy.' The harvest of human peace can never be reconciled with treachery, hate, lust, or greed. Form no truce with weeds, and He who in mystery makes you strong by the odds you have to face will prosper your battle."

Then why does God allow evil to become rooted? The tares are not merely unsightly, or their presence could more easily be tolerated; in hostile energy they crowd out the good life. Should they not be uprooted and cast away? When we see unrighteousness rampant we are all for summary measures.

> "Man's inhumanity to man
> Makes countless thousands mourn." [6]

Then why allow the colossal misery to continue? Why abide so ramshackle an existence?

> "Ah, love, could you and I with Him conspire
> To grasp this sorry scheme of things entire,
> Would we not shatter it to bits, and then
> Remould it nearer to the heart's desire." [7]

If we could conspire with God, we would sweep away wickedness with a strong hand and make an instant paradise. But— we are not God. We are very far from Godlike. . . .

If the unrighteous were to be uprooted, could any of us hope to be spared? When we consider the light that has shone, not once but often, on our path; and when we remember how, not once but often, we have quenched the light, can we be sure that we are "children of light" and not children of darkness? There have been numerous doctrines of election. There have

---

6 Robert Burns, "Man Was Made to Mourn."
7 "The Rubáiyát of Omar Khayyám." Edward Fitzgerald.

never been wanting those ready to declare that "few shall be saved." But when did it occur to these ready souls to be dubious of their own election? Such a one, self-assured of heaven, plied Jesus with the question: "Lord, are there few that be saved?"; and Jesus answered that man sharply: "Agonize to enter in at the narrow gate. . . ."[8] A proper humility will allow God to determine which are the tares and which the wheat.

"Let both grow together until the harvest"—because it is not until the ear has formed that the nature of the grain becomes evident. Many a movement persecuted in its beginnings for being "lawless" has later come to genuine fruit. A wise man will "judge nothing before the time."[9] The first protests against slavery were not in good repute. "Every new thing which appears in the life of the Spirit . . . looks dangerous. . . . Even Christ with His apostles appeared to the Jews and heathens as an impious rebel against Divine and human right."[10] The wild theory of a minority has grown before now into the accepted conservatism of the majority. It is well to give men and movements a chance to prove themselves. Analogies of human life drawn from nature are never fully analogous, and men are not exactly like wheat and tares. Men—to cite an instance—can change their nature under stress of experience. There is tenderness in the injunction: "Let both grow." They will proclaim themselves in the time of harvest!

Moreover, to pluck away the tares jeopardizes the wheat. A son may be worthless, but the sword that cuts him off enters the mother's soul. The roots of human lives are interwoven. None is so lonely but some one would be made lonely by his destruction. This truth holds in the realm of virtue as in the realm of affection. When has the church undertaken to uproot her heresies without uprooting also her gentleness and her courageous quest for truth? No church can adopt a settled policy of "Thou shalt not" toward others, without sacrificing several "thou shalts" in itself. Even in the region of private character (insofar as any character is private) the penalty in-

8 Luke 13: 23, 24.
9 I Corinthians 4: 5.
10 Arndt quoted by Bruce, *op. cit.*, p. 61.

flicted on violent measures is not suspended. The roots of individual good and evil are intertwined. Drastic uprooting may at times be necessary—"If thine eye cause thee to stumble, cast it out"; [11] but even within the limits of single consciousness the law holds—the destruction of tares must come by the strong growth of the wheat, or both must be allowed to grow until the harvest.[12]

"Until the harvest"—hopeful, yet ominous words! What do they mean? That God's control is never usurped! Even though weeds have entered the field, it is not rebelliously "out of hand." His ways may seem slow, but they are not therefore impotent. Neither politicians doling out "patronage," nor frenzied preachers thumping their pulpits, can determine the destinies of mankind. There is a wise and patient law of growth—"until the harvest"! Events, though slow to occur and seemingly of trivial import, move ever to their culmination. Life has its climacteric. That which for years has been whispered in the inner chambers is suddenly "proclaimed upon the housetops": [13]

> Some great cause, God's new Messiah, offering each the bloom or blight,
> Parts the goats upon the left hand, and the sheep upon the right." [14]

Life frequently reaches such a crisis of harvest. Death, the dissolving of life's "insubstantial pageant," must also be such an unmasking of our souls. The so-called good and the so-called bad may frequently be confused in the period of growth; but in the time of harvest it becomes clear that the "set" of one life, despite many lapses, is towards light, and the "set" of another life, despite many compunctions, is toward darkness.

"Gather up first the tares and bind them in bundles to burn them." [15] This is figurative language, but not on that account

11 Mark 9: 47.
12 Bruce limits the application of the parable to "other men" and holds it does not apply to the individual. (Op. cit., p. 57.) Its main teaching is undoubtedly social, but the individual aspect need not be excluded.
13 Luke 12: 3.
14 James R. Lowell, "The Present Crisis." ("Poems," Houghton Mifflin Co.)
15 It will be noticed that this exposition is based on the words of the parable itself rather than on the "interpretation." There is no sufficient data for a dogmatic opinion on the genuineness of Matthew 13: 36-40. W. C. Allen, while admitting apocalyptic elements, thinks this interpretation "is characterized throughout by phrases which are probably due to the Logia." ("I.C.C.," Matthew, p. 146.)

empty of meaning. Sin lights the fires of hell in this world: why should we deny a hell eschatological? We cannot conceive of God as permitting to wickedness a permanent place in His universe. A God tolerant of unholiness is a contradiction in terms. In every crisis of character here we realize the heaven of our aspiring and the hell of our consciousness of sin. That hell becomes real in the stab of remorse, in the awareness of a gulf set between us and those whose faith we have betrayed, and in the sense of alienation from God.

"Hell? If the souls of men were immortal as men have been told,
The lecher would cleave to his lusts, and the miser would yearn for his gold,
And so there were Hell for ever! But were there a God as you say,
His Love would have power over Hell till it utterly vanished away." [16]

But would God's love "have power"? It shone uncloudedly in Jesus, but did not "have power" over Caiaphas or Pilate. That His love persists unchanged and unchangeable in the next world as in this, we may well believe; for God is God and in Him there is "no variableness." But we must also hold that human freedom likewise persists; for when freedom ends, essential humanity ends. If hell be defined as the concomitant and consequence of sin, it endures while sin endures, is eternal if sin is eternal, and ceases when sin ceases. As to the possibilities of moral change hereafter, who can speak? We may say that the Good Shepherd will seek His sheep "until He find it"; [17] or we may say, "if so be that He find it." [17] We may protest, "His love will have power over hell"; or we may argue, "It is lame logic to maintain the inviolable freedom of the will and at the same time insist that God can, through His ample power . . . bring the soul into a disposition which it does not wish to feel." [18] Some of us, listening for the soul's deepest accent

"The sons of the kingdom" is a phrase with an authentic ring. But, as G. H. Box ("Century Bible," Matthew, p. 228), has pointed out, there are many phrases which are typical of the "apocalyptic" outlook of the early church. "The end of the world," "furnace of fire," "then shall the righteous shine forth" are all the conventional language of apocalypse. There still remains, however, the vexed question of how much Jesus Himself employed the apocalyptic language widely current in His day. We incline to believe that the "interpretation" is of later origin than the parable. At least there is enough ground to doubt the genuineness of the "interpretation" and to trust the genuineness of the parable, to make us cleave to the latter in our exposition.
16 Tennyson, "Despair."
17 Luke 15: 4, Matthew 18: 13.
18 Shedd, "Dogmatic Theology," ii, 669.

> ". . . can but trust that good shall fall
> At last—far off—at last, to all,
> And every winter change to spring," [19]

but we may not dogmatize where Jesus is silent. He leaves us in no doubt concerning the cruciality of our present life. The days move toward their harvest! Meanwhile He is patient past all dreaming or deserving. His hand is stretched over us in blessing. Whether we call ourselves "tares" or "wheat," "The Son of man hath power on earth to forgive sins." [20]

19 Tennyson, "In Memoriam," LIV.
20 Matthew 9: 6.

THE CHILDREN OF THE KINGDOM OF GOD

CHAPTER VII

THE CONDITIONS OF DISCIPLESHIP

THE PARABLE OF THE EMPTY HOUSE

"But the unclean spirit, when he is gone out of the man, passeth through waterless places, seeking rest, and findeth it not. Then he saith, I will return into my house whence I came out; and when he is come, he findeth it empty, swept, and garnished. Then goeth he, and taketh with himself seven other spirits more evil than himself, and they enter in and dwell there: and the last state of that man becometh worse than the first. Even so shall it be also unto this evil generation."

(Matthew 12:43-45)

(Parallel passage: Luke 11:24-26)

THE PARABLE OF THE UNCOMPLETED TOWER

"Now there went with him great multitudes: and he turned, and said unto them, If any man cometh unto me, and hateth not his own father, and mother, and wife, and children, and brethren, and sisters, yea, and his life also, he cannot be my disciple. Whosoever doth not bear his own cross, and come after me, cannot be my disciple. For which of you, desiring to build a tower, doth not first sit down and count the cost, whether he have wherewith to complete it? Lest haply, when he hath laid a foundation, and is not able to finish, all that behold begin to mock him, saying, This man began to build, and was not able to finish." *(Luke* 14:25-30)

THE PARABLE OF THE KING'S RASH WARFARE

"Or what king, as he goeth to encounter another king in war, will not sit down first and take counsel whether he is able with ten thousand to meet him that cometh against him with twenty thousand? Or else, while the other is yet a great way off, he sendeth an ambassage, and asketh conditions of peace. So therefore whosoever he be of you that renounceth not all that he hath, he cannot be my disciple."

(Luke 14:31-33)

THE CONDITIONS OF DISCIPLESHIP

The Parable of the Empty House
The Parable of the Uncompleted Tower
The Parable of a King's Rash Warfare

It is a mark of a great leader that he should clearly state the terms of his discipleship. Garibaldi offered his followers hunger and death—and the freedom of their beloved Italy! King Arthur bound his knights

> "by so straight vows to his own self,
> That when they rose, knighted from kneeling, some
> Were pale as at the passing of a ghost,
> Some flushed, and others dazed, as one who wakes
> Half-blinded at the coming of a light." [1]

But no leader required such "straight vows" as Jesus. Uncompromisingly He warned His followers against heedless discipleship. The cost was complete self-commitment; and they must face the cost, lest by renegade loyalty they bring contempt on themselves and on a cause too hastily espoused. Nor could the choice go by default. To drive out false masters from the soul and leave the house of personality unoccupied might be a policy of disaster. This warning is the pith of the Parable of the Empty House. The "straight vows" of His discipleship are plainly declared in the twin parables of the Rash Builder and the Warring King.

The Parable of the Empty House [2]

Can neutrality ever be dangerous? The answer of Jesus is unqualified: moral neutrality is everywhere in imminent peril.

---

1 Tennyson, "The Coming of Arthur" ("Idylls of the King").
2 This parable is very loosely joined to its context in both Matthew and Luke, a fact which seems to indicate that it is not merely descriptive, but originally existed in its own right as a parable.

To abstain from self-commitment is not safe; it is beset by danger. Negative virtue is not a city of peace; it is beleaguered on every hand. . . .

In Jesus' day the belief in demons was widespread. The prevalent cosmology assigned to God a realm of calm above the sky, and intervening between God's dwelling-place and man's earth was the demon-filled air. A man's most fearful foes pressed about him invisibly. Many sicknesses were but demon-possession.[3] Calamities were brewed in the cauldrons of that same grim realm. Paul hints that the malice of the Cross was inspired by demonic agency;[4] and elsewhere he declares that the Christian's hardest battle is "not against flesh and blood, but with the angelic Rulers, the angelic Authorities, the potentates of the dark present, the spirit-forces of evil in the heavenly sphere."[5] He warns us of the "prince of the power of the air."[6] Human life in that day was demon-ridden. *We* see the sky filled with light, but *their* sky was infested with unseen malignities. That the Christian faith could conquer the demons and drive them into oblivion is a striking tribute to its power. Jesus alludes to the exorcists who claimed control over the demons.[7] Probably the claim was not proved. Not until He spoke did the demons flee.

The popular belief in demons provides the setting[8] for the Parable of the Empty House. A demon is expelled from a man's life. Thereafter he wanders, a grisly presence, through "waterless places," seeking rest but finding none. (For it was supposed that exorcised spirits made their unquiet dwelling in the wilderness or in forbidding ruins.)[9] He resolves to return

---

3 Mark 9: 38, and many such references.
4 I Corinthians 2: 8.
5 Ephesians 6: 12 excellently translated by Dr. Moffatt.
6 Ephesians 2: 2. See article on demons in Hastings' "Dictionary of the Bible," and an interesting chapter, "The War with the Dæmons," in Dr. T. R. Glover's "Jesus in the Experience of Men."
7 Luke 11: 19. The interesting phrase "by the finger of God" in Luke 11: 20 probably is an echo of a formula of the exorcists: "I adjure thee by the finger of God."
8 This does not imply that Jesus accepted or endorsed the belief. Our instinctive reverence for Him does not require that we attribute to Him the scientific knowledge of to-day or of a thousand years hence. Neither does it require the assumption that He shared all the superstitions of His own day. We see Him at times taking direct issue with those superstitions, as, for instance, when He contradicted the theory that blindness always came from a man's sin or the sin of his parents. (See John 9: 2, 3.)
9 See Isaiah 13: 21; 34: 14.

to the life from which he was banished. He still calls it "my house" (for evil yields stubbornly), and is overjoyed to find it "empty, swept, garnished." No better tenant had replaced him! Thus he takes new possession of the house; and, lest his tenancy should be again disputed, he brings seven other demons to live with him.[10] With these horrible reinforcements he can defy any new attempt to dispossess him. So, says Jesus—clinching the grim story in a sharp proverbial phrase—"the last state of that man becometh worse than the first." [11]

Could the peril of neutrality be more dramatically shown, or the folly of a merely negative virtue be more relentlessly pilloried! The Jewish nation had been "swept" clean of idolatry, and "decorated" with all the ritual of the law; but it was "empty." It could not remain empty, for human nature (as well as that nature of which science speaks) "abhors a vacuum." It was empty—like a whited sepulcher; and demons came to live among the tombs! There was no divinely positive life, no lofty enthusiasm, no indwelling of God.

Succinctly the parable describes our frequent human course. Harried by our sins, we vow amendment. The devil of wrongful habit, tearing and befouling our life, can no longer be endured. We make short shift of our sins. Straightway we begin a careful, but still superficial reformation. The house is "swept"—cleansed of its worse defilements; "garnished"—with some attempt to make it seemly; but it is *"empty"*! The tragedy told by this parable turns upon the pivot of that word —"empty." An empty house, however it may be decorated, is always desolate. There are ghostly shadows at the windows. The floors creak. Every footfall echoes ominously. In the hollow distance there is the slamming of a door. Moreover, an empty house never remains empty. Spiders spin their webs, vermin claim the forsaken rooms, rats run behind the wainscotting. . . . So our house of life left empty invites undesirable tenants. Former evil habit, seductive circumstance, and weakened will prey upon it. Finally, overcome with disappointment over our failure in reform, we deliver the house to

10 Seven devils was the worst state of demondom. That was why the plight of Mary Magdalene was so desperate. See Luke 8: 2.
11 Compare Matthew 27: 64.

the abandon of despair—and our last state becomes worse than the first!

The peril of neutrality is in its emptiness. Ill health must be driven out by the incoming of nature's own vitality. Otherwise, the expulsion is not permanent, and a relapse must be feared. Medicine now concerns itself, not only with the process of cure, but with the establishment and maintenance of health. Again, modern methods of child training recommend that parents should eschew the "don't do that" kind of discipline, and substitute for a wrong activity a new and proper interest. Recent psychology reiterates the truth. What is to be done with a dark memory or a cherished grudge? It must be driven out. The demon must be exorcised. To bury a dark memory (to let it remain as an evil tenant) is to spread its balefulness.[12] But expulsion of the malign presence is not enough. That conquest is merely preliminary; the obsession, bitterness, or remorse must then be "reassociated." It must be absorbed in a legitimate and more passionate purpose; it must be linked with a new and sound attitude of life. The house must be occupied by its rightful tenant!

But though many voices conspire to proclaim this truth, religion is slow to hear and heed. There are pulpits quick to indulge in orgies of denunciation but tardy to preach the positive tidings of life abundant. There are ministers' associations and reform organizations more eager to expel disintegrating forces than to engage in the less spectacular task of constructive goodwill. So ready to banish the demon—so loathe to welcome Jesus! Yet, if we would but know, when He comes to rule the demon flees of himself!

No neutrality can remain neutral. A moral issue settled by default is settled wrong. Nature abhors a vacuum. Life demands its mastery. Bobbie Burns sang blithely of

> ". . . the glorious privilege
> Of being independent," [13]

but he knew in hours of insight that the world had him in a halter. Some men are mastered by their bodies, some by hard

12 See J. B. Streeter's "Reality," Chapter VII.
13 In "Epistle to a Young Friend."

circumstance, some by gold; but others, like Paul, are "the slaves of the Lord Jesus."[14] Some, boasting their freedom, are the lackeys of any trivial lordship—compelled to walk in the retinue of any passing whim or fancy! The man who "does as he likes," every time he likes, is slave to his likes, whatever may be his loud pretence of liberty.

For every man has some master! We have no choice between self-commitment or neutrality, for devils possess the home which invites no worthier tenant. Our only choice is the choice among many masters. We are compelled to serve. In the course of human history there is but one service which has proved a "perfect freedom":

> Holy Spirit, right divine,
> King within my conscience reign;
> Be my law, and I shall be
> Firmly bound, forever free.[15]

The Parable of the Uncompleted Tower
The Parable of the Rash Warfare

Neutrality is encompassed by dangers. Men must swear allegiance, or in the default some unworthiness will make them slaves. As for the Christian allegiance, its terms are clear! But were ever terms so startling, so harsh?—"If any man cometh unto me, and hateth not his own father, and mother, and wife, and children, and brethren, and sisters, yea, and his own life also, he cannot be my disciple. Whosoever doth not bear his own cross, and come after me, cannot be my disciple." Were ever followers "bound by such straight vows"?

Evidently the sight of "great multitudes" flocking to Him provoked Jesus to this plainness of speech. His fame had spread like a prairie fire. The inquisitive came gaping, just as they would have come to an accident or a dog fight. The self-seeking resolved to take the tide of His popularity at the flood, and ride on to fortune. Patriots, restive under the dominion of Rome, were eager to use Him as a firebrand of revolution.

---

14 Ephesians 6: 6.
15 Samuel Longfellow's "Holy Spirit, Truth Divine." ("Poetical Works"; Houghton Mifflin Co.)

Many were stirred to impulsive enthusiasm. A few were conscious of the brooding of the Spirit. . . .

"And He turned," and looked out over the sea of faces. They were following, but did they know what "following" might mean? He had no earthly kingdom, not even a kingdom large enough to rest His head. His way would never make Him princely in Church or State. A King? Nay, a pariah!— a crucified Man! Had they forgotten their own proverb: "Cursed be the one who hangs on a tree"? Did they understand that His discipleship meant feet cut by jagged stones, and shoulders raw from the chafing of a cross?—"Whosoever doth not bear his own cross, and come after Me . . ." So "He turned and said, If any man *hate* not his father and mother . . ." It was a staggering word—but then, it was intended to stagger! It was a flail to sift the motley crowd. Also—it was a brave facing of realities. Jesus would not hide the sharp flint, nor gild the shadows, nor cloak the cross. If life spelt tragedy, even the Golgotha kind of tragedy, He would see life steadily and see it whole. He would insist that other men face realities with the same unflinching eyes. No man must embark on His venture without counting the cost!

Hence the twin parables [16] of the Rash Builder and the Rash King. The Herods had a passion for erecting imposing buildings. Doubtless many who tried to imitate their extravagance came to grief. Pilate had begun the building of an aqueduct which, from lack of funds, was left incomplete. Perhaps Jesus was daringly hinting at notable instances of unfinished towers. Perhaps He was leading the laughter against a folly which began what it could not end! For a tower which begins in challenge to the sky, and ends as the poor stub of an abortive venture, is always a target for general scorn. So, also, is an extinguished enthusiasm! Therefore Jesus demands that His followers shall count the cost. Can they build a tower accord-

16 G. H. Hubbard, *op. cit.*, p. 244 ff., again draws a sharp distinction between these twin parables. The story of the Tower Builder (he says) points to the soul's essay for saintliness, while the story of the Rash King concerns the altruism of the Christian life. The distinction is based on the claim that "architecture always represents that" (*i.e.*, the struggle for saintliness) "when used as a type of the spiritual." The claim is too uncertain to be made the line of cleavage between two parables which are so clearly conjoined. The difference between them is in the simile. Life (individual and social) may be pictured as a building and also as a warfare. Each figure is rich in suggestion.

ing to the blueprint of the "Sermon on the Mount"? Can
they live by a higher law than the law of retaliation? Can they
endure the hostility of their kinsfolk?—the ostracism of the
church? Can they complete the building? Failure will only
give occasion for such taunts as are always flung at·apostate
vows. "This man began—and was not able to finish." [17] That
bitter scorn, having struck the man, glances from him to dis-
credit his deserted cause!

The other simile is as pungent. For the age was one of reckless warfare no less than of reckless building. Herod the
tetrarch, having divorced his first wife, the daughter of Aretas,
king of Arabia, was attacked by Aretas and soundly defeated.
A wise king counts the cost, appraises the odds, and does not
rush headlong into battle. Even so, a wise disciple will not venture heedlessly upon the Christian warfare. He will face the
disparity of forces, and consider "whether he is able with *ten*
thousand, to meet him that cometh against him with *twenty*
thousand" lest the campaign end in irretrievable disaster. (That
Jesus should so state the odds of battle is further proof of His
challenge to the heroic!) He does not mean that it is better
never to begin, than to begin and fail—for no one dealt with
failure more tenderly than He. But He *does* mean that it is
better (both for the man and for the cause) not to begin, than
to begin in the jaunty heedlessness that invites defeat. The
conditions of His discipleship must be understood and pondered—and then courageously espoused.

The conditions are clear. They remain vividly focussed in
the word "hate." That word must not be whittled down. On
the other hand, we must not explain it in bald literalness.
Renan declared that Jesus is here "trampling under foot everything that is human—blood and love and country" . . . "despising the healthy limits of man's nature" . . . "abolishing all
natural ties." But Galilean fishermen could be trusted to interpret Jesus better than the learned critic! They were not afraid
of a startling paradox. In their minds, one word sternly
spoken in stern purpose would not distort His truth uttered
winsomely in every deed. *He* bidding them hate their parents,

---

[17] Notice the satirical force of *"this* man" in the Greek version.

Who taught them to love their enemies? *He* advocating trea-
son to their country Who Himself wept in compassion over
Jerusalem? *He* recommending that they count their brethren
as detestable, Who had taught that the spirit of anger is a kind
of murder.[18] *He* counselling a disregard for little children,
Who Himself took children in His arms to bless them? Nay,
they knew Him better! One of them preserved this saying in
a form which robs it of its paradox: "He that loveth father
or mother more than Me is not worthy of Me and he that
loveth son or daughter more than Me is not worthy of Me" . . .

Plainly stated, the condition of discipleship is this: *Jesus
must come first.* It is an amazing claim! In regal humility He
confronts the race of men: "My spirit is to be your law and
your life. You will be wise to die, if need be, for My name's
sake." What is equally amazing is the fact that it does not
occur to us to question either His sanity or His lowliness. We
look on Him, and know His claim is just. We know that
genuine love for parent, wife, child, or comrade, will never
conflict with our love for Him. We know, by some unerring
intuition, that if it *does* conflict—if there is a clash of claims—
the human love by that very token is unworthy! The earthly
must exist within the heavenly (such is the condition), or it
must be renounced as if we hated it. If it does exist within
the heavenly, it gains such radiance, such depth of joy, as to
be itself transmuted to a thing divine. Did not Jesus renounce
His home, and thereafter wander homeless?

John Galsworthy with consummate art has shown us the
heartbreaking confusion caused by our conflict of loyalties.[19]
In a dramatic play of character and circumstance he portrays
one man true to his race, another true to his social group, and
others, in their respective challenges, refusing to be faithless to
profession, home, wife, or child. He shows that these various
fealties do not cohere. Their issue is tragedy. The conclusion is stated with sudden, poignant insight: "Prejudices—
or are they loyalties—I don't know—criss-cross—we all cut
each other's throats from the best of motives." At the play's
end comes the terse comment. A suicide's letter says, "A pistol

18 Matthew 5: 21, 22.
19 In the play, "Loyalties." (Charles Scribner's Sons.)

keeps faith." Whereupon one reading it remarks, "Keeps faith! We've all done that. It's not enough." The chaos of our lesser loyalties cries aloud for some regal loyalty to rule them. Oh, for some transcendent passion—as pure as purity, as loving as love—to gather all other worthy passions beneath the healing of its wings! "If any man cometh unto me, and, in the conflict of allegiances, will not hate the whole world for my sake . . ." Is He—the Galilean Carpenter—the rightful, only King? Is love for Him the regal passion that can bring order in the troubled realm of our lesser loyalties? If we "kept faith" with Him, would that be "enough"?

Such is the amazing claim He makes! The twelve disciples, even on such absolute conditions, were constrained to follow. What of their homes, their parents? We do not know—except that they left all and followed. They followed this Galilean who presumed to lay His law upon the world, this Fanatic who kissed little children, this Idealist who, deeming His *ideal* the only *real,* suffered real nails to be driven through His hands! . . .

We may say that His conditions of discipleship are preposterous. But if we refuse to accept them, what of the alternative? Did He not state it in words that writhe?—"Or else, while the other is yet a great way off, he sendeth an ambassage, and asketh conditions of peace." Is that the alternative?—the surrender of the soul's honor, before our enemy is even near? —an unworthy peace on terms dictated by the foe? Is that the alternative?—that we enthrone Him in unquestioned regnancy, or that we live in the haunting sense of a coward's compromise? It is well that we should "count the cost," not only of His discipleship, but of that other choice! "So therefore whosoever he be of you that renounceth not all he hath, he cannot be my disciple."

CHAPTER VIII

The Marks of Discipleship (I)

HUMILITY

THE PARABLE OF THE CHIEF SEATS

"And he spake a parable unto those that were bidden, when he marked how they chose out the chief seats; saying unto them, When thou art bidden of any man to a marriage feast, sit not down in the chief seat; lest haply a more honorable man than thou be bidden of him, and he that bade thee and him shall come and say to thee, Give this man place; and then thou shalt begin with shame to take the lowest place. But when thou art bidden, go and sit down in the lowest place; that when he that hath bidden thee cometh, he may say to thee, Friend, go up higher: then shalt thou have glory in the presence of all that sit at meat with thee. For every one that exalteth himself shall be humbled; and he that humbleth himself shall be exalted."

(Luke 14:7-11)

THE PARABLE OF THE PHARISEE AND THE PUBLICAN

"And he spake also this parable unto certain who trusted in themselves that they were righteous, and set all others at nought: Two men went up into the temple to pray; the one a Pharisee, and the other a publican. The Pharisee stood and prayed thus with himself, God, I thank thee, that I am not as the rest of men, extortioners, unjust, adulterers, or even as this publican. I fast twice in the week; I give tithes of all that I get. But the publican, standing afar off, would not lift up so much as his eyes unto heaven, but smote his breast, saying, God, be thou merciful to me a sinner. I say unto you, This man went down to his house justified rather than the other; for every one that exalteth himself shall be humbled; but he that humbleth himself shall be exalted."

(Luke 18:9-14)

CHAPTER VIII

HUMILITY

The Parable of the Chief Seats
The Parable of the Pharisee and the Publican

The story of the Chief Seats is more than counsel in social deportment. Otherwise, it would have no claim to the title of parable. Under the guise of a lesson in table manners, Jesus explains that in heaven's household humility is a lovely and essential grace. Thus the final sentence is doubly final; it is an axiom of the kingdom: "For every one that exalteth himself shall be humbled; and he that humbleth himself shall be exalted." [1]

The story of the Pharisee and the Publican teaches the same truth in sharper etching. The same unqualified dictum (with an emphatic "I say unto you") concludes it, to make clear beyond cavil that humility is an indispensable virtue.

The Parable of the Chief Seats

Jesus "marked how they chose out the chief seats." No smallest turn in the drama of our daily life escaped Him. He "spake a parable unto those which were bidden." It was a daring parable to tell at the table of Simon the Pharisee where He has just witnessed the unseemly scramble for prominence. The story speaks, indeed, of a "marriage-feast," a more formal occasion than that at which Jesus was a guest and one demanding on the host's part a careful appraisal and acknowledgment of the rank and prestige of his guests. But if the story's setting served to coat the pill, the patient was not spared the dose. Were "social ambitions" ever more neatly punctured, or the pushings and elbowings of the place-seeker impaled on

---

[1] The repetition of the phrase may be the work of the evangelist. In any case it is appropriate. But there is no need to assume that Jesus did not repeat His sayings, especially those of aphoristic nature.

a shrewder scorn? The satire, kind yet keen, paints an almost ludicrous picture. See this gentleman, affable and self-important, taking a high place at the feast. Sitting there he swells with pride like Æsop's frog. See him now requested by his host, because a guest of real honor has arrived, to take a lower place. But all the lower seats are filled. Red-faced and mortified he goes to the table's farthest end. It would have been wiser to have begun at the meanest station. Then the host might have singled him out, expressing surprise and offering apologies that one so great should have been so humbled, and might have conducted him conspicuously (amid the deference of all the guests) to a place of glory.[2]

It is a trenchant commentary on the old proverb: "Put not thyself forward in the presence of the king, and stand not in the place of great men: For better it is that it be said unto thee, Come up hither; than that thou shouldest be put lower in the presence of the prince whom thine eyes have seen."[3] Dante and Vergil in their upward journey through Paradiso came to the Angel of Humility who called them to the steps of ascent and beat his wings on Dante's forehead. Then Dante heard voices singing, "Blessed are the poor in spirit," and noticed that, though he was climbing, progress was easier than it had been on level ground. Why? Vergil explained that one of the seven sin marks, that of pride, had been erased from Dante's forehead by the Angel's wings, and that in consequence the other six had become much fainter. (Is not pride the deadliest foe of human virtue?) Whereupon Dante felt his brow —for true humility is unconscious of being humble. The story reads aright the mind of Jesus!

> "He that is down needs fear no fall,
> He that is low, no pride;
> He that is humble ever shall
> Have God to be his guide."[4]

"For every one that exalteth himself shall be humbled." The dicta of Jesus play havoc with our common verdicts. The

---

2 The fact that "that he may say" in v. 10 is not necessarily purposive does not forbid the interpretation here suggested. The glints of humor—a humor pregnant with meaning—seem to me unmistakable.

3 Proverbs 25: 6, 7 which seem to have been in the mind of Jesus as the theme of the parable.

4 John Bunyan, "The Shepherd Boy Sings."

Beatitudes, for instance, are forthright denials of accepted valuations. Is it blessed to be poor in spirit? Nay, surely a man must hew out his own course in a world which receives men at their own reckoning. Is it blessed to mourn? Not in an age which believes that "a good time" is mankind's inalienable right! Is it blessed to be persecuted? On the contrary, "single thought is civil crime," and persecution is proper punishment for the temerity which flouts a standardized opinion. Some one has suggested that the Beatitudes, because they prescribe an unobtrusive virtue, would not furnish in actual character any materials for a thrilling biography. The retort is obvious: The Beatitudes once became incarnate, and the resultant Biography is the most thrilling known to men. We try to forget Him and cannot. When His presence becomes too awkward, we shuffle Him off to some new Calvary. But He reappears, the world's unquiet Conscience, to Whom soon or late we must surrender. He is the curse of our orderly selfishness—and our only Peace. The Beatitudes not thrilling? If we dared to apply them they would explode like a mine beneath the careful trenches of a success-worshipping generation.

The day of Jesus did not believe that "every one that exalteth himself shall be humbled," and still less that "he that humbleth himself shall be exalted"; nor do we to-day believe Him. It is a duty, we think, that every man should strive to gain the public ear and eye. And imagine a government being humble! Imagine a nation so concerned with her duties toward other nations as to be forgetful of her rights! We do not accept His teaching, but in our illumined hours we become uneasy about our boasted civilization and surprise ourselves in the forbidden thought that perhaps He is right. . . .

For humility is not cowardice; no man is craven who dares to look first on an eternal splendor and then upon his own littleness.[5] "The meek are they who have consented to receive the knowledge of themselves." It is a brave consent. Nor is humility mean-spiritedness, or self-depreciation, or lack of enthusiasm.

Humility has one root in a sense of indebtedness. What have

5 Bruce, *op. cit.*, p. 322, quotes Arndt in a pretty turn of phrase: "Das Wesen der Demuth ist Muth," "the essence of humility (Demuth) is courage (Muth)."

we that we have not received? The food on our table, the words in our mouth, the liberties which overarch our days are in largest measure gifts to us from invisible helpers in past or present. The cult of the "self-made man" is an unlovely and ungrateful cult. The first fact in the history of the self-made man is that a mother went down to the gates of pain that he might be born. Nor is the least portion of our debt that which comes from the faithfulness of "common" folk. "Common," in this regard, has often its first meaning: "com-munis"— "ready to be of service." There is vast cheer and goodness in average humanity (a cheer and goodness not less real, but more, because they do not flow into theological molds), and they are bestowed upon us "without money and without price." We are in overwhelming debt to life—and a man overwhelmingly in debt cannot afford to be proud!

The other root of humility is in reverence and the sense of need. The scientist confronts the æonian daring, the patience and perfection of the created world, and knows full well that his own power and learning are, as Isaac Newton confessed, but a few pebbles on the shore of an infinite ocean. The artist sees the beatific vision, and asks as he takes palette and brush in hand, "Who is sufficient for this splendor?" In his own tongue he chants with seraphim around a throne: "Holy, holy, holy; the whole earth is full of Thy glory." From this contrast between the Divine Excellence and the human frailty there flows a sense of human need and a fountain of prayer:

> "And chiefly Thou, O Spirit, that dost prefer
> Before all temples the upright heart and pure,
> Instruct me, for Thou know'st. . . .
>
>   . . . : what in me is dark
> Illumine, what is low raise and support;
> That to the highth of this great argument
> I may assert Eternal Providence,
> And justify the ways of God to men." [6]

It is said of George Frederick Watts: "There is always in his work a window left open to the infinite, the unattainable ideal." [7]   That open window is also in the homage of a Coper-

6 Milton, "Paradise Lost," Book I.
7 Mary S. Watts' "George Frederick Watts," i., 299.

nicus as he reads the unfolding epic of the skies. It is in the
music of Mozart as he confesses:

> "I heard a sound
> As of a silver horn from o'er the hills. . . .
>
> "O never harp nor horn,
> Nor aught we blow we breath or touch with hand,
> Was like that music as it came. . . ." [8]

It is in the prayer of Saint Francis as, with awakened conscience, he bows adoringly before the holiness of God. One
who lives in face of an "unattainable ideal" cannot be proud.
Neither will he be cowardly, mean-spirited or bereft of enthusiasm. He will be humble.

When we see a man inflated with pride and worshipping at
the poor altar of himself (such a man as we, a drowned debtor
to life and encompassed by perfection), some instinct tells us
that he is an outrageous freak, a cardboard figure on stilts,
who will soon be blown away by the winds of reality. The
instinct is just. One who was "meek and lowly of heart" endorsed it. "Every one that exalteth himself shall be humbled;
and he that humbleth himself shall be exalted."

The Parable of the Pharisee and the Publican

The Pharisee was a pillar of the Church, an ardent patriot,
and respected in his community as a citizen of highest character. The publican, on the other hand, was almost untouchable.
That Jesus should tell a story condemning the one and approving the other was a staggering and unpardonable assault on
accepted judgments. He committed the assault. Therein is
proof enough of His conviction that self-righteous pride is as
noxious a sin as penitent humility is an essential grace. [9]

8 Tennyson, "The Holy Grail" ("The Idylls of the King").
9 Dr. Montefiore has said of this Pharisee that he is "a ludicrous caricature of
the average Pharisee, a monstrous caricature of the Pharisaic ideal." George Murray, *op. cit.*, p. 3, agrees; but defends Jesus on the ground that His method was
that of *tour de force* and so demanded pictures bordering on the extravagant. Jesus
did at times employ figures verging on the grotesque (as, for instance, that of a
camel passing through a needle's eye), but it is doubtful if He ever indulged in
"monstrous" travesties of human types. He was too kind for such unbridled scorn.
There are enough artless hints as to the Pharisaic character scattered about the
Gospels (Matthew 19: 24, 23: 6, etc.), to defend the belief that this picture is not
"overdrawn" except in the minor measure necessary to sharpen the contrast between
the Pharisee and his opposite.

There is nothing in the story to suggest that either the Pharisee or the publican was insincere in his self-estimate. They were not praying for public consumption or to curry public favor, the one man by exaggerating his virtues and the other by the "pride which apes humility." They had ascended Mount Moriah to the Temple of their fathers. Their prayers may have been inaudible,[10] but whether audible or inaudible they were unfeigned. The Pharisee in his own eyes and by common consent was a virtuous man, while the publican by the same tests was a sinner. But—and this is the inescapable, revolutionary teaching of the story—the Pharisee's virtue was so cankered by pride that it was almost rotten, and the publican's sin was so saved by humility that it came near to the gates of the kingdom of God.

Every line is drawn to emphasize the contrast between the one man's self-righteousness and the other's penitence. The Pharisee prayed "I thank Thee," but his prayer was such only in name. He had no real thanksgiving to offer, for he was under no sense of blessings received. He had no plea to make, for he was unconscious of any lack or need. He used the word "God," but it was only a glance in the general direction of heaven to prelude a pæan of self-praise. He first congratulated himself on his virtues of omission. He was not "as all other men"—the rest of mankind! He was not an extortioner, not unjust, not adulterous, nor even "as this publican." (The poor publican, standing at a distance, is thus dragged into the "prayer" as a dark foil for the Pharisee's gleaming whiteness.) Measured by other men, he towered aloft. It had not occurred to him to measure himself by the sky. A mountain shames a molehill until both are humbled by the stars. Thomas Carlyle has a dramatic passage in which he conducts the heedless Louis XV of France to the eternal judgment-seat: "Yes, poor Louis, death has found thee. No palace walls . . . or gorgeous tapestries . . . could keep him out. Time is done and all the scaffolding of time falls wrecked with hideous clangor round thy soul; the pale kingdoms yawn;

10 The indefinite phrase "stood and prayed thus *with himself*" seems to imply not aloofness of location but rather that the prayer was spoken within himself. See v. 11.

there thou must enter naked, all unkinged. . . ." Then with sudden change of front Carlyle turns upon his readers: "And let no meanest man lay flattering unction to his soul. Louis was a ruler; but art thou not also one? His wide France, looked at from the fixed stars, is not wider than thy narrow brickfield, where thou too doest faithfully or unfaithfully." [11] But the Pharisee had forgotten how to look at the stars, and therefore his virtue was a "wide France" and that of other men was "a narrow brickfield."

His abstentions from wrong having been listed, the Pharisee next informed heaven of his virtues of commission. By the test of omission or commission he was equally justified. He fasted twice in the week, even though the law might have been fulfilled if he had fasted but once a year.[12] He gave tithes of everything he gained, even of "mint, anise, and cummin" which the law did not require him to tithe.[13] Then what was wrong with him? His virtue was negative! His goodness was mummery! He lacked the essential spirit of goodness— that spirit which has as a necessary element "an humble and a contrite heart." All his righteousness was vitiated by that lack.

Every stroke in the picture of the publican deepens the impression of humility. He "stood afar off" as one unworthy to be the neighbor of a righteous man. His posture was well-nigh abject: he dared not raise so much as his eyes to heaven. He smote repeatedly upon his breast in an agony of self-condemnation. His prayer was a piteous outpouring of shame and entreaty: "God be propitiated to me, *the* sinner." The Pharisee was self-separated from the "rest of men" by his righteousness; the publican by his own confession was infamously separated from all others by his sin. *"The* sinner"— as if the sin of others were negligible by comparison!

Then the terse conclusion of the matter: "I say unto you"— Jesus claims to know both the secrets of men and the judgments

11 Thomas Carlyle, "The French Revolution."
12 See footnote on p. 4, and an interesting comment in the "I.C.C." (St. Luke), p. 417.
13 For the ancient law of tithing, see Deuteronomy 14: 22. It required the giving unto God of a tenth of the yield of the cattle and of the fields. Garden produce was exempt from the tithe. See the comment of Jesus on "mint, anise, and cummin" in Matthew 23: 23. The Talmud inveighs against the Pharisaism of those "who implore you to mention some more duties which they might perform."

of God, and states both emphatically "in low, deep tones, and simple words of great authority"—"I say unto you, This man went down to his house justified rather than the other." A publican "justified"?—pronounced right by God?—forgiven? He was traitor to his country (like a Pole selling himself to the Russians in the days of Poland's dream of liberty to collect Russian taxes!). He was apostate to his church, his friends, his self-respect. Some men are traitorous in one black deed, but he was traitorous all day long and every day. A publican "justified"? Yes!—it is the emphatic word of Jesus. Not that his misdeeds were suddenly condoned, not that he was lifted by some swift magic to permanent heights of godly character, not that his struggle was cancelled, but rather that he had Humility—that lowly postern by which alone the King of Heaven comes in lowly guise.

Our precious pharisaisms appear bedraggled in this parable's merciless light. What of our pharisaism of race—that new gospel of our time, preached with invincible (?) arguments from biology, heralding the white man as the only chosen of God? (It was heaven's egregious blunder that Jesus was not born an occidental!) What of our pharisaism of class—that amazing pride which assumes that a man whose chairs are upholstered in velour can have no dealings with a man whose chairs are upholstered in plain board? What of our pharisaisms of intelligence—that arrogance which talks in terms of morons and is so blind as not to see that one super-intelligence lacking goodwill may be far more pestilential than a gross of morons honorable in motive? What of our continuing pharisaisms of religion? This parable thrusts home! Perhaps the racial, social, educational, and even theological imprimatur upon our life is a poor substitute for the justification pronounced by God.

Pharisaism has no romance, no quest for a "city that hath foundations," for it accounts its own achievement a perfect city. Pharisaism has no friends and no friendliness, for it is cursed by the inward-turning eye and looks not on "the things of others"[14] except to feed its own conceit of character.

14 Philippians 2: 4.

Pharisaism has no hope, for it has already attained. It has no God, for it feels no need of God. Unconscious of defect, it raises no cry to that Completeness "which flows around our incompleteness," and thus misses heaven whose strength is made perfect only in our weakness. Concerning Pharisaism Jesus spoke two of the most desolating words that ever passed His gracious lips: "They have their reward" (the future holds no promise!) and "Let them alone," as if to say "They are beyond the help of man and God until the crash of calamity has brought their pride to ashes"!

But humility has its city of desire (a city all the lovelier that its spires are seen in far distance), because it counts itself not to have attained. Humility has friends because it looks ever on the common life with sense of gratitude and ever strives to pay its debt. Humility has God, for its very sense of sin comes of its vision of a white throne. It cries "Woe is me" just because its eyes have seen the King.[15] It knows the jangling discord of its life just because it has heard sphere-music. It is cursed by unrest because it knows, if only in dim surmise, the "peace that passeth understanding." Heaven bends low to the soul that feels its need. They that mourn for their sins are comforted, and the poor in spirit are enriched by the kingdom of God.

15 Isaiah 6: 5.

CHAPTER IX

The Marks of Discipleship (II)

FORGIVEN AND FORGIVING

THE PARABLE OF THE TWO DEBTORS

"And Jesus answering said unto him, Simon, I have somewhat to say unto thee. And he saith, Teacher, say on. A certain lender had two debtors: the one owed five hundred shillings, and the other fifty. When they had not wherewith to pay, he forgave them both. Which of them therefore will love him most? Simon answered and said, He, I suppose, to whom he forgave the most. And he said unto him, Thou hast rightly judged. And turning to the woman, he said unto Simon, Seest thou this woman? I entered into thy house, thou gavest me no water for my feet: but she hath wetted my feet with her tears, and wiped them with her hair. Thou gavest me no kiss: but she, since the time I came in, hath not ceased to kiss my feet. My head with oil thou didst not anoint: but she hath anointed my feet with ointment. Wherefore I say unto thee, Her sins, which are many, are forgiven; for she loved much: but to whom little is forgiven, the same loveth little. And he said unto her, Thy sins are forgiven. And they that sat at meat with him began to say within themselves, Who is this that even forgiveth sins?" *(Luke* 7:40-49)

THE PARABLE OF THE UNMERCIFUL SERVANT

"Then came Peter and said to him, Lord, how oft shall my brother sin against me, and I forgive him? until seven times? Jesus saith unto him, I say not unto thee, Until seven times; but, Until seventy times seven. Therefore is the kingdom of heaven likened unto a certain king, who would make a reckoning with his servants. And when he had begun to reckon, one was brought unto him, that owed him ten thousand talents. But forasmuch as he had not wherewith to pay, his lord commanded him to be sold, and his wife, and children, and all that he had, and payment to be made. The servant therefore fell down, and worshipped him, saying, Lord, have patience with me, and I will pay thee all. And the lord of that servant, being moved with compassion, released him, and forgave him the debt. But that servant went out, and found one of his fellow-servants, who owed him a hundred shillings: and he laid hold on him, and took him by the throat, saying, Pay what thou owest. So his fellow-servant fell down and besought him, saying, Have patience with me, and I will pay thee. And he would not: but went and cast him into prison, till he should pay that which was due. So when his fellow-servants saw what was done, they were exceeding sorry, and came and told unto their lord all that was done. Then his lord called him unto him, and saith to him, Thou wicked servant, I forgave thee all that debt, because thou besoughtest me: shouldest not thou also have had mercy on thy fellow-servant, even as I had mercy on thee? And his lord was wroth, and delivered him to the tormentors, till he should pay all that was due. So shall also my heavenly Father do unto you, if ye forgive not every one his brother from your hearts." *(Matthew* 18:21-35)

FORGIVEN AND FORGIVING

The Parable of the Two Debtors
The Parable of the Unmerciful Servant

The full mind of Jesus concerning forgiveness has not been understood; or, if understood, not courageously expounded. We think we know Him better than our forbears; we claim "the rediscovery of Jesus." We have rescued His social gospel, for instance, from the oblivion to which it was consigned by a disproportionate individualism in religion. We preen ourselves as His true interpreters. Then some word of His, long known by rote, affrights us by its sudden newness; and we wonder if we are more comprehending than the twelve, or if we can follow any better than they the flaming meteor of His thought. Ever and again the realization strikes us that His truth, if we dared apply it, would rend the fabric of our age.

Part of His message about forgiveness has not lacked proclamation. That God's pardoning grace is full and free has been preached—with such jaunty irreverence at times, and with such reckless ignoring of its Divine cost and human conditions, as to make it cheap. But what of the felt need of pardon which must precede forgiveness, and the sense of gratitude which must follow it? Jesus addressed Himself to that question in the Parable of the Two Debtors. And what of our own willingness to forgive? On that score the Parable of the Unmerciful Servant has teaching so new, so little heeded as to prompt again the question, "Have I been so long time with you, and dost thou not know me?"

The Parable of the Two Debtors

Jesus was dining at the home of Simon the Pharisee. Neither high rank nor low barred the outgoing of His friendliness.

1 John 14: 9.

Simon appears to have been typical of his caste; but his willingness to entertain Jesus, though with condescension, betokens a
measure of open-mindedness. He was at least curious about
the new Teacher. Suddenly, during the dinner, a woman of
notorious name is found anointing the feet of Jesus with costly
balm. Thus arose a situation as dramatic as the most dramatic
sense could crave. Behold the three players in the drama.

There was Simon, curious, half-friendly, patronizing, whose
loveless virtue knew no humility. Unconscious of moral lack,
he had no reverence either for perfect heaven or for broken
earth.

There was Mary,[2] of generous but unstable emotion, who,
falling into fleshly sin, had become sin's slave. Yet she hated
herself for her bondage. She hungered for her lost purity,
without hope until she saw Jesus. The caste of Simon had not
saved her from despair; as they passed her in the street, they
had drawn holy ropes of condemnation tight about them lest
they should catch her leprosy. But Jesus had saved her.
Standing on the edge of the listening crowd,[3] she had felt His
love. Through Him God's peace had fallen in healing on her
driven and self-tortured soul.

There was Jesus held in this interplay of varied moods and
motives.

Access to Simon's house was easy. The rules of hospitality
in the Orient were surprisingly free. Strangers could come and
go during the progress of a meal; and cushions were provided
for them against the wall, so that they might recline there and
converse with the guests. But that Mary should come—a
woman whose reputation was the village scandal—was an un-
believable temerity. Yet she came to Jesus, and, as she was
about to anoint His feet, she burst into tears. The weeping
was all unpurposed; the mingled memory of her shame and His

2 The weight of scholarship is against the view which would identify the Mary
of this story with either Mary of Bethany who anointed Jesus before His passion
(see Matthew 26: 6, Mark 14: 3, John 12: 3) or with Mary of Magdala (see Luke
8: 2). The three women appear dissimilar in character, and it is quite improbable
that Luke would confuse two women so unlike as Mary of Bethany and the Mary
of this story. The fact that a Simon appears in both anointings argues little. There
are eleven Simons mentioned in the New Testament. See "I.C.C." (Luke), p. 209.

3 That Mary had prior acquaintance with Jesus seems to be clear not only on the
ground of probability but also in the word of forgiveness in v. 48; "Thy sins *have
been and remain forgiven.*" The verb is in the perfect tense.

mercy broke the seal upon her eyes. Spontaneously she released her tresses—an act considered immodest—and, so shielded, she kissed His feet again and again,[4] and used her hair to wipe away the flood of contrite tears. There is not a more affecting scene in the Gospels.

The effect on Simon was instant. He spoke within himself, "If this man were a prophet . . ." It had occurred to him that Jesus might be a prophet, but now the surmise was impossible. A prophet would have known this woman's character, and would have indignantly disowned her clinging homage. Either He did not know her,[5] or He was morally insensible; and by either alternative, so Simon reasoned, His claim to be a prophet was belied. But Jesus quickly proved His power to read not only Mary's character but Simon's thoughts: "Simon, I have somewhat to say unto thee." It was so seriously spoken that Simon answered with some instinctive deference, "Teacher, say on." Against that tense and dramatic setting Jesus told the little Parable of the Two Debtors:

There were two debtors. One owed five hundred pence and the other fifty.[6] When they had nothing with which to pay, the money-lender—far more genial than most in his trade—absolved them both. Which would love the creditor the more? Which, when they passed him on the street, would greet him with more grateful cheer?

Simon answered the question half superciliously: "I suppose he to whom he forgave most." Jesus confirmed the answer. "Thou hast answered right"—almost in the Socratic manner, as though Simon had been led into a fatal admission. Why did Mary love intensely, and why this lavish outpouring of her love? Because she had been forgiven much! Why did Simon love penuriously? He had been forgiven little!

The Christian message of forgiveness is here—never more

4 *Kai katephelei*—"continued to kiss affectionately."
5 It was a necessary gift or power in a prophet that he should be able to read character. See Isaiah 11: 3, 4 and 1 Samuel 9: 19.
6 Bruce suggests that the smallness of the sums may indicate the prevalent poverty of Judea, and quotes Hansrath ("History of New Testament Times") to the effect that Jesus frequently used the images of creditor, debtor, usury, and debtors' prison. (*Op. cit.*, pp. 243, 4 footnote.)

compassionately spoken. Whether the sin of Mary was more
blameworthy than other sins is not the primary question. It
was blameworthy enough—though Jesus treated guilt of emotional excess with less sternness, it would seem, than guilt of
Pharisaic pride or of deliberate calculation. He had pity for a
harlot, but withering invective for "whited sepulchers." [7] But
Mary's sin was not condoned; it was with full cause that her
name was a shadowed password. Yet she found forgiveness.
Jesus made her feel that she could rise above her evil past
and her bondaged present. This is the perennial, redeeming
hope of the gospel.

But the emphasis of the story is not mainly on forgiveness
as a saving assurance, but rather on the relationship between
forgiveness and love. The measure of forgiveness received
at God's hands and the measure of consequent love are in direct
ratio—such is the crux of the parable. Then goodness is under
penalty? Then it were wisdom to "continue in sin, that grace
may abound"? [8] No, because the measure of our forgiveness
rests upon another factor, namely, the measure of our *conscious need* of forgiveness. Mary *felt herself* overwhelmingly
in debt, and her love was commensurate with her conscious
need of pardon. Simon, on the other hand, was not deeply
penitent, not sharply stricken by remorse; and so, since he
deemed his sins slight, his slight forgiveness issued in slight
love. Yet Simon did not lack sufficient sin! Who among the
sons of earth suffers any such lack? His very complacency,
his indifference to the wreck and woe of such as Mary, were
sin enough. He lacked a *consciousness* of sin, the writhing of
a moral sense which has seen the White Throne.

> "For none, O Lord, has perfect rest
> For none is wholly free from sin:
> And they who fain would serve Thee best
> Are conscious most of wrong within." [9]

Jesus proceeds to lay bare in Simon's life the need to which

7 See a discussion of the list of cardinal virtues and vices in connection with the
interpretation of the Parable of the Prodigal Son, p. 195, 196.
8 Romans 6: 2. There is only one answer to Paul's question, and he himself
makes it: "God forbid." Yet love and forgiveness are in direct ratio and causal
union. The antinomy has frequently been discussed. *Vide, e.g.,* a chapter on redemption in Dr. G. A. Gordon's "Aspects of the Infinite Mystery."
9 Henry Twells, "At even, ere the sun was set."

his self-righteousness had made him blind. The phrases bite.
Simon had grown no rank weeds—he had been too arid!—but
he had grown no flowers. Mary's nature was rich soil and
had brought forth poisonous weeds in dark profusion, but her
garden was not bereft of beauty. The courtesies [10] are a test
of the generosity of character.

> "For manners are not idle, but the fruit
> Of loyal nature and of noble mind." [11]

Let the test be applied to Simon and Mary—however Simon
may resent the comparison! "Thou gavest me no kiss upon my
cheek"—a common sign of oriental welcome; "but she has not
ceased to kiss my feet"—token of lowliest homage! "Thou
gavest me no water for my feet"—in patronizing condescension
even that most customary act of hospitality had been neglected;
"but she has given me the water of her weeping"! "Thou
gavest me no oil for my head"—and oil was plentiful and always at a guest's disposal; "but she has anointed my *feet* with
costly balm." The items of hospitality seem of small significance, but the aridness or generosity of a nature is revealed in
them; and Mary, in Simon's house, had done the honors to
Simon's guest.[12]

There is enough of sin in any Simon to prompt the penitent
cry, which, then answered, issues in its turn in fullness of devotion. The master spirits in every age have had moments of
such consciousness of guilt that their confession has been with
strong crying and drops of blood. St. Paul was, in his own
eyes, the chief of sinners,[13] and St. Francis, when told by
Brother Masseo that "all the world runs after thee," replied
that there was nowhere "a greater, more miserable, poorer
sinner than I." [14] Sensitiveness to sin is one side of that shield

10 The courtesies meant more and still mean more in the Orient than in our
western world. See Trench, *op. cit.,* p. 305.
11 Alfred Tennyson, "Guinevere."
12 Murray, *op. cit.,* p. 31, asserts that Jesus would not thus upbraid Simon in
his own house. "Would He pillory His host as stingy, at his own table?" Perhaps the application of the parable was spoken by another voice than His at another
time. Yet Jesus, when offence was given to "one of these little ones," could speak
with flaming wrath; and on this occasion Mary was being pilloried by the contempt
of the whole table, and His concern was for her. We are inclined to believe that
the objection is not sustained.
13 I Timothy 1: 15.
14 J. Törgensen, "St. Francis of Assisi."

whose other face is sensitiveness to the undimmed radiance of God. Mary knew her own darkness, and thereby proved that she had seen the light "in whom there is no darkness at all"; but Simon, blind to his own stain, was blind to heaven's purity. "Seest thou this woman?" Nay, Simon had not seen. "Her sins, which are many, have been forgiven, for she loved much; but to whom little is forgiven, the same loveth little." [15] Did Simon yield to the strong yet tender rebuke? We may cherish the hope, for there is no mention of his murmuring. As for Mary, she heard her Master change the words of the oriental salutation: He said, not "Go in peace," but "Go *into* peace." What mercy and hope are in the change! Our eyes follow her as she goes from grace to grace, from glory to glory, ever deeper into that peace which is too deep for understanding, until, folded in light she passes beyond our mortal sight.

The Parable of the Unmerciful Servant

Has the Church seriously faced and courageously preached the assertion of Jesus that Divine forgiveness and human willingness to forgive are joined together? What can a reverent mind say of a pardon so indiscriminate as to require only that a man walk down a sawdust trail and shake hands with a preacher? If forgiveness is so cheap, wrong-doing cannot be so costly! If pardon is by "wave of hand," sin cannot be heinous! Should we not study the conditions of forgiveness, among which the will to forgive is always and necessarily included?

The message of Jesus in this regard is unequivocal. "If ye forgive men their trespasses, your heavenly Father will also forgive you. But if ye forgive not men their trespasses, neither will your Father forgive your trespasses." [16] . . . "Forgive us

---

15 On this verse has been built the Roman Catholic doctrine of salvation by love, as distinct from the characteristically Protestant doctrine of salvation by faith. Whatever truth there may be in the Roman Catholic doctrine *per se* (and some day we shall learn of conflicting theological views that truth is more often reached by their synthesis than by their opposition), that doctrine is not taught in this parable. A theory cannot be established on an abbreviated phrase or on the juxtaposition of words. The teaching here is "much love is the consequence of much forgiveness" as the concluding phrases of v. 47 and the clear purport of the whole parable manifestly show.
16 Matthew 6: 14, 15.

our debts as we forgive our debtors." [17]   (How can we pray
that prayer so glibly?) . . . "So shall also my heavenly Father
do unto you, if ye forgive not every one his brother from your
hearts." [18]   The message is too frequent and spoken with too
sharp an emphasis ever to be denied. It comes close to home.
There may be irenic souls who cherish no grudges and nurse
no bitterness. In one of Gladstone's early letters to his wife
he remarks, "I seem hardly to have any daily pressure . . .
no strokes from God; no opportunity of pardoning others, for
none offend me." But such unruffled goodwill is rare. Most
men have opportunity for the exercise of forgiving grace, and,
if the offence is slight, most men are ready to forgive; but stern
rebuffs are remembered with resentment and sometimes with
revenge. Thus the Parable of the Unmerciful Servant strikes
deep as it gives warning that our unwillingness to forgive one
another bars the door against God's willingness to forgive us.

The parable arose from Peter's question: "How often shall
my brother sin against me and I forgive him?   Till seven
times?" The Jewish law appears to have required forgiveness
until three times. [19] Presumably it allowed a man who had forgiven his enemy three times, to regard him thereafter with
implacable hostility. Perhaps Peter with his "till seven times"
was eager to appear magnanimous. [20] Jesus swept the suggestion aside, and asserted that forgiveness is not cheese-paring
arithmetic but an overflowing spirit: "I say not unto thee until
seven times; but, until seventy times seven." [21] The parable
is spoken to illuminate the command.

The leading character is a man who being left in charge of
a king's realm proved so unfaithful to the trust that at the day
of reckoning he owed his ruler ten thousand talents. Even one
talent was a considerable sum. The total annual taxes of
Judea, Idumea, Samaria, Galilee and Perea amounted to only

17 Matthew 6: 12.
18 Matthew 18: 35.
19 See "I.C.C." (Matthew), W. C. Allen, p. 199. The Jewish rabbis quoted such
passages as Job 33: 29, Amos 2: 6, as their authorities in teaching this threefold
forgiveness. Therein is a curious revelation of the rabbinical mind.
20 Or perhaps he was echoing Jesus' words as recorded in Luke 17: 4. Seven,
it must also be remembered, was a sacred number.
21 Dr. Moulton thinks this phrase is deliberately in the language of Genesis 4: 24
which breathes out revenge "until seventy times seven."

eight hundred talents.[22] It is written of Amaziah [23] that he
hired "a hundred thousand mighty men of valor" as trained
levies in war for "a hundred talents of silver." All the gold
used in the ark of the covenant was worth less than thirty
talents.[24] By any reckoning, ten thousand talents was a fabulous debt—about two million dollars. The debtor might plead
his resolve to pay "all," but he could not possibly fulfil the vow.
His only hope was that his royal master "being moved by compassion" might forgive him. So it befell in the story. The
king's clemency saved him and his family from that slavery
into which, as utterly insolvent debtors, they might lawfully
have been sold.

Why did Jesus instance "ten thousand talents"? A smaller
sum would not only have served the purpose of the parable but
increased its verisimilitude. But—is our human debt to God
payable? Can we ever "make good" our sins? We think
they have spent their force and then we stumble over some
new havoc they have wrought. "Ten thousand talents" is
true to psychological fact. If the Church neglects that truth,
then fiction and the drama preach it and become our evan-
gelists. The "Second Mrs. Tanqueray" [25] deplores the fact of
her failure to escape the consequences of an early misadven-
ture: "The future is but a door into the past." Macbeth
confesses that moral solvency is hopelessly beyond his reach:

> "Will all great Neptune's ocean wash this blood
> Clean from my hand? No, this my hand will rather
> The multitudinous seas incarnadine,
> Making the green one red . . ." [26]

"Ten thousand talents" justly describes not only our bank-
ruptcy of soul, but also the measure of Divine compassion.
Forgiveness is defined by the dictionary as "to give up re-
sentment or claim for requital for an offence or wrong." But
God's forgiveness is of another kind. He is above resentment.
He makes no "claim for requital." His pardon is a sorrowing

---

22 "Century Bible," *in loco.* A slave in the "flower of his youth" could be
bought for one talent (see Hastings' "Bible Dictionary," article on "Money").
23 II Chronicles 25: 6.
24 Exodus 38: 24.
25 In Sir Arthur Pinero's play of that title.
26 Shakespeare, "Macbeth."

over those who by their wrong are self-deceived, and a sharing of the shame and consequence of wrong with intent to redeem. Such forgiveness is not easy. A cross was raised to silence the blasphemy that forgiveness is easy. "Ten thousand talents" hints the dire cost of forgiveness.

The second scene of the parable reveals the debtor of ten thousand talents in the rôle of creditor. There was a man who owed him a hundred shillings. The obligation was not two million dollars now, but twenty. It could have been met, granted a reasonable respite. But though the large debtor had just been blessed by a compassion which cancelled his overwhelming liability and though the small debtor pleaded his case in identical entreaties to those which he had used, he took him by the throat and flung him into prison.

Mercy received ought to issue in mercy shown. Wrongs we suffer should weigh with us as negligible compared with wrongs we commit.

> "Earthly power doth then show likest God's
> When mercy seasons justice. Therefore, Jew,
> Though justice be thy plea, consider this—
> That in the course of justice none of us
> Should see salvation. We do pray for mercy;
> And that same prayer doth teach us all to render
> The deeds of mercy." [27]

Our concern for our sins, if it were sincere, would leave small zeal to demand justice for our injuries. The sins would appear as "ten thousand talents," and the injuries as the sixtieth part of one talent. But imagine any party in a labor war minimizing injuries received, and remorsefully confessing sins! Imagine a nation so occupied in contrite sorrow for its "reeking tubes" and "frantic boasts" as to have no heart to protest its "rights" against affronts. So far are we from being the true interpreters of Jesus, that His counsels still seem wildly quixotic.

The closing scene in the drama of the Unmerciful Servant is darkness unrelieved. Every stroke in the picture is of angry doom—the king's uncontained wrath on finding that his erstwhile debtor had played the hard-hearted creditor, his unsparing condemnation, and the stern fate he finally pro-

27 Shakespeare, "Merchant of Venice."

nounced: "And his lord was wrath and delivered him to the tormentors."

This description of the fury of the king is not to be construed as true to the nature of God. The closing verse is indeed emphatic: "So also shall my heavenly Father do unto you"; but only a gross literalism could assign the vindictiveness of the parable's conclusion to the ways of heaven.[28] The scenery of the story is not to be treated as though it were inerrant symbolism. We need not believe that God deliberately revokes a pardon once granted, still less that He consigns debtors to a vengeful torment. It is we ourselves who, by our unforgiving spirit, bar the door against Him who is always ready to forgive —such is the parable's piercing truth. Forgiveness implies one to receive as well as one to give. Forgiveness flows in upon us when life is reopened to the dealings of God, but no life is open to God which bitterly nurses its resentments. Such a life revokes its own pardon.

"Revenge is sweet," but the sweetness is short-lived. Soon revenge becomes acrid and miserable. It drives deeper the chasms of cleavage; it makes of every foe an implacable foe; it turns the days to gall. While God stands at the door in mercy and knocks, revenge broods over injuries and magnifies them, and so becomes deaf to God's knocking. Revenge is not sweet; it is burning poison. Revenge delivers itself to the tormentors.

But there was One who into earth's brackish waters of enmity and hate poured a crimson flood to make them sweet. Never was any man more unjustly smitten. The world He loved drove nails into His hands and feet. Yet He prayed, "Father, forgive them." The servant is not above his Lord!

28 G. H. Hubbard, *op. cit.*, p. 141, rightly issues this warning.

CHAPTER X

The Marks of Discipleship (III)

PRIVILEGE AND DUTY

THE PARABLE OF THE BARREN FIG TREE

"Now there were some present at that very season who told him of the Galileans, whose blood Pilate had mingled with their sacrifices. And he answered and said unto them, Think ye that these Galileans were sinners above all the Galileans, because they have suffered these things? I tell you, Nay: but, except ye repent, ye shall all in like manner perish. Or those eighteen, upon whom the tower in Siloam fell, and killed them, think ye that they were offenders above all the men that dwell in Jerusalem? I tell you, Nay: but, except ye repent, ye shall all likewise perish.

"And he spake this parable; A certain man had a fig tree planted in his vineyard; and he came seeking fruit thereon, and found none. And he said unto the vinedresser, Behold, these three years I come seeking fruit on this fig tree, and find none: cut it down; why doth it also cumber the ground? And he answering saith unto him, Lord, let it alone this year also, till I shall dig about it, and dung it: and if it bear fruit thenceforth, well; but if not, thou shalt cut it down.'

(*Luke* 13:1-9)

THE PARABLE OF THE BONDSERVANT

"But who is there of you, having a servant plowing or keeping sheep, that will say unto him, when he is come in from the field, Come straightway and sit down to meat; and will not rather say unto him, Make ready wherewith I may sup, and gird thyself, and serve me, till I have eaten and drunken; and afterward thou shalt eat and drink? Doth he thank the servant because he did the things that were commanded? Even so ye also, when ye shall have done all the things that are commanded you, say, We are unprofitable servants; we have done that which it was our duty to do." (*Luke* 17:7-10)

PRIVILEGE AND DUTY

The Parable of the Barren Fig Tree
The Parable of the Bondservant

A fruit-tree's reason for existence is to bear fruit. It has no claim to live if, exacting man's labor and the soil's fertility, it yields no harvest. Responsibility is the price of privilege. Such is the teaching of the story of the Barren Fig Tree.

The story of the Bondservant carries this caveat to its ultimate limit. The discipleship of the kingdom sometimes wears the harsh aspect of duty unrelieved by privilege. Then duty must be the disciple's watchword and his sole reward.

The Parable of the Barren Fig Tree

The life of Jesus sometimes seems to us idyllic in its simplicity, and Palestine a land of pastoral calm. But Jesus often moved through turbulence. Experience for Him was of a complicated and sometimes broken pattern. Roman legions were a sore provocation to the Jews. On occasion the yoke chafed until it became unendurable. Then the goaded compatriots of Jesus would hurl themselves vainly against an iron foe, and reap straightway the savage penalty. An echo of that troublous time is heard in the report brought to Him concerning certain Galileans "whose blood Pilate had mingled with their sacrifices." There is no other record of this incident, but Josephus cites many such and it is doubtless trustworthy. The rebellious were attacked by the legionaries in the midst of their religious rites. Animal blood and human flowed in one stream.

The reporters of the outrage apparently hoped to receive

from Jesus an endorsement of their conviction that the victims
had induced this violent death by their sins. It was a current
doctrine that misfortune was the nemesis of transgression.[1]
Job's comforters earned their satirical title by enlarging on
that doctrine to Job in the midst of his calamities. The theory
is inviting—at least to those spared by adversity, for it exempts
them from the pain of sympathy and reckons them among the
virtuous. No form of self-complacence is more noxious.[2]
Jesus meets it with ruthless truth: "Think ye these Galileans
were sinners above all the Galileans? I tell you, Nay: but, except ye repent, ye shall all likewise perish." To secure the
reply against misunderstanding *He* proceeds to quote to *them*
an example of disaster fresh in their memory, a disaster which
occurred not in Galilee[3] but in Judea. Eighteen workmen,
engaged perhaps in building Pilate's aqueducts, had been buried
beneath the falling of a tower at the Pool of Siloam. "Think
ye that they were debtors[4] above all the men that dwell in
Jerusalem? I tell you, Nay: but except ye repent, ye shall all
likewise perish."

This comment is not to be construed as a denial on Jesus'
part that wrongdoing has tangible consequences. Sin's aftermath of misfortune is too conspicuous to be gainsaid, and Jesus
often recognized it in sadness.[5] But He flatly refused countenance to the theory that calamity is *necessarily* induced by the
sins of its victims. Of an instance of affliction so directly
traceable as blindness His remark was categorical: "Neither did
this man sin, nor his parents."[6] He recognized nature's ap-

---

[1] Cf. John 9: 2.

[2] Joseph Addison takes issue with it and remarks wisely: "There is no calamity
. . . supposed to have happened as a judgment to a vicious man, which does not
sometimes happen to men of approved . . . virtue." (*The Spectator*, September,
1712.)

[3] Josephus writes that the Galileans were industrious and brave. They were particularly restive under Rome's dominion. The Judeans affected to disparage them
because their blood was partly admixed through heathen marriage, because they
were less orthodox, and because they spoke in a harsh and sometimes almost unintelligible dialect. Cf. Matthew 4: 15 ("Galilee of the Gentiles"), John 7: 52, and
Matthew 26: 69, 73. (See footnote, Trench, *op. cit.*, p. 348.)

[4] It has been suggested that the word "debtors" is used in this connection because the workmen were being paid by Pilate from the Temple treasury, *i.e.*, from
money considered as sacred to God.

[5] When, *e.g.*, He said to the man sick of the palsy, "Thy sins are forgiven thee."
See Matthew 9: 2.

[6] John 9: 3.

palling impassivity which makes her seemingly careless both of
vice and virtue:

> "O mother, praying God will save
>   Thy sailor,—while thy head is bow'd,
>   His heavy-shotted hammock-shroud
> Drops in his vast and wandering grave." [7]

Yet He bade us have confidence in the irrefragable love of
God. The apparent strife between God and nature He did not
explicitly reconcile. That strife remains. Along with the
mystery of sin and of sin's havoc among the innocent it con-
stitutes the heaviest odds of faith. Jesus met those odds at
their most diabolical—and conquered. "Be of good cheer: I
have overcome the world." [8] But having asserted a realm of
misfortune not ascribable to sin, He asserted also the fact that
sin carries with it the seeds of grim consequence. All affliction
is not due to wrongdoing, but all wrongdoing brings affliction:
"Except ye repent, ye shall all likewise perish." The very
self-complacence which prompted His informants to detail a
calamity visited on others would bring a similar calamity upon
them. Could they but see, the times even now were ominous!
    Such is the setting which Luke supplies (from actual occa-
sion or from striking sense of fitness) for the Parable of the
Barren Fig Tree. The tree was planted in one of the irregular
patches of a vineyard.[9] It was on a sunny slope. No other
trees cast shade upon it or crowded its branches. It rose above
the garden. The sky was all its own. Doubtless it received the
individual and painstaking care which the vinedresser gave to
his vines. But it bore no fruit: for three years it had been
barren. What right had it to live? "Cut it down; why doth it
also cumber the ground?" We are to notice that word "also." [10]
It implies recognition on the owner's part that the barrenness
of the fig tree was not the full extent of its unfitness: it "nulli-

[7] Tennyson, "In Memoriam," Canto VI.
[8] John 16: 33.
[9] Bruce suggests that a vine is a more winsome emblem of Jewish national life
than a fig tree, and that Jesus in employing the latter symbol was intent to lower
the pride of His hearers. (See Bruce, *op. cit.*, p. 431.) But the force of the
symbol seems to point rather to special privilege.
[10] The word "also" is omitted mistakenly from the Authorized Version but is
restored in the revisions.

fied" the soil. It robbed the vines of sunlight and sustenance. On every count it was self-sentenced to destruction.[11]

Clearly Jesus had His own nation in mind. Jewry had prospered on a sunny hillside of God's favor, not indeed in worldly bounty or in political dominion, but in the richer blessing of prophetic guidance. What other nation had been blessed by so noble a succession of lighted souls? Abraham, Moses, David, Isaiah, Jeremiah, Amos, Hosea, John the Baptist—and Jesus! No land great or small, in ancient or modern times, can match that galaxy of inspired leadership. Their insight is still the chart and compass of our voyaging world. But this intensive privilege had produced no good result in character. Nor was Israel's barrenness the end of her mischief. Privilege might have been bestowed upon another nation to good purpose. Israel had nullified the soil of earth. Year after year she had impeded high achievement.

The wonder arises how Jesus would fare nowadays if He came in flesh and spoke in such untrimmed language to a modern nation. "Jeremiad!" would be the smallest taunt flung at His message. Speakers at luncheon clubs would tell Him to "throw away that hammer and buy a horn," or would offer advice equally fatuous. Self-appointed custodians of other people's patriotism would call His loyalty into question and place His name on a black list! Fashionable churches would dismiss Him as a gloomy crank peddling a gospel of calamity. But we may be sure that He would insist as of old that uselessness in nations or men invites disaster. He would declare with undiminished zeal that to be unserviceable is not merely a negative good but a positive ill: it nullifies life like a blight. . . .

Each tree must bring forth its *own* fruit. Each nation has its genius—Judea with a monotheistic and most holy faith, Greece with a quickening sense of beauty, Rome with a mind for ordered government—and must yield from its fiber its

11 It has been suggested that this parable is the origin of the miracle of the withering of the fig tree. (Cf. Matthew 21: 18-21, Mark 11: 11-14.) But the latter incident is described so circumstantially that the suggestion seems arbitrary, as the "Century Bible" (Luke, p. 212), and the "I.C.C." (Luke, p. 430), rightly maintain. Those who find grave difficulty in the miracle in question (and there are many) must delete it on different cause.

appropriate contribution to the commonwealth of nations.
Each man has his distinguishing trait and gift, which, with the
manner of his opportunity, will determine his tribute to mankind's stock of goodness, beauty and truth. Copernicus sweeping the sky and discovering a vaster music of the spheres,
Millet fleeing Paris for a village plainness to show us how
haunting beauty can live in sepia, Captain Scott dying like "a
very gallant gentleman" in Antarctic snows, Thoreau regarding the passing show of business and pleasure with unenvious
eyes because he chose to live beneath the face of eternity—
each spoke in his own tongue and bore fruit after his own
kind. If any one of these had been untrue to his own word,
to that measure he would have failed. A fig tree is not expected to produce grapes. Each life is under fee to bring forth
spontaneously its inherent treasure.

The barrenness may run for three years,[12] but still the
worthless tree has its intercessors. "Let it alone this year also,
till I shall dig about it, and dung it." The law that uselessness
induces death is savingly entangled with a deeper law of pity-
ing grace. At least the tree is green. Its rich foliage is a
sign of the fruit it might have borne. Perhaps the spade of
varying experience digging about it (thrust through its roots,
perchance, in merciful harshness), and the fertilizing strength
of high example will make it fruitful. Thus the intercession
was raised—as Abraham interceded nobly for Sodom,[13] and
Moses offered his own life with strong tears and utter self-
abnegation for his idolatrous people.[14] So Jesus Himself (even
while He spoke stern warning) made ready to carry His Cross
and by His righteous death to plead the cause of an unrighteous people.

Beneath the simple rigor of the story there is the throb of an
intense emotion. Would this little land, so headstrong yet so

12 The allegorizers have been very busy with the "three years." They represent,
according to Augustine, the dispensations respectively of natural law, written law,
and grace. According to Theophylact they hint at Moses, the Prophets, and Jesus
or (in the individual) at childhood, manhood, and old age. (See Trench, *op. cit.*,
p. 354.) We may accept the three years as part of the verisimilitude of the story.
Similarly we need not follow Bruce (*op. cit.*, p. 433) when he draws conclusions
from the "one year" of grace and claims that this "indicates Christ's own sympathy with this Divine rigor."
13 The noble story in Genesis 18: 22-33.
14 The nobler story in Exodus 32: 30-32.

dearly loved, justify His plea to God? Would it heed His
admonition of approaching doom? "One year more!"—for
grace cannot brook perpetual fruitlessness. Leaves of ritual
and vain oblation cannot indefinitely serve as substitute for
fruitful deeds. "One year more!"—thus the story ends, hurling
its challenge! Never was inconclusiveness more dramatic! It
has left us with a philosophy of history and a rationale of
life.

We wonder if the men who brought tidings of that Galilean
tragedy were trapped in Jerusalem when Roman battleaxes
flashed in the streets, and when the Temple fell like that tower
at the Pool of Siloam? We wonder if our modern world with
all its facility for reading laws of nature has read the deeper
law that requires fruit of useful living—doing justly, loving
mercy, walking humbly with God—at the penalty of destruction? "Except ye repent, ye shall all likewise perish."

The Parable of the Bondservant

There are sayings of Jesus that strike the ear harshly. Frequently they concern the terms of His discipleship. "Follow
me; and leave the dead to bury their own dead." [15] . . . "If
any man cometh to me, and hateth not his own father, and
mother, and wife, and children, and brethren, and sisters, yea,
and his own life also, he cannot be my disciple." [16] There was
a terrifying quality in His character. When He set His face
like a flint to go to Jerusalem "they that followed were
afraid." [17] The fierceness of His own struggle is reflected in
the peremptory and inflexible demands which He made on His
disciples.

Jesus is never more severe than in the story of the Bondservant.[18] God is a slave-driver, and man is a slave whose work

[15] Matthew 8: 22.
[16] Luke 14: 26. See Chapter VII of this book.
[17] Mark 10: 32.
[18] The parable is unrelated to the verses which precede it. Vv. 1, 2 (Luke 17)
speak of the sin of causing others to sin; vv. 3, 4 of the duty of forgiveness; vv.
5, 6 of the power of faith. Matthew and Mark give these precepts in different
connections. (See Matthew 18: 6, 7; Mark 9: 42. Also Matthew 17: 19, 20; Mark
11: 23.) These fragments throw a most interesting light on the manner in which
the Gospels were compiled. Godet says of Luke 17: 1-10 that it is composed of
remnants found "at the bottom of the portfolio."

is endless. Though he has toiled a full day in the field plough-
ing or tending sheep, when he reaches the homestead footsore
and weary he must gird himself and serve at his master's table.
Can he expect to eat in his master's company? Can he satisfy
his hunger before his master is fed? Can he plead his flagging
strength? No, he is but a slave! Acknowledgement is not due
him, still less thanks. When he drags his tired body to his
couch, only this can he say: "I am but a slave; I have done
no more than my duty." [19]

The story is not to be interpreted as a full picture of God.
The Father of mankind is not a slave-driver. The story is a
story, and its appeal is to human custom and not to the Divine
Nature: "But who is there of *you*." . . . Nevertheless it is
doubtful if Jesus could have told it except under a sense of the
awe and majesty due to God. He is "our Father," but not an
indulgent or doting Father. He is also our "great Taskmaster."
The heaven "is His throne" and the earth "is the footstool of
His feet." [20]

> "Know that the Lord is God alone,
> He can create and He destroy. . . ." [21]

Man cannot bring anything into being—his creations are from
materials given to his hand. Man cannot cause anything to
pass out of being, for if he blow a mountain into dust, the dust
remains—he can only change its form. But God can create
and destroy. We are the creatures of His might.

> "Wide as the world is Thy command." [21]

But, lest we should wrench a truth out of due proportion, this
also is true:

> "Vast as eternity Thy love." [21]

The whole scale of Deity cannot be sounded in one story,
but only a dominant note. So with the scale of human life.

19 The word "unprofitable" seems to be used in a literal sense. In II Samuel
6: 22 it means "vile," but here it means "leaving no margin of profit or merit."
The emphasis is on the noun which means not "servant" but rather "bondservant"
or "slave."
20 Matthew 5: 34, 35.
21 Isaac Watts' noble hymn to which the tune "Old Hundredth" seems fitly
wedded.

Our experience does not always make us bondservants, but sometimes it does come in the guise of a taskmaster.[22] The parables of Jesus sprang directly from His reflection upon our human lot which He intensely shared. Were there not days and moods when He felt His work was never ended? Toil as He might with a recalcitrant earth, there were always tasks as stern awaiting Him! He never overtook the kingdom's demands. At the end of the day He must gird Himself as if the day's toil had just begun. When such a mood possessed Him, He flung the brave challenge: "A man must do His duty. He must toil and toil while it is day. When the hours are a treadmill he must repudiate the mocking insinuations of doubt; and ask, if need be, no other reward than the sense of duty done." This story is an echo of His brave soliloquy. So regarded its message is clear.

It is a challenge to endurance. The disciples fondly hoped that hardship was only for a season; then they would sit on thrones. An arduous kingdom now made them as despised slaves, but soon angel hands would wait on them. "No!" said their Master, "it is an unending labor!" Even in the lengthening shadows they must still toil. Even when the flesh became darts of weariness they must gird themselves as in the morning hour. The kingdom would brook no sluggard mood, no effeminate self-pity, no hankering after silks and crowns. They must be as slaves—in the kingly spirit that knows no servitude! . . . Such a recruiting never fails of volunteers!—

> "God, if this were enough,
>   That I see things bare to the buff
> And up to the buttocks in mire,
>   That I ask nor hope nor hire,
> Nut in the husk,
> Nor dawn beyond the dusk,
> Nor life beyond death:
> God, if this were faith? . . .
>
> "To thrill with the joy of girded men,
>   To go on for ever and fail and go on again,
> And be mauled to the earth and arise,
>   And contend for the shade of a word and a thing not
>   seen with the eyes:

---

[22] The attempts of Grotius *et al* to invert the story, *i.e.*, to find in it a condemnation of the servile religion of the scribes, need not be followed. The teaching of Jesus is as fluid and varied as life itself—and as true!

With the half of a broken hope for a pillow at night
That somehow the right is the right
And the smooth shall bloom from the rough:
Lord, if that were enough?" [23]

We can imagine that courage sang within many a heart as
Jesus told this story. Let a bugle sound the crusade with a
coward call: "We must seek the city. Its spires are just
beyond the hilltop. Soon there will be banqueting and song"
—and few will follow. But let the bugle say: "The city is far,
the way hazardous, and we may die before we see it"—and
there will be an instant upstarting of heroes. Jesus always
sounded the heroic call. . . .

For strong souls duty is a sufficient recompense. The doctrine of works of supererogation has no standing in life and
therefore no standing with Jesus. The ideal flames down
upon us. We cannot match its splendor, much less surpass it.
If we *could* match it, we would no more than fulfill its demands; we would do no more than "that which was our duty."
Is the work of him who seeks a purer social order ever fin-
ished? Politicians still shuffle their greasy cards, the dema-
gogue still trades upon the credulity of the mob, and there is
no gain save through eternal vigilance. Is the ascent of him
who seeks the white peaks of character ever complete? If
one range is conquered, another gleams above him! The
kingdom grants no respite. Sometimes it seems to yield no
reward except the reward of duty done. Let that be recompense enough! Hardy spirits will ask none better! For them
the spoils of battle will be inward—they have kept faith with
life's inflexible demand! Therefore they seek no golden isles:
they have done their duty! Duty—

"Stern Lawgiver! yet thou dost wear
The Godhead's most benignant grace;
Nor ask we anything so fair
As is the smile upon thy face. . . .

"I myself commend
Unto thy guidance from this hour;
O let my weakness have an end!

23 Robert Louis Stevenson, "If this were Faith." ("Poems," Charles Scribner's Sons.)

Give unto me, made lowly wise,
The spirit of self-sacrifice;
The confidence of reason give;
And in the light of truth thy bondman let me live." [24]

Without this story the message of Jesus would not have been full-orbed. Here is His antidote for the disease of self-pity and the conceit of merit. Let a man be at the beck and call of the ideal life! When he has toiled until limbs are cramped and the sunset beckons to rest, let him gird himself to bear new burdens through the dark! And when he has done all, let him know himself but a poor slave of heaven and say: "I am but bondman of the truth. I have done no more than duty!" So shall he prove his royal blood!

But, since duty does not always wear an inexorable mien, the story holds but a partial truth. There is a fragment of another parable of Jesus which is this parable's twin brother with a brighter face. It tells of a master who in gracious heart girded himself and, bidding his slaves sit down to the feast, came and served them: "Blessed are those servants, whom the lord when he cometh shall find watching; verily I say unto you, that he shall gird himself, and make them sit down to meat, and shall come and serve them." [25] If His command is as wide as the world, then vast as eternity His love!

24 William Wordsworth, "Ode to Duty."
25 Luke 12: 37.

CHAPTER XI

The Marks of Discipleship (IV)

RESOURCEFULNESS AND FORESIGHT

THE PARABLE OF THE UNJUST STEWARD

"And he said also unto the disciples, There was a certain rich man, who had a steward; and the same was accused unto him that he was wasting his goods. And he called him, and said unto him, What is this that I hear of thee? render the account of thy stewardship; for thou canst be no longer steward. And the steward said within himself, What shall I do, seeing that my lord taketh away the stewardship from me? I have not strength to dig; to beg I am ashamed. I am resolved what to do, that, when I am put out of the stewardship they may receive me into their houses. And calling to him each one of his lord's debtors, he said to the first, How much owest thou unto my lord? And he said, A hundred measures of oil. And he said unto him, Take thy bond, and sit down quickly and write fifty. Then said he to another, And how much owest thou? And he said, A hundred measures of wheat. He saith unto him, Take thy bond, and write fourscore. And his lord commended the unrighteous steward because he had done wisely: for the sons of this world are for their own generation wiser than the sons of light. And I say unto you, Make to yourselves friends by means of the mammon of unrighteousness; that, when it shall fail, they may receive you into the eternal tabernacles."

(Luke 16: 1-9)

CHAPTER XI

RESOURCEFULNESS AND FORESIGHT

Parable of the Unjust Steward

Did this master "commend" a servant who had defrauded him? Did Jesus use the rogue "to point a moral and adorn a tale"? Many commentators have felt that to give this parable a straightforward meaning is to cast a cloud, if not on the radiant name, then certainly on the good judgment of Jesus.[1] The Emperor Julian, becoming apostate from the Christian faith, made capital of this story as being contrary to high morality. To escape the seeming impasse the critics have coined interpretations which are miracles of ingenuity. Some have regarded the Unjust Steward as a symbol of Jesus, and others have found in him a representation of Satan—two views which ought to be mutually destructive! This versatile character has been made the type also of Paul, Pilate, and Judas.[2] He has been allegorized by opposing schools of thought, as on the one hand, Christ's warning to the Pharisees and, on the other, an example suggested by Him for their imitation![3] The different expositions offered would comprise a considerable and very self-contradictory library.

The story is a parable and not an allegory. It is as far from allegory as any of the parables—a fact which cuts the ground away from a multitude of mistaken renderings. We need not ask who is intended by the steward or who by the "Lord"; or what esoteric meaning is hidden in the drama of "dismissal." We need not search for finespun analogies. The story is its own best evidence—as bold and challenging a story as Jesus ever told.

---

1 Thus Keim cited by Bruce, *op. cit.*, p. 357, as believing that such "gross morality of prudence" could not come from the lips of Jesus.
2 See Trench, *op. cit.*, p. 352.
3 Tertullian thinks the story is aimed not solely at the Pharisees, but at the whole Jewish nation.

But did this lord commend the deceitful underling? Verily, but not for his deceit! He commended him for his astuteness.[4] Every one at times singles from an unprincipled character some trait for admiration. If a man comes to our door with a "hard luck story" and persuades us by his plausibility to a foolish charity, and if we find the next day that he is a rank impostor, we are apt to say ruefully: "Why doesn't he earn an honest living? He is shrewd enough!" Or if we see a criminal in the dock, his misdeeds proved to the red hilt, facing sentence of death without a tremor, we pay tribute to his courage though we stand in horror at his crimes. This parable approves not the fraudulence of the Unjust Steward, but his foresight. Its language is quite explicit—"because he had done shrewdly." The *thievery* was visited, we are left to surmise, with summary dismissal.

Then did Jesus use such a man as an example? Yes—as an example in resource, not as an example in point of corruption. It is not reverence, but merely stiltedness, which bestows on Jesus an unnatural halo and robs Him of keen-humored interest in the chequered interplay of human life. Admittedly Jesus could have chosen a more respectable character to grace a parable, but not one more piquant and striking. He crowded His canvas with a motley array of types, not all of them unsmirched. An earthly story even for the purpose of a heavenly meaning must use earthly people, and earthly people are not paragons:

"... not too bright or good
For human nature's daily food." [5]

Jesus told another story of a heartless judge [6] before whom a widow pleaded her cause with ceaseless importunings. He let her go, not for the sake of either justice or mercy, but to be rid of her, and because he was weary of her pestering. Jesus pointed the moral: If a heartless judge forgave that woman because of her importunity, you may trust a Fatherly God to vindicate His elect if they offer ceaseless prayers. But a

4 Thus an older Latin version seems to have had *"astutiores"* ("wiser") in v. 8. See Trench, *op. cit.*, p. 442, footnote.
5 William Wordsworth, "She was a phantom of delight."
6 Luke 18: 1-8. See p. 167 of this book.

heartless judge, one might think, is not particularly appropriate in the rôle of God. But he is appropriate in an argument from little to great, from bad to good,[7] and he can be counted on to grip and hold the attention of the hearers. The mind once gripped can be trusted to separate the wheat of the story from its chaff. The Parable of the Unjust Steward must have electrified those who first heard it. The theme is daring, the dramatic turns sudden and surprising, and the final challenge leaves the soul without defence.

This steward was the trusted overseer [8] of his master's estate, but he betrayed the trust. The nature of the perfidy we are not told. Perhaps he enjoyed hilarious evenings with his cronies while his master's money paid the bills. Soon the betrayal came to the master's ears. "Why do I hear this of thee? Give an account of thy stewardship." There was no convincing account to be given, and a rascal faced the threatened ruin of his career. He took counsel with himself: "What shall I do? My master is about to take away my stewardship. I cannot dig; I have been in my cups too often, my flesh is too soft for manual labor. I cannot beg; my pride rebels at the thought of whimpering at thresholds. What shall I do? I have it![9] I know what I will do, that, when I am put out of the stewardship, they may receive me unto their houses."

Into whose "houses"? What will he do? Mark the clever scheme! Precautions had probably been taken to forestall any attempt by the steward to decamp with a bag of gold. So he called one of his master's debtors.

"How much do you owe?"

"A hundred measures of oil."

This debtor held the tenancy of an olive grove, and paid rent in kind—one measure of oil for every ten the grove produced.

"Take thy voucher [10] and sit down quickly and write fifty."

---

7 Jesus was very fond, as many instances in His teaching plainly show, of the *a fortiori* argument.

8 Like the Scotch bailiff or factor; a position similar to that described in Genesis 39: 5, 6.

9 The Greek (*egnon*) has the force of an exclamation, and expresses the sudden birth of the idea.

10 Literally, "writing"—the bond or deed declaring the terms of the tenancy, and, possible, the indebtedness paid or due.

Note the word "quickly." The steward was not flustered (he was too cool a customer!) but simply prompt. Another debtor was called: "How much do you owe?" He owed a hundred measures of wheat—a tenth of the thousand measures which the land had yielded. "Write eighty" was the instruction. Did the percentage of reduction vary because our inspiring hero knew each man's price, or was the variation simply a flair, part of the splendid highhandedness of the plan? But the scheme was not clever enough to elude his master's ears and eyes, and once more he was hailed into the condemning presence. "And his master"—imagine the gasp of surprise as Jesus spoke the words; for the disciples [11] were sure, as the story reached its climax, that the steward would be consigned to outer darkness—"and his master *commended* the unjust steward because he had done shrewdly!"

This "commendation" does not mean that the "master" pronounced any formal eulogies. (When will we concede the glow and tang of the human in the speech of Jesus?) The "master" had suffered the pangs of a man deceived; he was not surprised or unduly hurt at news of further fraud. Himself a man of the world, he was probably curious to know how his steward would wriggle out of a corner from which there seemed to be no escape. He pronounced no formal eulogies (he was not in the mood!), but his admiration was won in spite of himself. He knew deftness, quick thinking, unflustered action when he saw them. "You rogue!" he exclaimed; "of all the impudent coolness! I'm bound to admit you're clever. There's something almost magnificent about you!"

While the disciples were chuckling over the surprising issue of the story, Jesus turned on them—humor in His eyes, and love, and holy purpose—and drove home the sharp truth: "For the sons of this age are wiser toward their generation than the children of light." [12]

11 Luke says the story was told to the disciples. "Disciples" does not necessarily mean only the twelve disciples.
12 There is an alternative interpretation which deserves careful consideration, namely, that based on the idea that the steward had been extortionate with his master's debtors, and was now squaring with them, bringing forth fruits of repentance. The "commendation" bestowed by the "master" is thus justified, and the moral becomes clear. Trench, *op. cit.*, p. 439 footnote, takes note of this

It is a challenge to resourceful zeal. The worldling in pursuit of money shows a consuming eagerness. He labors early and late. He allows himself few vacations. When the hard day is ended, he gives himself with the fervor of a saint to the study of "the psychology of salesmanship." Barriers do not daunt him; they are erected to be overcome. His devotion to the quest of wealth is all-absorbing. But what of the quest of "the enlightened ones" for God? The "sons of this age" in pursuit of *pleasure* show no lack of ardor. They will tax body and mind to their limit to win the goal. Is golf their pleasure? They will stint no money for clubs or instruction. They will study the mysteries of stance, grip, swing, "follow." They will recite the incantations of the game ("Keep your eye on the ball") with a faith as of celebrants of some high ritual. Disappointment must not conquer them. If they fail a hundred times, they return with courage renewed, resolved to achieve. But what of the "enlightened ones," who are the children of eternal tidings, in their quest for truth?

These have received the truth of a new age. They have become disciples, for example, to the immemorial insight of the Bible. But do they pursue the truth of the scriptures as the "sons of this age" pursue business or pleasure? That the Book is supremely worth studying admits of no question. If a book can maintain itself in public regard for a century it has worth; not many of the books of to-day are likely to stand that test. If a book lives for several centuries it has claim to greatness. But what of a Book which lasts thousands of years, crosses oceans and mountains, is translated into several hundred languages, and overleaps every obstacle of caste and color? —a Book which Ruskin confessed to be "the one essential part" of his education; of which Carlyle declared, that "for thousands of years the spirit of man has found light and

interpretation as advanced by Schulz in 1821. Recently Latham ("Pastor Pastorum," pp. 386-398) has revived the view in slightly different form. His exegesis is written with charm and persuasiveness. The steward, he said, had been extortionate in his master's interests, and the reduction of indebtedness was a token that he finally recognized the rights of (poor) tenants. The parable is thus a warning against that holy zeal which forgets human kindness. But will the parable abide any such construction? The steward is described as "unrighteous." The motive of the reduction of the indebtedness seems to be made clear: "that they may receive me into their houses." He was feathering his nest against the approaching storm! Furthermore, the whole mood and tempo of the story seem to us in keeping with the interpretation I have suggested.

nourishment" in its pages? Yet this is the Book which in the homes of the "enlightened" lies unopened! They do not steep themselves in its radiant verities as another man steeps himself in the barrenness of stock exchange quotations! It is treasured indeed, but only as a sacred horseshoe—in the vague hope that it will bring good luck. "For the children of this age" are more zealously resourceful towards their generation, than "the children of light" towards God.

The parable is a challenge to reality. The Unjust Steward took stock of his situation and faced facts. He refused to live in a fool's paradise. He reckoned assets and liabilities with frank and fearless eyes. Rogue that he was, he was at least honest with himself: "To dig I have no strength. To beg I am ashamed." The "sons of this age" are in their own way the sons of reality.

But are the "enlightened ones" similarly real? How many hoary lies in theology have endured because the should-be "children of light" have stubbornly closed their eyes to new discoveries of truth? And what of unreality in the wider realm of the art of living? Do the "illumined of God" insist on findings of fact, and do they order life according to the findings? Fame is a bubble, money a gilded hollowness, and comfort a stagnation. There is enough of history to prove and doubly prove that indictment; the logic of human experience is on that score irrefutable. But are "Christians" characterized in their manner of life by the frank facing of this data? Do they take honest stock of their life-situation? John Masefield has enumerated his sources of joy!

> "London has been my prison,
> But my books, hills and great waters, laboring men and brooks,
> Ships and deep friendships, and remembered days
> Which even now set all the mind ablaze . . ." [13]

Others have garnered similar insight from the fields of human joy and tears, and have counselled with their fellows regarding the shadow and the substance of our peace. The vast calm of nature—the distilled wisdom of great books—the handclasp of a friend—a few unshadowed pleasures—a spirit sensitive to

[13] John Masefield, "Biography." ("Collected Poems," The Macmillan Co., 1921.)

beauty in music and all art, and more sensitive to human
cheer and courage—the rapture and the loyalty of human love
—a soul kept clean to serve the common good—the printing
of the radiant image of Jesus on the retina of our eyes so
that we see all things through Him—the daily linking of our
mortal pool with God's ocean by the simplicity of prayer; these
are "the things which belong unto our peace." Ages of human
travail supply the evidence. Then why evade the facts? (A
business man does not blink business facts!) Why succumb
to the unenlightened standards of the world? Why surrender
the quest when driven into a corner of difficulty? But "the
children of this world" are more real in matters that pertain
to "their generation" than the "children of light" in matters
that pertain to life.

The parable is a challenge to foresight. The Unjust Steward considered his future. He resisted the temptation to thrust
from his mind his imminent dismissal. "When the blow falls,"
he said, "I still must live, and I must decide now how I shall
live." But what of the "children of light"? Do they so plan
that they may be received "into their houses"? [14] There is a
world beyond this world,—or, rather, a world holding this
world in its spiritual ether as the universe holds a planet.
Jesus assumed this wide realm of immortality: "If it were
not so I would have told you." [15] In our liberated hours we
also assume it. It is hard to believe that a child of ours born
in travail and reared in love will one day, soon or late, become
a white powder in the ground. Our refusal to believe in ex-
tinction may be in face of the facts of sight, but it keeps faith
with facts deeper than sight. The idea that compassion is a
mere titillation of the flesh, or that Jesus is long ago indis-
tinguishable from Syrian dust, evokes from the soul an instant
challenge and rebuttal. The soul's scorn for the doctrine of

14 There is obviously a transition in the parable beginning with v. 9. The
emphasis up to that point has been on the contrast between the "wisdom" of the
world and the "wisdom" of the enlightened. Then the emphasis shifts from
"wisdom" (resource) to "faithfulness." V. 9 has a point of definite connection
with the parable, as the interpretation above given attempts to show; but its mood
is different. Some commentators think the parable originally ended with v. 8.
If so, vv. 9 ff., it would seem, are in themselves supplied from teaching of Jesus
given on other occasions; or are a direct reflection of His message. As such, and
because of their similarity of theme, their conjunction with this parable is justified.
15 John 14: 2.

annihilation is comparable with the scorn of science for the doctrine that the universe is chaos; it has the same validity for it moves in the same realm of faith; either doctrine makes life a farrago of nonsense. There is a future, we invincibly surmise, beyond the bounds of mortality. Do the "children of light" prepare for it, with a foresight as clear as that which marks the dealings of the world?

"Make friends to yourself by the mammon of unrighteousness." [16] Is money unrighteous? Verily, since no human wealth is without blemish. What a story a coin could tell, if it had speech! How do we know that the clothes we wear were not made by sweated labor, or woven by dishonest hands? How do we know that our houses did not involve some sharp practice, or that the printing of our Bible did not implicate some unfaithfulness in employer or employee? We are "bound up in the bundle of life," and the taint in one life tinges us all. But the mammon of unrighteousness can, nevertheless, be dedicated to the cause of friendship. Our substance of earth may be compelled into molds of pity and love. It may be enlisted in the service of world peace. It may provide enlightenment for dark minds, healing for broken bodies, and shelter for the fatherless. If we make *such* use of "the unrighteous mammon" the future will be homelike; "that they may receive you into eternal tents." [17]

"Eternal tents"—what a description of heaven! A tent is a symbol of impermanence: "My dwelling is removed, and is carried away from me as a shepherd's tent . . ." [18] "I know that if this earthly tent of mine is taken down . . ." [19] A tent is pitched at sunset and struck again at dawn. But "eternal" involves, as one of its meanings, "that which endures." "Eter-

16 We cannot say if Jesus meant more by this phrase than that money is a snare: "the deceitfulness of riches." The above suggestions are at any rate in keeping with the facts of experience.
17 This must not be construed as an appeal to selfishness. The reasoning is again *a fortiori* as v. 11 shows. It is an argument from an unjust steward to the children of light, from "unrighteous mammon" to "genuine wealth," from a selfish feathering of one's own nest to the instinctive and serviceable joy of friendship human and divine.
18 Isaiah 38: 12.
19 II Corinthians 5: 1 as Dr. Moffatt beautifully and accurately translates it. The verse contrasts the impermanence of a tent with the permanence of a home. The influence of the tented wanderings of Israel strongly persists in Biblical metaphor and simile. Two especially lovely references may be found in Hebrews 9: 11 (see Moffatt's translation) and Revelation 21: 3.

nal tents" is a contradiction of terms, or, rather, a communion of opposites. Heaven is a "tent" because its peace is not idleness, its rest is not stagnation; it has the hope of the unattained, the zest of the ongoing. Heaven is "eternal" because its energies bring no poison of fatigue, its journeys no disappointment; because its hope is always brimming eagerness. Heaven's progress is still an abiding; its tents *are* a home. "Eternal tents"—surely it is Jesus' gracious word!

Heaven becomes homelike as earth becomes homelike—by the glow and confidence of love. "They shall receive you"—who are "they"? The poor who have been succored, the sorrowing who have been comforted, the little children who have been won to laughter! "They shall receive you into their houses."

Are the "children of this world" really wise? No, for their wisdom is only "towards their generation"! They draw the "circle premature." They have no horizon city. They do not see "the king in his beauty" or "the land that reacheth afar." [20] But there are elect souls (Jesus is their Captain) who pursue God with as consuming a zeal, as fearless a reality, as resourceful a foresight, as a miser pursues wealth, or a worldling his world. We look into their faces—these "sons of light"—and we know they are rich in "genuine wealth." Even now, in the frail canvas of this flesh, they are dwelling in "eternal tents."

[20] Isaiah 33: 17.

CHAPTER XII

The Marks of Discipleship (V)

LIFE—AND "MUCH GOODS"

THE PARABLE OF THE RICH FOOL

"And one out of the multitude said unto him, Teacher, bid my brother divide the inheritance with me. But he said unto him, Man, who made me a judge or a divider over you? And he said unto them, Take heed, and keep yourselves from all covetousness: for a man's life consisteth not in the abundance of the things which he possesseth. And he spake a parable unto them, saying, The ground of a certain rich man brought forth plentifully: and he reasoned within himself, saying, What shall I do, because I have not where to bestow my fruits? And he said, This will I do: I will pull down my barns, and build greater; and there will I bestow all my grain and my goods. And I will say to my soul, Soul, thou hast much goods laid up for many years; take thine ease, eat, drink, be merry. But God said unto him, Thou foolish one, this night is thy soul required of thee; and the things which thou hast prepared, whose shall they be? So is he that layeth up treasure for himself, and is not rich toward God."

(Luke 12:13-21)

LIFE—AND "MUCH GOODS"

The Parable of the Rich Fool

What did Jesus teach about material wealth? Concerning money the anathemas of the moralists are always easy, often thoughtless, and sometimes insincere. When all anathemas have been hurled, the fact remains that we inhabit material bodies and must meet the demands of a material world. We live, not in a vacuum, but in a realm of things. The Word became flesh; the Invisible is revealed through that "which is made." Faith and science may one day resolve the apparent duality of matter and spirit, but for purposes of daily living that duality remains. A wise religion will not ignore either of its terms.

It is evident that possessions are needed to enhance man's freedom. It is even doubtful if character in this world can be complete without them. Things are the tools of living; a workman is helpless without tools. "No man," said a wise old law, "shall take the mill or the upper millstone to pledge; for he taketh a man's life to pledge." [1] If life is constantly threatened in physical tenure, character is also threatened; though in courage it may defy the threat. An unequal struggle for daily bread saps mind and spirit as well as body. When a man who is accustomed to live from hand to mouth finally achieves property, he has reached a critical fork in the road; thereafter he will walk either in sturdier manhood or in the folly of an acquisitive life. Possessions may fulfill their perfect work, or they may smother him. It is a brave sight to see a man stake out his own claim in the common freehold and thereby learn independence, responsibility, and the joy of giving. Communism in the extreme Marxian meaning does not commend itself

[1] Deuteronomy 24: 6.

as a social goal. It "taketh a man's life to pledge." Owner-
ship seems a desirable, if not an essential, aid of character.

Jesus did not indiscriminately condemn wealth. It is true
that He bade the rich young ruler "sell all " [2] and follow; but
He was then prescribing an individual surgery, not a universal
rule. He did not require indigence as indispensable in discipleship. His first followers were called not from penury, but
from homes of some comfort. They followed a homeless Man,
but He did not sentence them to ascetic poverty; He came
"eating and drinking." The well-to-do centurion,[3] who built a
synagogue for the town in which his soldiers were stationed,
won favor in His eyes. The Bethany home, in whose hospitable friendliness He found sheltering joy, appears to have
been a home of "substance." The robe of Jesus for which the
soldiers cast lots may not have been of "fine linen," but it was
worth owning. Dr. George Adam Smith has argued force-
fully,[4] and not without historical evidence, that "a certain degree of prosperity, and even of comfort" is necessary for the
free exercise of religious faculties: "Poverty and persecution
. . . put a keenness upon the spirit of religion, while luxury
rots its very fibres; but a stable basis of prosperity is indispensable to every social and religious reform, and God's Spirit
finds fullest course in communities of a certain degree . . . of
freedom from sordidness." Thus social reform, though it may
pride itself on being irreligious and be condemned as such, may
be the necessary precursor of a revival of genuine faith. Certain it is that Jesus made no sweeping indictment of material
wealth.

And yet!—who has issued warnings half so forthright as His
against the devastating effect which "much goods" may have
on character? "How hardly shall they that have riches enter
into the kingdom of God!" [5] . . . "Ye cannot serve God and
mammon." [6] These warnings were not spoken in railing or bitterness. They were not the invective of a rebel against the eco-

2 Luke 18: 22.
3 Luke 7: 2, 9.
4 In his exposition of Joel 2: 28-32 in "The Book of the Twelve Prophets" (Expositor's Bible).
5 Luke 18: 24.
6 Luke 16: 13.

nomic order. Such rebels, when pressed to the wall, frequently offer no worthier proposal than that the poor should have the rich man's luxuries, in which the rich man has found no peace. Jesus' warnings are spoken gravely and from a depth of pity. He had little earthly wealth. He desired little. He saw men faring sumptuously, and felt no tinge of envy. From some depth of peace He gave account of His frugal lot: "I have meat to eat that ye know not of." [7] It is that deliberate renunciation of the world's goods for the sake of a hidden kingdom which gives point and power to His warnings against material wealth. His lowly way haunts a mercenary and ostentatious generation—and convicts it. We cannot forget how a Galilean Peasant looked one day at a man whom we would call eminently successful, and said of him—"Thou fool!"

"Teacher, bid my brother divide the inheritance with me." [8] The man's mind was so full of his inheritance that he broke rudely upon a message to a "multitude." The multitude could wait! Here was One who seemed to be taken for a prophet; he would "use" Him. Some word from Him might fulfill his grasping ambition where other means had failed. But Jesus refused to be a "petty magistrate." He had higher work than that of legal and industrial arrangements. His not to write economic regulations! His to live a life and speak a truth which would be a fountain-head of ever purer laws and ever worthier institutions to the end of time. We would not exchange His cross for a treatise on property rights. "Who made me a judge over you?" Then turning to the multitude: [9] "Keep clear of covetousness in every shape and form, for a man's life is not part of his possessions because he has ample wealth." [10] And He told them another story. . . .

The "Certain Rich Man" appears to have come by his wealth honestly. His farm yielded heavy crops. He did not "add

7 John 4: 32.
8 There is no ground to assume that the "brother" had treated the complainant unjustly. Perhaps the quarrel was against the ancient law of inheritance which gave the older brother two-thirds of the property and the younger brother one-third. (See Deuteronomy 21: 17.)
9 The connection between the incident and the parable seems to have been historical. If it is due to Luke's arrangement of material it is extraordinarily natural and apt.
10 Moffatt's translation which admirably conveys the distinction which Jesus drew between a man's life and his goods.

field to field" by oppression, or "devour widows' houses" by fraud, or cheat the hireling in his wages. Nor was he a miser; he said to himself with a certain *bonhomie*, "Take thine ease, eat, drink, and be merry." He was foresighted and practical; he had all the marks of a good business man. When his harvests taxed the capacity of his barns he built greater barns. In the realm of finance he thought in big terms and moved with sure step. He had definitely "arrived." His neighbors greeted him with the deference due to the "successful." In a modern city he might be one of the "key men"; but Jesus called him a fool. He failed to keep a clear space between himself and his possessions!

A man must keep things at their distance. He must be *in* the material world, but not *of* it. He must say to his possessions: "You are not my life. You never can be my life. There is a gulf set between you and me." The gulf is proved because his possessions cannot even answer him! But the Rich Man thought so persistently and with such concentration about his "goods" that the necessary line of distinction between *him* and *his* was erased. His life was lost in his livelihcod.[11] He (the self of the man) was absorbed into his ownings. The essential "within" of his nature was swallowed by the world "without."

Of course he was an egotist. Things are a jealous god; they brook no rival. His soliloquy as translated in our version occupies sixty-one words.[12] "I" occurs six times in that brief monologue, and "my" or "thine" (addressed to himself) six times. He had no thought for God. "*My* fruits," he called them; "*my* grain." But in what sense were they his? Could he command the sap in the tree, the fertility in the soil? Were sunrise and sunset under his control? Was the faithfulness of returning seasons his merit? If the rain had been withheld, where then would have been his wealth? "The *ground* brought forth plentifully"; all the man could do was to take nature's tides at the flood. He was carried to fortune on a fecundity,

11 This distinction is in the Greek. When Jesus says, "A man's *life* consisteth not in the abundance of the things," He employs the word *zoe*. But in Mark 12: 44, Luke 8: 43, 15: 12, 21: 4, "living" means "livelihood," and the word used is *bios*.
12 In the Greek there are only forty-six words, and the egotism is even more apparent.

a light, a heat, a constancy in nature's cycles, which are bound-less mysteries of blessing—and he called them "mine"! His title was earned—"Thou fool!"

Of course he was bereft of fellow feeling. Other men had enriched him; for he did not plough, reap, and build barns sin-gle-handed. Always wealth is more an achievement of society than of the individual. Society maintains and enforces laws without which separate industry would be impossible. Society provides that bulwark of common honesty which, in the last resort, is the only guarantee of investments. The sources of income are land, labor, and ideas. However resourceful and industrious the individual may be, his contribution is slight compared with the vast fund of labor and ideas which the living and the dead pour out for him "without money and without price." The rich man reached affluence mainly by reason of the *commonwealth*. Yet he had no gift of sympathy. "What shall I do, because I have not where to bestow my fruits?" Was there no sickness to heal, no nakedness to clothe? Were there none on whom a sharper problem pressed, who were compelled to ask, "What shall I do, because stark poverty has come to be our guest?" Deliberately this man proposed to spend the rest of his days on the pleasure of his body: "Soul, thou hast much goods laid up for many years; take thine ease, eat, drink, be merry." He was heedless of his comrades of earth, even as he was heedless of God.

Of course he was in reality a pauper. He lost even his phys-ical life. We are not told that his sudden death came because the grind of getting had sapped his strength. It is a fair as-sumption. Many such men do die in what should be the prime of manhood. Their friends remark on the mysterious Provi-dence which brought them to an early grave, when, in fact, there was nothing mysterious about it—except the mystery of folly which drives men to burn themselves out for things. The minister intoned over their graves, "forasmuch as it hath pleased God"; but we can be reasonably certain that it did not please God. They died by their own act. They gave their physical life to gain a world.

But his pauperhood did not consist in the loss of his physical life; there was a far more tragic loss. Jesus sacrificed His physical life when He was a young man. He invited death by fealty to the ideal far more wittingly than other men invite death by their slavery to things. He taught His disciples that the cessation of breathing may be a minor calamity: "Be not afraid of them that kill the body, but are not able to kill the soul." [13] The tragedy of the Rich Man was that the sudden death of the body brought realization of a *soul* sick unto death. All the "within" of his nature had been stolen from him by his property.

He had forfeited intellectual joy. Once his mind had made alert response to the multitudinous messages of earth and sky, and to the vital touch of other minds. But in the amassing of things he died while he lived, as trees sometimes die—from the top downwards. The woodland "flecked with leafy light and shade" found him blind. The majesty of stars left him unmoved. Poets and prophets had no truth for him. Thus Rudyard Kipling's words describe his complacent doom:

"And because we know we have breath in our mouth and think we have
     thought in our head,
We shall assume that we are alive, whereas we are really dead . . ."

"The Lamp of our Youth will be utterly out, but we shall subsist on
     the smell of it,
And whatever we do, we shall fold our hands and suck our gums and
     think well of it.
Yes, we shall be perfectly pleased with our work, and that is the
     perfectest Hell of it!" [14]

Spiritual joy likewise had been quenched. Walt Whitman offered his confession of faith, "I love God and flowers and little children." That love made him rich beyond reckoning. But the so-called Rich Man had no such love. His money had cheated him of those memories, ideals, and affections which are life's veritable treasure. Ultimately our choice lies between a world within ourselves and a world outside; the crux of character is in that decision. What is wealth? A conscience void of offence, cleansed by frequent prayer, made virile by high resolve and noble deed—the glad outgoing of human love—compassion's

13 Matthew 10: 28.
14 Rudyard Kipling, "The Old Men" ("The Five Nations," Doubleday, Page and Company).

springs kept quick and warm—obedience to ideals which brood over our mortal journey like a galaxy of stars—the quest for a soul washed white, worthier homes, kindlier industry, purer patriotism, a planet spinning in destined righteousness and peace—the finding of the Great Companion Whose love atones for our mistakes and sins . . . herein is wealth beyond all price, the treasure of the world within!

This was the wealth which a "certain rich man" exchanged for barns. He erased the definitive line between life and livelihood, between the soul and things. He failed to keep his possessions at their menial distance. But the line which he obliterated death retraced! "This night they require thy soul of thee![15] and the things which thou hast prepared, whose shall they be?"[16] The line between self and possessions now became a gulf. The man travelled one way; his property travelled another way, beyond his control. Bereft of the world without, his only treasure was a world within. That treasure he had despised; and he was destitute! The fact that his death came suddenly in the heyday of material prosperity adds dramatic force to the truth of the story, but the truth would have remained had the Rich Man died full of years. He was dead while he lived; the cessation of breathing was but the belated announcement of his earlier demise. So Jesus ended the story in a terse sentence which once more sharply drew the line between the "within" and "without" of our lives. We must choose, He said, between a mundane treasure and being "rich towards God."

This is revolutionary teaching. We do not believe it, except in certain moments of piercing insight. If we did believe it, it is doubtful if we would have courage to obey; for it would make havoc of an age that is cluttered with things. Our standards of success are almost fatally entangled with the lust for acquisition, but we are not yet ready to abandon them. We

---

15 The impersonal phrase, "They are demanding thy soul," and its present tense, are very impressive. There is no need to assume that "they" means the angels of death, or that the man came to a violent end at the hand of robbers. The Gospel of Luke frequently uses this impersonal plural, *e.g.,* 12:48; 16:9; 23:31.

16 "Whose shall they be?" underscores the parable's contention that life is distinct from things. The fact that wealth of a man's careful hoarding may be wasted riotously by his heirs serves to emphasize the folly of living for wealth. Cf. Psalm 39:6; 49:6; Ecclesiastes 2:18-23; Job 27:17-22.

pay Jesus the doubtful compliment of lip-service, but by our deeds we exclaim: "What will this babbler say?" He is still absurdly quixotic. Yet our "much goods" have not brought peace. An oriental writer, who is by no means blind to occidental virtues, lays this charge at our doors:

"You call your thousand material devices 'labor-saving machinery,' yet you are forever 'busy.' With the multiplying of your machinery you grow increasingly fatigued, anxious, nervous, dissatisfied. Whatever you have, you want more; and wherever you are, you want to go somewhere else. You have a machine to dig the raw material for you . . . , a machine to manufacture (it) . . . , a machine to transport (it) . . . , a machine to sweep and dust, one to carry messages, one to write, one to talk, one to sing, one to play at the theater, one to vote, one to sew, . . . and a hundred others to do a hundred other things for you, and still you are the most nervously busy man in the world. . . . Your devices are neither time-saving nor soul-saving machinery. They are so many sharp spurs which urge you on to invent more machinery and to do more business." [17]

The charge is difficult to refute. Since the dawn of the "industrial revolution" we have been absorbed in the exploitation of the material resources and powers of the planet. We have assiduously enlarged our bodies. The telescope is our larger eye; the telephone our stronger voice and ear; the automobile our swift, mechanical legs; heavy artillery our longer arm and more destructive fist. We wake o' mornings and don this larger body as easily as we don our clothes. We do not pause to ask if accumulation of things represents advance or retrogression; but Jesus looked at a man intent on barns and more barns, and called him a fool. There are plenty of lives to support the contention that the amassing of property, without an accompanying growth of love Godward and manward, is suicidal.

Materialism in practice has reached the proportions of an overwhelming and sinister threat. Materialism in theory we need not fear; *that* is a figure of straw which the mere breath of vital thinking will overturn. Possibly the doctrine of materialism could not have gained credence except as the plausible excuse for our conduct. Theories are frequently symptoms of the life we lead. If it is true that life is only galvanized flesh, that thought is only a temporary product of grey matter, and

17 Abraham Mitrie Rihbany, "Wise Men from the East and from the West," p. 137. (Houghton Mifflin Co., 1922.)

that personality is only a phosphorescence from certain chemical reactions, *then it follows* that materialism has no more validity than any other doctrine. In company with other theories (idealism, for instance) it has been ground out of the machine. It is not more true or more false than idealism. There is no true or false; there is only the grinding of the machine. The vital synthesis of human experience may be trusted to deal becomingly with such folly of materialistic theory.

But materialism in practice remains a present menace. No one can wisely suggest the turning back of the clock. The power-loom will not abdicate in favor of the spinning-jenny, or the tractor in favor of the hand-plough. But our moral and spiritual "lag" must be redeemed! Increasing material powers are not safe except with proportionately improving character.[18] A drunken man afoot is dangerous; but the danger is multiplied if the drunken man is permitted to drive a car. An angry man can work damage enough with two fists; but the damage becomes calamity if the two fists hold a bomb. Enlarged powers spell enlarged peril, if the soul does not grow. If the soul lags behind the advance of the body, the advance of the body must be temporarily stayed. If the "world without" takes the bit in its teeth in mad flight and drags the "world within" bruised and bleeding at the end of entangled reins, the runaway must be stopped until the driver takes new control. Society can endure for a time without new inventions; it is doubtful how long it can endure without a better spirit. When livelihood absorbs life, when the "without" breaks bounds and subjugates the "within," the day darkens in folly.

Is the "certain rich man" our acquisitive generation? Can we hear a Galilean, Who possessed treasures of peace which our clutter of things cannot bestow, saying as of old, "Thou fool!"? There is a word of His which seems now like the play-candle of a little child, but which one day we will know to be the Lantern of Truth: "Make for yourselves purses which wax not old, a treasure in the heavens that faileth not. . . ."[19]

---

18 Dr. William Heard Kilpatrick has discussed this "lag" (or a comparable "social lag") as it concerns education, in "Education for a Changing Civilization," p. 45.
19 Luke 12:33.

CHAPTER XIII

The Marks of Discipleship (VI)

THE SPRINGS OF SYMPATHY

THE PARABLE OF THE RICH MAN AND THE BEGGAR

"Now there was a certain rich man, and he was clothed in purple and fine linen, faring sumptuously every day: and a certain beggar named Lazarus was laid at his gate, full of sores, and desiring to be fed with the crumbs that fell from the rich man's table; yea, even the dogs came and licked his sores. And it came to pass, that the beggar died, and that he was carried away by the angels into Abraham's bosom: and the rich man also died, and was buried. And in Hades he lifted up his eyes, being in torments, and seeth Abraham afar off, and Lazarus in his bosom. And he cried and said, Father Abraham, have mercy on me, and send Lazarus that he may dip the tip of his finger in water, and cool my tongue; for I am in anguish in this flame. But Abraham said, Son, remember that thou in thy lifetime receivedst thy good things and Lazarus in like manner evil things: but now here he is comforted, and thou art in anguish. And besides all this, between us and you there is a great gulf fixed, that they that would pass from hence to you may not be able, and that none may cross over from thence to us. And he said, I pray thee therefore, father, that thou wouldest send him to my father's house; for I have five brethren; that he may testify unto them, lest they also come into this place of torment. But Abraham saith, They have Moses and the prophets; let them hear them. And he said, Nay, father Abraham: but if one go to them from the dead, they will repent. And he said unto him, If they hear not Moses and the prophets, neither will they be persuaded, if one rise from the dead."

(Luke 16: 19-31)

THE SPRINGS OF SYMPATHY

The Parable of the Rich Man and the Beggar

A drama in two scenes entitled, "The Rich Man and the Beggar." Could any theme be more hackneyed?—or more liable to bathos and a cheap emotion? Yet the Playwright has drawn character with such insight, given the threadbare plot such strange but convincing turns, provided "lines" of such human self-revealing, that it leaves us to this day unmasked and defenceless. Whence came our word "lazar"? The story is scored indelibly on language and life.

Jesus regarded our contrasts of wealth and poverty with troubled eyes. Otherwise this story could never have been written. His swift reproof for unfeeling wealth and swift pity for the uncomplaining poor [1] had their birth in His pain. He marvelled that people blessed with abundance could be deaf to the plea of distress. So do we marvel that medieval barons could glut themselves cheerily while captive wretches rotted in dungeons below the banquet-hall. Perhaps the year 3000 A.D. will marvel that our civilization could tolerate extremes of inordinate wealth and abject penury, and still call itself "Christian." No one has depicted the opposites of human estate more remorselessly than Jesus.

The first scene in this drama is cast in Palestine in the first century. It is a tableau—for not a word is spoken. There are two main characters: the unnamed Rich Man and Lazarus, [2]

---

[1] The Lucan version of the Beatitudes (which some scholars believe to be an earlier version than that of Matthew) will occur to mind. See Luke 6: 20-25

[2] The name "Dives" is merely Latin for "rich man." "Lazarus" is from the Hebrew *Eleazar*, meaning "he whom God helps." It is the only instance in the parables of the naming of a character. Ambrose and Tertullian believed the story to be historical, and a late tradition that the Rich Man was called Nineus gives some slight countenance to the view. The suggestion that the miracle of the raising of Lazarus is a plagiarization of this story seems quite arbitrary. The other suggestion that the beggar was named Lazarus (after Jesus' time) because Lazarus of Bethany *did* come back from the dead but by his coming did *not* persuade men

the beggar at his gates. We see the Rich Man richly clothed—his outer garment was dyed in the costly purple of the murex; his inner garment was woven from Egyptian flax. We see him richly housed—"gates" betokens the portico of a palatial home.[3] We see him richly fed and living merrily.[4] Then Lazarus enters in ghastly contrast. He is daily carried to the Rich Man's porch. His rags do not cover his ulcerated body. Unclean dogs which infest the street come to lick his sores,[5] and he has no strength to drive them off. He counts it good fortune to be fed with scraps from the Rich Man's table.[6]

Dives was not unscrupulous; the story gives no hint that he came by his wealth dishonestly. He was not penurious; no miser lives "merrily." He was not cruel in the word's accepted meaning. Doré's picture shows servants whipping Lazarus from the door, but that assumption is unwarranted. The fact that a beggar was brought there daily implies that he had been fed. An oriental beggar is shrewd in choosing his "pitch." Dives dispensed the customary charities; he was no more unfeeling than fifty other men in his town. But his love (if such it could be called) was so thin and perfunctory as to be almost an offence. He passed Lazarus several times a day, but he never really *saw* him. He felt no genuine compassion. Rags and ulcers left him unmoved; they were merely part of life's familiar and accepted scenery. Dives went his carefree way, selfish and essentially heartless. Being rich was not his crime; being rich, the story hints, was his opportunity. His crime was worldly self-love.

The second scene in the drama is cast daringly in the next world. Lazarus died. There is no mention of his burial. Per-

---

to repentance, has more to commend it; but there is no sure ground on which to assert a connection between the parable and the miracle (however the latter is interpreted). Accepting the name as original in the story, it is not necessary to give it character-content, as if it implied saintliness in the beggar. It is more probably intended to point to his helplessness—nobody but God helped him.

3 See Matthew 26: 71.

4 The R. V. translates "faring sumptuously" into "living in mirth and splendor every day." "Splendor" is the secondary meaning of *lampros* but it is the probable meaning in this case.

5 Some commentators (*e.g.*, Arnot and Hubbard, *op. cit., ad loc.*) have assumed that the ministrations of the dogs were an alleviation of the beggar's sufferings, and in contrast with Dives' inhumanity. The likelihood is rather as above suggested. Dogs were regarded as unclean.

6 "Crumbs" is possibly an echo of the word in Matthew 15: 27. The accurate translation is "pieces of bread," *i.e.*, which in such a home were used for table napkins.

haps he was left to the mercy of dogs in his death as in his life.
But there is mention of angel hands bearing him to unwonted
joy. Dives also died. It is expressly written that he was
"buried"—doubtless with elaborate ritual and display. But
for him there were no ministering angels: "And in Hades he
lifted up his eyes, being in torments." It is as if the first scene
had been swung on a pivot to reverse the parts. Lazarus is
now affluent; he leans on Abraham's bosom at the Celestial
Banquet. Dives is now in wretched need; he craves one drop
of water at Lazarus' hands. He sees the erstwhile beggar
across the gulf which separates his anguish from heaven's
radiance, and beseeches Abraham to send Lazarus to relieve
his woe.

Let it be remembered that the story is a parable. Its symbols are symbols, not literal facts. Jesus took for granted a
Hereafter, but did not describe it. He gave no instruction in
the flora and fauna, the history and geography, of the land
beyond death. We must be faithful to our ignorance and to
His reticence. Such descriptions of heaven as are offered in
the name of spiritualism impress healthy minds as being but
second-rate projections of this world to make another world
of dreary sameness. It is doubtful if we have faculties to
understand a true portrayal of the realm that lies beyond "our
bourne of Time and Place." Did not Jesus say, "I have yet
many things to say unto you, but ye cannot bear them now"? [7]
That which is pre-natal cannot comprehend the wonders of our
natal earth. A man born deaf is dead to the music of the Fifth
Symphony. A man born blind cannot conceive the miracle of
sunset. So our dull mortal ears are ill-attuned to celestial harmonies; our dust-filled eyes see spiritual realities only "as trees
walking." "Eye hath not seen, nor ear heard, neither have
entered into the heart of man the things which God hath prepared for them that love him." [8] Jesus spoke in symbols.
"Abraham's bosom" was the customary phrase for the bliss of
heaven. "Hades" [9] means in this story a place of punishment.

[7] John 16: 12.
[8] I Corinthians 2: 9 (A.V.)
[9] "Hades" generally corresponds to the "Sheol" of the Old Testament. The R. V.
rightly changes "hell" (A.V.) to "Hades." "Sheol" is the shadowy realm of the
dead. Good and bad are there without distinction or separation incident on judg-

It appears to be synonymous with "Gehenna," "where their worm dieth not, and the fire is not quenched."[10] Jesus added nothing to conventional Jewish imagery; except in the instance of the "gulf,"[11] which is a somewhat significant change. To use this story as warrant for a doctrine of a brimstone hell, or to deduce from it the dogma of the absolute and irrevocable separation of the good and the bad hereafter, is to transplant it violently from its native soil of parable to a barren literalism where it cannot live.

Nevertheless, symbols are the flung shadows of realities. Men do not picture a hell of endless burning except they have known in experience a torment without respite. Nor do men picture a heaven of jasper walls and golden streets except they have known in experience an unspeakable joy. Any one who, quenching the pride of self, has given even a "cup of cold water" to a child has found an inner heaven more radiant far than any heaven of jewelled gates. Let all symbols be swept away; the realities remain, and will promptly fashion new symbols.

> "I sent my soul through the Invisible
> Some letter of that After-life to spell:
> And by and by my soul returned to me,
> And answered, 'I Myself am Heaven and Hell.'

> "Heaven but the Vision of fulfilled Desire
> And Hell the shadow of a Soul on fire
> Cast on the Darkness into which ourselves
> So late emerged from, shall so soon expire."[12]

ment. The good, it would seem, are worse off, having exchanged light for shadow (see Ecclesiastes 9: 10); while the bad are better off, being relieved of the pains of transgression (see Job 3: 16-19). But "Hades" in this parable has a meaning which involves the idea of punishment. Dr. Plummer maintains ("I.C.C.," p. 394) that the word means "Sheol" in the original sense (cf. Genesis 37: 35, Job 14: 14): "Dives lifts up his eyes, not to look for help, but to learn the nature of his changed condition." But Dr. Grieve is surely nearer the true interpretation when he says (Peake's Commentary, p. 736) that the word "Hades" is here "equivalent to Gehenna, not simply a place of shades, but of torment, which is emphasized by Paradise being within sight." The context of the story and its deliberate staging of contrasts require this latter interpretation.

10 "Gehenna" is also a Jewish symbol. See Mark 9: 48. Gehenna was the Vale of Hinnom, on the southeast of Jerusalem, and was regarded as accursed because it was the scene of the sacrifice of the children to Moloch—the worse excesses of idolatry. It was used for the refuse and garbage of the city. There worms consumed dead matter and the fires were kept burning.

11 The Rabbis taught that heaven and hell were separated only by "a wall," or a "palm-breadth." See Bruce, op. cit., p. 395.

12 Omar Khayyám, "The Rubáiyát," translated by Edward Fitzgerald.

There are piercing realities behind the symbols of this parable. Self-consciousness remained in that Hereafter both for the Rich Man and Lazarus. Memory remained—and for Dives it was a flame. Recognition remained; they knew each other across the "gulf." Moral decision remained with its alternatives of selfishness and love. Heaven was not a realm of automatic goodness or untroubled peace for Lazarus; the plea of Dives was his problem. Nor was Hades a realm of automatic evil or relinquished responsibility for Dives; confronted by his earthly record, he tried to condone it. Self-consciousness (without which we cease to be human), memory (without which we have only the shreds and semblance of personality), mutual recognition ("Shall we be greater fools in paradise than we are here?" asks George Macdonald), and moral decision between selfishness and love (that power of choice which is the core of character)—these remained. They are the realities behind the trappings of the story, as they are the realities of life.

The drama, thus far consisting of two strangely contrasted tableaux, suddenly breaks into speech: "Father Abraham, have mercy on me, and send Lazarus, that he may dip the tip of his finger in water, and cool my tongue; for I am in anguish in this flame." Lazarus now becomes a minor character in the play. Even in the first scene he is hardly more than a pitiable foil of Dives' self-love, a living symbol of Dives' opportunity.[13] We must assume his piety, for he was carried to Abraham's bosom. The point at issue, however, is not his piety, but his need. Dives could not have condoned his heartlessness by saying of Lazarus, "I did not know he was a good man." The court within himself would have replied at once: "Yes, but you knew he was ragged and diseased; and you knew you had power to clothe and comfort him." So Lazarus retires from the foreground of the scene while Abraham, whose rôle is that of heaven's advocate, makes answer to the plea of Dives:

13 Bruce says pertinently, *op. cit.*, p. 390, "In real life men go to heaven because they are good; in parables they may go there because the motive of the story requires them to be there. . . . Lazarus has to perform two rôles with conflicting qualifications. On earth he represents the objects of compassion, who are the miserable, saintly, or otherwise: in heaven he represents the friends who receive the benevolent into the eternal tents, who could not themselves be there unless they had been saintly as well as poor."

"Child," [14] (the voice is gentle, but inexorable), "remember that thou in thy lifetime receivedst thy good things." The emphasis is on the pronoun—"*thy* good things." Fine apparel, soft divans, and merry feasting had been *his* "good things." How blind he had been to what was really "good"! All his days he had grasped at shadows. Now he could have said of his "good things" as Jacob Marley, speaking from the shades of death, said remorsefully of the business-profits which had absorbed him:

"Business! Mankind was my business. The common welfare was my business; charity, mercy, forbearance, and benevolence, were, all, my business. The dealings of my trade were but a drop of water in the comprehensive ocean of my business." [15]

Dives had turned his light to darkness. Instinctively he had known that "charity, mercy, forbearance, and benevolence" were the best of earth's "good things," but he had chosen to live an ingrowing life. Lazarus had been laid daily at his gate —a beggar on whom "evil things" had come; not because he had chosen them, not because they were "his," but because tragic circumstances had thrust on him rags, ulcers, and gnawing hunger. The sight of Lazarus at his gate had quickened a heaven of pity within his breast, but that heaven had perished under the blight of self-love.

"And in all these things," [16] Abraham continues (his voice a voice of eternal verities), "between us and you there is a great gulf fixed." Who had dug that gulf? It was of Dives' own digging. Lazarus was his brother man, but he had denied their brotherhood. Lazarus had come through the same mysterious gateway of human birth, into the same adventure of mortal life

14 Brouwer, quoted by Bruce, *op. cit.*, p. 392, footnote, contrasts the mild terms of this reply with the harsh language used in similar settings in the Talmudic parables. The rigor of Jesus lives on the edge of gentleness.

15 Charles Dickens, "The Christmas Carol."

16 This is a much better translation than, "And besides all this." The gulf was not merely an additional reason why the request of Dives could not be granted; it was *the* reason. Some commentators argue that the parable originally ended at v. 25, the remainder being an addition by the early church. There is no final evidence to prove or disprove the view. The story seems, however, to be self-consistent and the teaching of the later sentences is harmonious with the strong message of Jesus.

—but he would not own him kin. They were one in human joy and human woe, but Dives forswore the blood-bond. He drove the wedge of selfishness between them. As selfishness hardened into habit, and habit hardened into fixed character, the wedge was driven ever deeper to form a "great gulf." The sin of Dives was not his wealth. Was not Abraham himself a rich man? His sin was that he had quenched compassion. For the sake of his "good things," he had cut himself off from the common brotherhood of man as by a chasm. Chasms of ingrained character are not easily bridged. Dives had driven a cleavage wide and deep—"that they that would pass from hence to you may not be able, and that none may cross over from thence to us." [17]

The story offers no support to the glib assumption that Dives would have fulfilled all duty had he dressed Lazarus' sores and fed his hunger. True charity is more than flinging a coin to a beggar; it is not spasmodic or superficial. Ameliorations such as food and medicine are necessary, but there is a more fundamental neighborliness, "These ought ye to have done, and not to have left the other undone." [18] Compassion will play the Good Samaritan on life's roadside, but that will be only an initial act. Soon compassion will learn to look uneasily on our glaring contrasts of poverty and wealth. Soon it will lay hands of imperious love on industry and say: "This is not altogether kind. This monotony of machine labor (which a changing world almost of itself has brought upon us) is not kind. The aloofness between employers and employees is not kind. The threat of unemployment hanging over those who have nothing but mind and body to invest is not kind." Compassion will lay hands on the world-order and say of war: "This way of settling differences is not kind. This business of choking men with poison-gas, of pumping propaganda of

---

17 The symbol must not be press-ganged into the dogma of irrevocable joy and irrevocable doom hereafter. To make the story a brief for that dogma is one of many mistaken interpretations. Some commentators have allegorized the parable— Lazarus represents the ill-used Jewish nation; Dives and his five brothers are the Herods (though sons and grandsons become "brothers" for the nonce to satisfy the allegory). Trench, *op. cit.,* p. 475 *seq.,* following Augustine and Gregory, makes Dives the symbol of the Jews and Lazarus is the despised Gentile world. Strauss assumed that riches were the rich man's only crime, and felt that the parable was not fully just. It is hoped that the interpretation suggested here will approve itself as reasonable. Bruce's chapter on this story is excellent.

18 Matthew 23: 23.

hate into the veins of peoples normally humane, of darkening
a million homes in one campaign, cannot be reconciled with the
dictates of love." The Good Samaritan's work only begins on
the Jericho road. Soon he is seen molding a recalcitrant planet
with bruised hands until he has fashioned it into a brotherhood. And—always his greatest "charity" is the outgoing of
his own spirit!

The plea of Dives for his brothers—"lest they also come to
this place of torment"—is not so much an ebbing of selfishness as an attempt to justify selfishness. He implies that his
brothers were living under a handicap: they had not been prop-
erly warned. He implies that he himself had not had his full
opportunity; if he had been admonished, he would not have
walked in the way of self-love. But the answer of Abraham
has the accent of plain truth: "They have Moses and the
prophets; let them hear them." But Dives protests that the
witness of the past is not enough for the saving of men. God
has laid on humanity burdens of faith grievous to be borne.
Meanwhile the guarantee of human peace is in His hands, if
He will but use it! "Nay, father Abraham: but if one go to
them from the dead, they will repent." But the answer comes
with finality: "If they hear not Moses and the prophets, neither
will they be persuaded, if one rise from the dead."

But—we wonder! Dives' device for our salvation half wins
our approval. If only a thin veil divides our world from the
next, why are we kept in ignorance of the very existence of
that other country? Why does not God rend the veil, and end
the agony of our unknowing? Such an ambassador from
Eternity would surely conquer our waywardness. Suppose he
said to us, "There is no River of Lethe in the After-life;
memory abides, a living torment. I have seen the wicked in
pains and anguish; I have seen the just receive their radiant
reward"; we would straightway turn from darkness to the
works of light!

But—would we turn? If one should "rise from the dead,"
would we take him at his word? We might ask for his credentials; and what credentials could he give except the credentials of good character? Already Moses and the prophets have

that warranty! Would we believe our eyes and ears, if one
re-crossed the dark river?

> "If any vision should reveal
>   Thy likeness, I might count it vain
>   As but the canker of the brain;
> Yea, tho' it spake and made appeal
>
> "To chances where our lot was cast
>   Together in the days behind,
>   I might but say, I hear a wind
> Of memory murmuring the past." [19]

Moreover, even such a living sign would soon become commonplace; then we would demand a greater sign. If God
plucked a star from the sky at our behest, or removed a mountain suddenly into the sea, or halted the sun in its orbit, these
wonders would soon pall. Then a new and more stupendous
miracle would be required to validate past miracles. Each new
doubt would cry out for a greater marvel, until life would be
diseased by overweening curiosity and victimized by prodigies
of sensationalism. "An evil and adulterous generation seeketh
after a sign." [20]

An emissary from the shades of death might arouse our gaping wonder—but conscience lies deeper than the eyes. He
might fill us with sharp fear—but the fear would pass, and
fear has scant power to change the fiber of our motives. A
moral change demands a moral instrument. Only deep can
call to deep. Only love can quicken love; and love is its own
best evidence. The proof of an inner conviction is not an outer
marvel, but the courage to trust God and obey! When love
accepts its Calvary and dies, the just for the unjust, it has shot
its last bolt. Golgotha is the ultimate resource; if that entreaty
fails, nothing but flame and torment can bring the soul back to
reality.

So Jesus told a story on the trite and faded theme of the
Rich Man and the Beggar, but the story is not trite; it burns
with the white light of truth. He leaves us with the picture of

19 Tennyson, "In Memoriam," Canto XCI, aptly quoted by Marcus Dods in his
study of this parable
20 Matthew 16: 4.

a yawning gulf—the immemorial gulf which selfishness drives
between a man and his neighbor. Does the fixed and lifelong
habit of selfishness leave a man any power or inclination to
repent? Can God's love "to the uttermost" bridge that chasm?
We do not know. The curtain has fallen on the drama.

CHAPTER XIV

The Marks of Discipleship (VII)

TRUE NEIGHBORLINESS

THE PARABLE OF THE GOOD SAMARITAN

"And behold, a certain lawyer stood up and made trial of him, saying, Teacher, what shall I do to inherit eternal life? And he said unto him, What is written in the law? how readest thou? And he answering said, Thou shalt love the Lord thy God with all thy heart, and with all thy soul, and with all thy strength, and with all thy mind; and thy neighbor as thyself. And he said unto him, Thou hast answered right: this do, and thou shalt live. But he, desiring to justify himself, said unto Jesus, And who is my neighbor? Jesus made answer and said, A certain man was going down from Jerusalem to Jericho; and he fell among robbers, who both stripped him and beat him, and departed, leaving him half dead. And by chance a certain priest was going down that way: and when he saw him, he passed by on the other side. And in like manner a Levite also, when he came to the place, and saw him, passed by on the other side. But a certain Samaritan, as he journeyed, came where he was: and when he saw him, he was moved with compassion, and came to him, and bound up his wounds, pouring on them oil and wine; and he set him on his own beast, and brought him to an inn, and took care of him; and on the morrow he took out two shillings, and gave them to the host, and said, Take care of him; and whatsoever thou spendest more, I, when I come back again, will repay thee. Which of these three, thinkest thou, proved neighbor unto him that fell among the robbers? And he said, He that showed mercy on him. And Jesus said unto him, Go, and do thou likewise."

(Luke 10:25-37)

TRUE NEIGHBORLINESS

The Parable of the Good Samaritan

This story begins in a theological controversy and ends in a description of "first aid" at a roadside. It arises in a question of eternal life and works out to a payment for room and board at a hotel.

The question was asked by an expert in the Jewish law: "Teacher, what shall I do to inherit eternal life?"[1] It was not a captious inquiry. The scribe was not laying a trap; rather he was putting the new Teacher to the test. Perhaps he hoped that Jesus would recommend certain fasts and sacrifices—"what must I *do* . . . ?" Perhaps in self-confidence he was taking up the cudgels of debate. It was disconcerting to have Jesus reply, "What is written in the law? How readest thou?"[2] as if to say, "The law is *your* profession. You ought to know." But he rallied from the retort and recited smoothly: "Thou shalt love the Lord thy God . . . and thy neighbor as thyself." Then came the conclusive word: "Continually do that, and you *shall* live."

The scribe was placed in a poor light. He appeared to have asked a needless question, whose sufficient answer was the best-known pronouncement of the law in which he was an expert.[3]

1 The phrase "eternal life" was in use prior to Christian times and can be found in apocalyptic writings. In the Synoptics it is conceived as a possession to be claimed after death; to be "inherited." In the fourth gospel and notably in the Johannine Epistles it is described as the veritable life which a man may enter in this present world. See I John 3: 14.

2 It is conjecture to suppose that Jesus pointed to the scribe's philactery as He answered Him. The philactery would probably not contain the second part of the "great commandment." The first part was preeminent in Jewish law; the second was originally lost among a ruck of trivial rules, though later given higher standing. See Deuteronomy 6: 5 and Leviticus 19: 18.

3 It is natural that the scribe of this incident should have been identified with the scribe reported in Matthew 22: 34 *seq.*, and Mark 12: 28 *seq.*, where Jesus is represented as reciting the law in answer to the scribe's question, and where the scribe does not ask the second question, "Who is my neighbor?" These scriptures both hint plainly that the original questioning was asked in an insidious motive. Arnot, following Stier, protests that Luke's "scribe" is therefore not to be identi-

A sorry end to a promising debate! He must absolve himself in the eyes of the bystanders. He must show Jesus that he was not without discernment. Jesus' reply, as he would demonstrate, was far from conclusive. So, "desiring to justify himself," he said, "And who is my neighbor?"

It was a clever thrust, for it impaled Jesus on one of the sharpest questions of His age. The Jew did not regard a Gentile as a neighbor. Even if he slew the stranger within his nation's gates the Sanhedrin (so one writer asserts) [4] did not condemn the slayer to death. The law forbad a Jew to lift up his hand against his neighbor, but a "stranger" was not a neighbor. The Greeks held the "barbarian" in similar contempt; they denied the title "neighbor" even to the horde of Greek slaves (human goods and chattels) on which the City States were built. The glory of Greece, which we rightly acclaim, was built on a foundation of human servitude, which we wrongly ignore. How would Jesus define a neighbor? Was a Samaritan a neighbor?—was a publican?—or a sinner? Where did the line run? Jesus had shown, strangely enough, a friendship for outcasts: how would He define a "neighbor"?

So Jesus defined a neighbor in a story which age after age lays its constraint on the conscience of mankind. He lifted the question out of the atmosphere of controversy, since in that atmosphere real questions can never be settled, and set it down —where? He set it down on a dangerous road in Palestine!

"A certain man" (name and nationality not cited!) "went down from Jerusalem to Jericho." Jerusalem was some two thousand feet above sea level and Jericho over one thousand feet below it. The twenty miles between the cities wound through mountainous country, whose limestone caves offered ambush for brigand bands, and whose sudden turns exposed the traveller to unforeseen attack.[5] The road became known as the "Bloody Pass." Many among Jesus' hearers had trav-

---

fied with the "scribe" of Matthew and Mark. No final solution of the problem seems possible. The original question was basic and may easily have been asked of Jesus more than once. If Luke has taken the incident as related in Mark and attached the parable to it, the arrangement has the appropriateness of a living record.

4 See "I.C.C.," *ad. loc.*
5 See "I.C.C.," *ad. loc.*, for further facts about the red history and evil name of this particular strip of road. Perhaps Jesus was on the road when the story was told, for Bethany was located between the two cities.

elled it. They listened and saw the "certain man" stripped, beaten, and left half dead. Soon the scribe's wordy quibble was forgotten in the rough and bleeding facts. . . .

"And by coincidence a certain priest." The "coincidence" was in the parable, not in the purpose of the Teacher! *He* was moving with unerring intuition, dissecting with sure fingers the motives of men. The priest was a fellow Jew and withal a pillar of the Temple. By birth and by sacred calling he was a "neighbor" to the robbed and wounded man, but he left him to his fate. "And in like manner a Levite" [6] . . . a door-keeper in the house of God, a member of the hereditary order from which were chosen the singers in the Temple choirs—a "neighbor" to the life! Yet he passed by on the other side.

"But a certain Samaritan . . ." He was a half-breed, of a race which the Jews counted religiously in disrepute and with which they had "no dealings." But "when he saw him, he was moved with compassion." [7]

In print the conduct of the priest and Levite seems monstrous, but in the print of our own experience it assumes a different color. Can we be sure that we would never play their part? Perhaps they were "too busy" with other good works. Perhaps they shrank, as we naturally do, from "getting mixed up" in such a case. Moreover, it was better to cure injustice at the source; better, even if one man's wounds went untended, to lend voice and influence to secure strong military protection

---

[6] See Dr. Baudissin's exhaustive article on Priests and Levites in Hastings' "Dictionary of the Bible."

[7] It is generally believed that the Samaritans became a mixed race, after the overthrow of the "northern kingdom," by the intermarriage of the unexiled "poor" Israelites with the conquering Assyrians. Their religious offence was that they used only the Pentateuch as their Bible (thus denying canonicity to the other parts of the Old Testament), and Mount Gerizim (not the Temple) as the center of their religious zeal. See John 4: 20-21. Halévy (Peake's Commentary, *ad. loc.*) thinks the characters in the original story were Priest, Levite, and Israelite—a frequent grouping. He suggests that a Samaritan would be an unlikely traveller on the Jericho road, and that Luke, through his Gentile sympathies, is responsible for the "Samaritan." There is some show of reason to this conjecture, but it can be urged in rebuttal that the contrast of Jew and Gentile to the disparagement of the former is not unusual in the teaching of Jesus. See Matthew 11: 23, Luke 4: 25-27, Matthew 8: 10. The frequency of a grouping of characters is insufficient ground on which to question the authenticity of the story as Luke records it. In either event the message of the story remains intact. As Dr. Montefiore has written: "The Samaritan is in the parable now and the world will not easily let him go." Arnot, *op. cit.*, p. 351, footnote, warns us that not all priests and Levites were hard-hearted, nor all Samaritans generous. Some of the priests were not unfavorable to the Christian cause. Acts 4 is interesting in this connection. Jesus was teaching by a dramatic story a universal truth and was not launching a sweeping indictment against a race or a class.

thereafter along so dangerous a road. Besides, how were they
to know that the man was not himself a brigand, some victim
of a robbers' wretched feud? Wise men steer clear of ven-
dettas. There were a hundred good excuses for their callousness. If it was monstrous for them to quench the sudden uprising of sympathy, the monstrous mood is very commonplace.
Our diffused compassions are not often brought to the focus
of actual help in an actual need. We herald the dawn of a
new earth more easily than we lend our fingers to binding up
present and particular wounds. Our distributed sympathies
have the same sinister effect as our distributed conscience; as
responsibility is spread over the crowd the sense of personal
obligation grows faint. The priest and Levite felt cowardly
on the first few occasions of their "passing by," then cowardice
became indifference, until finally they deemed wounds and poverty an intrusion. The lament is not out of date:

> "Alas! for the rarity
> Of Christian charity
> Under the sun." [8]

"And who is my neighbor?" To ask the question is a condemnation. True neighborliness is not curious to know where
its boundaries run; it cares as little for boundaries as sun and
rain care for the contour lines upon our maps.[9] It seeks not
for limits, but for opportunities.

"Who is my neighbor?" Nearness does not make neighborliness. The priest and Levite were near both by race and by
office, and the Samaritan by race and office was remote. People may live divided only by a narrow wall, and yet not be
neighbors. People may live with no intervening wall, and yet
not be neighbors. Only the eyes and the spirit of the Samaritan
make neighborliness.

"Who is my neighbor?" "I do not know," Jesus retorts;
"but life will reveal him to you. He is not of one class or
nation. He is anybody—in need! You will find him as you
journey. You will come upon him 'by chance.' He is not of
this or that religious allegiance, he is not a 'sinner' or a 'saint,'

---

8 Thomas Hood, "The Bridge of Sighs."
9 Both G. H. Hubbard, *op. cit.*, pp. 428, 429, and Marcus Dods, *op. cit.*, p. 260,
have admirably expressed this implied teaching of the parable.

he is not brutish or refined. He is 'a certain man'—any man needy at your roadside." Thus Jesus replies not in a definition but by an instance. He gave us "truth embodied in a tale."

The neighbor had *insight of sympathy*. He was the only man travelling the Jericho road who really saw the victim of the robbers. The priest and the Levite saw a bruised and bleeding body, a vexatious interruption of the customary day, but they did not see a man made in their own likeness. Rarely do we see people; rarely do we wish to see. We are content to look upon the sheaths we wrap around them to excuse our ignorance or selfishness. We say, "He is an American," a "Japanese," a "negro"; it is astonishing how the "national" sheath can save our sympathies. We label him "catholic" or "protestant," the creedal sheath being more opaque even than the national. Rarely does our sight pierce beyond the accidents of wealth or poverty. Rarely do we discover a *human,* gifted with our meed of longing, broken by our wreck of grief. Perhaps we should allow merit of eyesight only to those who see in others the immemorial human realities—joy and pain, shame and longing, terror and hope. Max Mueller has written that to the Greek every foreigner was a "barbarian"; to the Jew, every stranger was a "gentile dog"; and to the Mahometan every alien was an "infidel." Then Jesus came, and erased these contemning titles from the dictionaries of mankind, and wrote in their stead, "brother." The stricken man was brother to the Samaritan because the stricken man also was human. It is required of a neighbor that he shall pull aside the sheaths long enough to see "a certain man."

The model neighbor rendered *a personal service.* It would have been easier to be compassionate by proxy—to have phoned the hospital and despatched an ambulance. But *he* bound up the wounds with his own hands. *He* himself poured in oil and wine. *He* placed the unfortunate on *his own* beast. He might have paid toll to the customary charities and held himself aloof. He might have sat on the committee and directed relief from afar. But in giving help he gave himself.

Philanthropy must be organized. Indiscriminate compassion quickly becomes a curse. Unguided pity like unguided water stagnates into a malarial swamp. Charity needs channels. The

State has its duty of neighborliness—a recognized duty as many state institutions prove. There are governments which have established old-age pensions so that the poor may receive at the end of their years, not a dole, but deferred wages from the commonwealth. All this is proper and commendable; Jesus organized His own disciples into itinerant bands. But the wellspring of neighborliness (as of everything that is human) is personality in the strictest sense of the word—the spirit of the individual! Not all the channels ever cut can atone for the freezing of that wellspring! Love radiates only as life touches life. The coin must be held in understanding fingers or it cannot transmit blessing. The committee must be instinct with compassion constantly expressed or it will be a "clanging cymbal." A card-index easily becomes a non-conductor. "If I give all my goods to feed the poor and have not love, it profiteth me nothing"—and it profits the poor hardly more! "I may hire a man to do some work, but I can never hire a man to do my work," said Dwight L. Moody.[10] A check may buy bread, but if the check is not written in the genuine ink of sympathy the bread which it buys will soon turn to ashes. Thus social problems move to a bitter climax just because each man fails to act the neighbor on his own roadside. Life holds us to no forfeit for our failure to realize the sorrows of the race. That failure is universal and only Jesus is without blame. Two hundred people die each day in greater New York, and it is not within the spirit of common man to carry in sympathetic realization the piled-up blackness of that woe—any more than to carry the piled-up brightness of commensurate joy. That burden life does not lay upon us. But life does demand that we choose our road through life (noble men choose a Jericho road) and act the neighbor to those who fall at our roadside.

The model neighbor rendered *a thorough service*.[11] Beginning to help, he "saw it through." Of spasmodic and inadequate relief it has been wittily said that it creates one-half of the misery it relieves, but cannot relieve one-half the misery it creates. But the Samaritan's love was painstaking and complete. He made himself responsible even for the prolongation

10 W. R. Moody, "The Life of Dwight L. Moody," p. 195.
11 G. H. Hubbard, *op. cit.*, pp. 426, 427, has clearly itemized it.

of help beyond the limits of probable need. "Whatsoever thou
spendest more, I, when I come back, will repay thee." Such
love is costly. His beast was wearied and his saddle stained
with blood; property rights surrendered at the demands of
love. His journey was broken and his business errand hin-
dered; profits capitulated to human need. The Samaritan suffered, but he counted the suffering all joy. . . .

Therefore his service was thorough in a manner which the
story does not straightway reveal. He bound up wounds of
the spirit as he bound up wounds of the body. He poured in
the wine of love as he poured in wine from a humbler flask.
He gave rest to a broken spirit as he gave rest to the broken
flesh. Bestowing charity, he bestowed "God, Freedom, Immortality," because he acted from the impulse of a Godlike,
free, and immortal soul. Altruism is merely fragmentary—a
morsel which but accentuates the hunger—if it fails to provide
(through the spirit of the giver) that meat "which the world
knows not of."

To be a neighbor with a thorough zeal answers both for "him
that gives and him that takes" the deeper question: "What shall
I do to inherit eternal life?" The inheritance is ours already;
it is the impulse to be neighborly. We realize the inheritance
when the impulse is translated into the better language of
deeds.[12] The spirit of the Samaritan does not come "by
chance." It is the bestowment of God—His best gift to us.
Though neighborliness may be suddenly proved (being invoked
by crises as we journey), it is not suddenly grown. Heroism
in the crucial test has its source in that habitual readiness to the
heroic, that courageous bent of soul, which is induced by minor
braveries day after day. Only so does neighborliness become
instinctive. Such a quality and "set" of character *is* eternal
life; the God-given heritage has been realized.

Nor is the Samaritan spirit to be conceived merely as hu-
maneness or as a substitute for religion. In truth religion in
its outworking *is* neighborliness, and neighborliness in its final
implications *is* religion. A religion which "passes by on the

12 The Greek reveals the emphasis which Jesus placed on His closing question:
"Which of them *proved* neighbor?" and also the emphasis of the answer: "He who
did mercy."

other side" is a mummery, not a faith. But let no man say, on the warrant of this parable, "Kindness is enough." Let him remember rather that Jesus fashioned the parable from the fibre of His own spirit; that Jesus died as a Good Samaritan at the world's dark roadside; and that the fountain-head of the motive of Jesus is found only in that mystic depth from which He said: "I and My Father are one."

"In Paradise," says Fiona MacLeod,[13] "there are no tears shed, though in the remotest part of it there is a grey pool, the weeping of all the world, fed everlastingly by the myriad eyes that every moment are somewhere wet with sorrow . . . or vain regret. And those who go there stoop and touch their eyelids with that grey water, and it is as balm to them, and they go healed of their too great joy; and their songs thereafter are the sweetest that are sung in the ways of Paradise." The Samaritan bathed his eyes in the "grey water" until the spirit sang within him. That singing spirit *is* eternal life.

[13] Quoted by Alexander Smellie in his introduction to the "Journal of John Woolman."

CHAPTER XV

The Love of God (I)

GOD'S APPRAISALS AND REWARDS

THE PARABLE OF THE LABORERS AND THE HOURS

"For the kingdom of heaven is like unto a man that was a house-holder, who went out early in the morning to hire laborers into his vineyard. And when he had agreed with the laborers for a shilling a day, he sent them into his vineyard. And he went out about the third hour, and saw others standing in the marketplace idle; and to them he said, Go ye also into the vineyard, and whatsoever is right I will give you. And they went their way. Again he went out about the sixth and the ninth hour, and did likewise. And about the eleventh hour he went out, and found others standing; and he saith unto them, Why stand ye here all the day idle? They say unto him, Because no man hath hired us. He saith unto them, Go ye also into the vineyard. And when even was come, the lord of the vineyard saith unto his steward, Call the laborers and pay them their hire, beginning from the last unto the first. And when they came that were hired about the eleventh hour, they received every man a shilling. And when the first came, they supposed that they would receive more; and they likewise received every man a shilling. And when they received it, they murmured against the house-holder, saying, These last have spent but one hour, and thou hast made them equal unto us, who have borne the burden of the day and the scorching heat. But he answered and said to one of them, Friend, I do thee no wrong: didst not thou agree with me for a shilling? Take up that which is thine, and go thy way; it is my will to give unto this last, even as unto thee. Is it not lawful for me to do what I will with mine own? or is thine eye evil, because I am good? So the last shall be first, and the first last."

(Matthew 20: 1-16)

GOD'S APPRAISALS AND REWARDS

The Parable of the Laborers and the Hours

"But many shall be last that are first; and first that are last."
These are impressive words—"that solemn sentence inscribed
by Scripture on the curtain which hangs down before the
judgment seat." [1] But it is doubtful if they carve from the
average mind any clear or true concept. We read them and
think of blind Fate playing havoc with our careful plans; of
Kismet lifting a beggar from his rags to a throne, and then
capriciously, inscrutably, flinging him down again to his beggar's mat; or of some Cynic Spirit delighting to prick the
bubble of human pride or success. But Jesus spoke the words,
and He granted no place in the universe either to blind Fate
or to a sneering Cynic.

We may beset this precept "behind and before," and reach
its meaning through the incident and parable which respectively
precede and follow it in the Gospel record. [2]

When the Rich Young Ruler inquired some formula or
rubric which would guarantee eternal life, Jesus saw that only
a relentless surgery would cure his ills: "Go, sell that which
thou hast and give to the poor . . . and come, follow me."
The sorrowful refusal awakened an answering sorrow in Jesus
—sorrow that a would-be disciple of such promise was lost to
the kingdom. But He could not abate the rigor of the terms:
"I tell you truly, it will be difficult for a rich man to get into
the Realm of heaven." [3] Then Peter interjected, "Well, *we*

1 Mozley quoted in the "Expositor's Dictionary of Texts," Vol. I, p. 911.
2 There is no certainty that the parable was spoken in reply to Peter's question
or to clarify the apothegm in Mark 10:31, Matthew 19:30. The most cursory
acquaintance with the synoptic problem scouts such dogmatism. But whether by
actual chronology, or by the Evangelist's arrangement of his material, the context
of the parable supplies a perfect setting. Peake's Commentary seems far too sweeping in its remark that Matthew 19:30 has no bearing on the parable that follows,
though it is convincing in its contention that there are discernible two interpretations of the parable, *viz.*, that intended by Jesus and that suggested by the Evangelist. See footnote on p. 162.
3 Matthew 19:23 (Moffatt's Translation).

have left our all and followed you"—there was emphasis on
the pronoun to imply contrast with the Rich Young Ruler;
"We have left our all. Now what are we to get?"⁴

It was a taut moment! How should Jesus reply? Peter and
the other disciples *had* forsaken their "all" for His sake, and
such an adventure of soul (He must make clear) would not
be without its splendid consequence. In the "new world"⁵
they would be enthroned. But there was a bargaining streak
in Peter's question and a complacent self-justifying at the expense of the Young Ruler. "You shall be enthroned," said
Jesus in effect, "if your sacrifice is a sacrifice and not a calculation. But it were wisdom not to judge either your own merit
or another's failure. The kingdom will show surprising reversals of human estimates. Many shall be last that are first;
and first that are last."

The parable which follows clarifies and illustrates the maxim.
Its hero is a vineyard-keeper. He will scarcely qualify as an
efficient business man. He might almost be called an eccentric
humorist. He engages workmen when the sun is setting, and
when the sun has set he pays them a full day's wage. Moreover, he seems to attach less importance to the "production-
capacity" of his workmen than to their motives and their need.
An efficiency expert would risk insanity by visiting this vineyard. Hiring help at the eleventh hour and paying them in
full! There have been those (in the bad old days now passing)
who thought it better business to dismiss employees and then,
when hunger began to pinch their homes, reengage them at
lower wages! But we run ahead of our story. . . .

Behold the master going into the market place at six o'clock
in the morning to hire laborers. If it is spring, soil must be
carried up the steep slope, or the ground dug, or an encom-
passing wall built. If it is summer, the vines must be pruned
and tied. If it is autumn, the golden vintage must be gathered.
He needs men, and, since it is early in the day, they can bargain with him at their own terms. He agrees to pay them a
denarius a day. Three hours later he engages others who,

---

4 Matthew 19: 27 (Moffatt's Translation).
5 "The regeneration" (Moffatt: "the new world") is an interesting term used by
Josephus to express the return of Israel from captivity. See Peake's Commentary,
in loc.

being in a less favorable situation to parley, accept his assurance that they will be paid a fair wage.[6] Twelve noon and three in the afternoon witness a similar hiring, on the strength of a similar assurance. Five o'clock finds him again in the market place. The shadows lengthen. A few men wait disconsolately for work. Appraising them with a quick glance (were they loafers or unemployed?) he flings the question, "Why are you idle?" They might have made excuses, pleading the sweltering heat. They might have cursed the economic order. But they reply with the ring of truth, "Because nobody has hired us." "You go too into my vineyard," was the curt instruction. Strange efficiency!

This parable is not an economic tract. Jesus did not attempt to lay the rails on which the trains of industry should run. He lived instead a life so divinely compassionate that industry must ultimately make peace with Him or suffer torment. But, though this parable does not prescribe industrial methods, we cannot read it, even casually, without seeing the fingers of Jesus probing beneath the surface of the vast realm of "business." Is a man out of work because he will not work? Jesus has no saving grace for such a man except the saving grace of adversity. Is a man out of work because of the callousness of a society which will not seriously grapple with the curse of unemployment? That tragedy smites Jesus to the core! He could never have told this story if He had not been moved with pity as He saw men idle in the market place. What would Jesus say, were He here in the flesh, to the corporation which dismisses men without direst necessity; or to a labor union which "strikes" on a negligible pretext; or to business brains too absorbed with profits to address themselves to the poor man's problem of insecurity of occupation? This is not an economic tract; but it is a demand that industry shall exist for man, and not man for industry.

At sunset the laborers in the vineyard receive their wages. Those who were hired last were paid first (the vineyard keeper's eccentric humor comes into play); and to their glad surprise they receive a denarius, a full day's wage. Those who

6 "Right" in v. 4 seems to mean "proportionate."

worked three hours, six, or nine, are given the same amount. Finally those who have worked all day—a denarius is their payment! The agreement is fulfilled; they bargained for a denarius. But the good fortune of those who have worked one hour, three or nine, excites their ill-tempered complaint: "These last have worked only one hour, but you have made them equal with us who have borne the brunt of the day's work and the heat." But the leader of the revolt is promptly singled out and silenced: "Friend" (the reproof is not less stern because it is kindly) "I am not wronging you. . . . Be off! . . . Can I not do as I please with what is mine? Have you a grudge because I am generous? So the last shall be first and the first last."

The parable does not mean that the kingdom is a realm of complete equality, or that good fortune is bestowed at the expense of faithful labor, or that God's verdicts are arbitrary. "Can I not do as I will with mine own?" is not a New Testament version of that Old Testament assertion which, in its primitive conception of God lauded His power at the cost of the ethical: "He hath done whatsoever He pleased." The judgments of God are not capricious, but they are based on tests radically different from ours; and because, "My ways are not your ways, saith the Lord," the kingdom plays such havoc with the world's appraisals that the first become the last, and the last first.[7] Those not of the Kingdom may continue to be self-centered in their judgments ("What shall *we get* therefore?"), or jealous of the good fortune of others, or bereft of sympathy; but God's judgments are not of such a kind.

---

7 Trench, *op. cit.*, p. 169 ff., enumerates various suggested interpretations of the parable. Some commentators have regarded the equality of reward as the clue to the meaning, some have found in it a variant of the fable of the hare and the tortoise, and many have taken the "hours" as its leading feature. The latter group has again been divided into smaller groups according to the manner of allegorizing espoused. To some the "hours" mean the successive dispensations of Adam, Noah, Abraham, Moses, and finally the Apostles; to others successive ages of individual man (youth, manhood through to death-bed repentance!); and to others the successive periods of Jew and Gentile or of early and later Church. There are evidences in the parable that the early Church took it as a warning against those who imagined that the fact of earlier discipleship would gain them greater reward than those who heard the good news later. The spurious sentence, "For many are called but few are chosen" (*i.e.,* "many" of the Jewish nation) may have crept in through this interpretation. The sentence does not occur in the Vatican or the Sinaitic MSS. Though some of the allegorizing just instanced may *illustrate* truth in the parable, Trench is right when he writes: "Better . . . to say that the parable is directed against a wrong temper . . . against which all men . . . have need to be . . . warned."

Thus the verdicts of heaven cause amazing reversals in the verdicts of earth.

The parable suggests the standards of Divine judgment. *It is a judgment according to motive.* If one worker bargains for a denarius he shall receive it: "They have received their reward." [8]   If another accepts the assurance of honorable dealing, and pins his faith on the goodwill of God, his faith shall be justified with "good measure, pressed down, running over." [9] Life, lived abundantly, despises the careful calculation of rewards. It does not ask, "What shall we have therefore?" God is not the Keeper of a ledger entering a credit or debit account, according as a man observes or fails to observe certain holy regulations, according as he registers or fails to register a certain quantity and duration of labor. God has subtler tests than the piece-measure and the time clock. Everlastingly the *motive* of a man's life proclaims his worth.

A man came to Jesus: "Teacher, tell my brother to give me my share of our inheritance." [10]   That title "Teacher" was an implied compliment to His wisdom; and was it not right that the estate should be divided? "Take heed, and beware of covetousness," was the stern reply. The man's "rights" were cankered by his motives! That witch of Alexandria, walking the streets armed with a pitcher of water and a flaming torch, and crying, "Would that I could quench hell with this water and burn heaven with this torch, so that men would love God for Himself alone," was mistress of a white magic, not of a black art! Church-going which goes to Church to be wrapped in a warm glow of emotion, or in the hope that Church-going may be counted unto it for righteousness, debases worship into gross selfishness. So many prayers—so much of heaven; so many good deeds—so much reward! The blasphemy of the *quid pro quo* in religion endures in the Pharisaism of every age! Small wonder that in the Reformation the world demanded an ampler doctrine of "grace" instead of the dreary rubric of "works!" The generous soul

> . . . "Throws himself on God, and unperplext
> Seeking shall find Him." [11]

8 Matthew 6: 2, 5, 16.
9 Luke 6: 38.
10 Luke 12: 13 (Moffatt's Translation). See Chapter XII of this book.
11 Browning, "A Grammarian's Funeral."

Such souls, in Wordsworth's eyes, were the donor and the architect of King's College Chapel, Cambridge. While penurious spirits wondered if such lavish outpouring of money and talent, on a chapel intended only "for a scanty band of white-robed scholars," would ever be warranted by commensurate returns, the poet rallied to the defence of people who are prodigal for God.

> "Give all thou canst; high heaven rejects the lore
> Of nicely calculated less or more." [12]

The lines summarize the message of the parable.

Divine judgment, furthermore, is according not alone to the measure of work done but also *according to the measure of opportunity.*[13] Rewards in heaven are bestowed for handicaps overcome, as well as for goals achieved. Some men in the rash hardihood of their powers can demand terms of the universe. They greet life at the sunrise, and seize the opportunity in resolute hands. They exact their recompense by splendid strength. But others drag crippling chains of inheritance, or beat against confining walls of circumstances. Who will hire them? They would fain serve God, but cannot serve Him as they would. "No man hath hired us." But their intention is accepted as their deed! Though they cannot kindle in a living flame of prophetic speech, though they cannot claim saintliness, though in unrealized hopes they must be content to offer hospitality to the prophet and saint, they are not forgotten in the appraisals of the kingdom: "He that receiveth a prophet in the name of a prophet shall receive a prophet's reward." [14]

In the meridian of his powers and dreams John Milton was robbed of sight. What more could he do than wait disconsolately in life's market-place, hoping that some employer, less efficient by reason of kindness than the rest, would hire him?

> "When I consider how my light is spent
> Ere half my days in this dark world and wide,
> And that one talent which is death to hide,
> Lodged with me useless, though my soul more bent

12 William Wordsworth, "Inside of King's Chapel, Cambridge."
13 G. H. Hubbard, *op. cit.*, p. 127, summarizes this thought ingeniously in the phrase "the equation of character." Opportunity is the denominator of the equation, service its numerator, and character or destiny its quotient.
14 Matthew 10:41.

> To serve therewith my Maker, and present
> My true account, lest He returning chide;
> 'Doth God exact day-labor, light denied?'
> I fondly ask. But Patience, to prevent
> That murmur, soon replies, 'God doth not need
> Either man's work or His own gifts; who best
> Bear His mild yoke, they serve Him best; His state
> Is kingly: thousands at His bidding speed,
> And post o'er land and ocean without rest;
> They also serve who only stand and wait." [15]

Some come to the adventure of life eternally young; others are crippled from the start. Some have negligible handicaps; others have a taint in the blood, a pressure of environment, a native feebleness of will, an early thwarting which has left for constant smart an ever open wound. One man leaps to victory; another stubbornly resists the foe a hundred times and then succumbs—and only God knows which of them has truly won the victor's crown! Those whose strength is sure despise the comrade hired at the eleventh hour. "These last—" they murmur; and forget that the "scorching heat" is harder on the man who waits despairingly than on the laborer who toils in assurance of his livelihood! Idleness in appearance may not be idleness in motive. But His judgments are "true and righteous altogether," [16] and it comes to pass that those who are "first" in the appraisals of men, are sometimes "last" in the verdicts of God.

If only the laborers of the morning hours had offered a part of their ample wage to comrades who, because of weakness, or "the inhumanity of man to man," or fettering circumstance, waited while no one hired them! Then they would have entered into the joy of their Lord, and realized the wise and gentle kingdom in their midst!

15 Milton's Sonnet on his blindness.
16 Psalm 19: 9.

CHAPTER XVI

The Love of God (II)

THE GOD WHO ANSWERS PRAYER

THE PARABLE OF THE FRIEND AT MIDNIGHT

"And he said unto them, Which of you shall have a friend, and shall go unto him at midnight, and say to him, Friend, lend me three loaves; for a friend of mine is come to me from a journey, and I have nothing to set before him; and he from within shall answer and say, Trouble me not: the door is now shut, and my children are with me in bed; I cannot rise and give thee? I say unto you, Though he will not rise and give him because he is his friend, yet because of his importunity he will arise and give him as many as he needeth. And I say unto you, Ask, and it shall be given you; seek, and ye shall find; knock, and it shall be opened unto you. For every one that asketh receiveth; and he that seeketh findeth; and to him that knocketh it shall be opened. And of which of you that is a father shall his son ask a loaf, and he give him a stone? or a fish, and he for a fish give him a serpent? Or if he shall ask an egg, will he give him a scorpion? If ye then, being evil, know how to give good gifts unto your children, how much more shall your heavenly Father give the Holy Spirit to them that ask him?

(*Luke* 11 : 5-13)

THE PARABLE OF THE IMPORTUNATE WIDOW

"And he spake a parable unto them to the end that they ought always to pray, and not to faint; saying, There was in a city a judge, who feared not God, and regarded not man: and there was a widow in that city; and she came oft unto him, saying, Avenge me of mine adversary. And he would not for a while; but afterward he said within himself, Though I fear not God, nor regard man; yet because this widow troubleth me, I will avenge her, lest she wear me out by her continual coming. And the Lord said, Hear what the unrighteous judge saith. And shall not God avenge his elect, that cry to him day and night, and yet he is long-suffering over them? I say unto you, that he will avenge them speedily. Nevertheless, when the Son of man cometh, shall he find faith on the earth?"

(*Luke* 18 : 1-8)

THE GOD WHO ANSWERS PRAYER

The Parable of the Friend at Midnight
The Parable of the Importunate Widow

These two stories are so strikingly similar in purpose that they might almost be termed twin parables. Though they are separated in Luke's gospel and assigned to different occasions, it seems probable that they were originally spoken in uninterrupted sequence. The one story reiterates the truth of the other, but with significant changes of emphasis—a fact which holds of other twin parables.[1] The colors of the one story are gay; of the other wellnigh black. The one has traits of whimsical good humor, almost of comedy; the other is saved from unrelieved tragedy only by a happy issue. The one stresses a genial teaching, with a sterner truth for shadow; the other stresses the hard fact, but has the brighter truth for a "bow in the cloud." Both stories are transcripts of life.

A man, travelling by dark to escape the glare and heat of the Palestinian sun, came at midnight to the home of a friend. His coming was unexpected; his friend had no food to offer him. But the simplest hospitality required that a host should break bread with his guest before they retired to rest. He was embarrassed. What could he do? He hurried to his neighbor's cottage and knocked on the door. "Who's there?" asked a gruff, half-sleepy voice. "Friend," answered the would-be host, "let me have three loaves; for a friend of mine has just come to my house after a journey, and I have nothing for him to eat."[2] There was no prefix, "Friend," to the impatient retort: "Don't bother me! The door is fastened, and my children

---

1 *E.g.*, the twin parables of the Treasure and the Pearl (see p. 26), and the Uncompleted Tower and the Rash King's Warfare (see p. 77), and others.
2 Quoted with one slight change from Goodspeed's "The New Testament—an American Translation." "Lend" means rather "allow the use of," a sense in which we sometimes employ the word.

and I have gone to bed;[3] I cannot get up and give you any."
Who would wish to be jerked out of sound sleep, and made to
grope round the room and fumble with the latch? The children would wake and begin to cry, and who knows how long
it would take to quiet them? We can almost hear the muttered
comment: "To come knocking at a man's door at this hour of
the night! Give him bread? Not I! If he got what he de-
served . . . !" But the petitioner was not so easily gainsaid.
Shamelessly[4] he ignored the refusal, and began again to bang
on the door. Soon the banging threatened to wake the neighborhood. No chance to sleep with such a racket! There was
the shuffle of feet in the cottage, a fumbling with the latch, a
hand thrust through the partly opened door: "Here! Take
your bread, and be off!" Surely Jesus' eyes twinkled as He
said: "I say unto you, though he will not rise and give unto
him because he is his friend (!), yet because of his shamelessness he will arise and give him anything he asks for." The
story is told to the life! Perhaps it came from life. Perhaps
Jesus was one of those children in bed on a memorable night
in Nazareth. Perhaps He had listened with eyes wide-open in
the darkness, while Joseph held gruff converse with a neighbor
banging on their cottage door.

The other picture is painted in sepia. It concerns a venal
judge such as was all too common in that eastern world. He
feared neither God nor man. As for God, he laughed at Him
and accompanied double-dealing with blasphemy. As for man,
what cared he for public opinion? To such a judge there
came a widow pleading her wrongs. The Bible's repeated
reference[5] to widows is proof enough that their fate was frequently pitiable. Many were browbeaten or cheated out of
their scanty ownings. Jesus' flaming wrath against the scribes
who "devoured widows' houses, and for a pretence made long
prayers,"[6] points to a form of rapacity that had become a

3 By "bed" we are to understand the wide, low divan or platform, which was
the family's sleeping-quarters and which occupied a considerable portion of the
room in a lowly Palestinian home. There was good reason why Jesus should paint
humble homes lovingly!
4 "Shamelessly" is the meaning of the Greek word.
5 See Isaiah 1: 23, Job 22: 9, Malachi 3: 5 among Old Testament references.
6 Mark 12: 40-44. It is to be noted that the widow's plea was that she might be
"avenged," not "revenged." We are not told the exact nature of her persecution.

public scandal. His tender tribute to the widow woman who gave her whole meager living as a Temple gift is another instance of His solicitude for widowhood. Perhaps that solicitude also grew in Nazareth soil. There is a firmly rooted legend that Joseph died while Jesus was young, leaving to Mary the care of the hungry brood. Perhaps the beginning of the public ministry of Jesus waited not only for the due preparation of His own spirit, but also for the fulfillment of His duty as a breadwinner for the family. Perhaps Mary was the "widow" of this parable. It is at least a permissible conjecture. There were only three ways of dealing with such a judge as is described; he could be bribed, bullied, or besought until he surrendered. The widow had no wealth with which to bribe him, and no power with which to threaten. She could only plead with the persistence of despair. So she pleaded even against hope. She entreated the judge at his tribunal. She waylaid him as he went home. Wherever he might go, there she would be, waiting to pour her intolerable tale of woe upon him. He could not escape her. At last, for his own comfort (he knew no law but his own gain) he did as she asked; it was the only way to be rid of her: "Though I fear not God, nor regard man; yet because this widow troubleth [7] me, I will avenge her, lest she wear me out by her continual coming."

What is the genial teaching which, we have asserted, is dominant in the story of the Friend at Midnight? It is the *a fortiori* plea which is summarized in that regulative word of Jesus: "If ye then, being evil, know how to give good gifts unto your children, how much more shall your Father who is

---

[7] The Greek word is derived from *upoopion*, meaning "the part under the eyes." Hence the import is "to hit under the eyes," *i.e.*, "to make black and blue," *i.e.*, "to annoy exceedingly." The same word occurs in I Corinthians 9: 27. Bruce, *op. cit.*, p. 161, urges that the word must be given its literal meaning in the story. The judge foresaw that the widow, if she were denied much longer, would become a raging fury and might strike him. He affected to be afraid of her fists. But this interpretation seems to place both the widow and the judge "out of character." In an interesting article on this parable in the *Expository Times* (June, 1927), Dr. A. J. Robertson suggests that the judge was not so black a villain as he wished others and himself to believe. "Though I fear not God nor regard man" was a display of bombast. The woman discerned the core of goodness in him and therefore persisted. But such an interpretation does not seem to accord with the explicit statement of v. 2, nor with the treatment accorded to widows in that age. The parable is given only in outline, and imagination must fill in what is lacking. Dr. Robertson's imaginative delineation of the judge is fully allowable, but such facts as are available seem to favor a sterner portrayal. The latter also appears to accord better with the didactic purpose of the story. The article in question is masterly in description and stimulating in interpretation.

in heaven give good things to them that ask him?" What is
the sterner teaching which is shadow to that light? It is the
implication that God cannot be found save by persistent plea—
"because of his importunity." In the story of the Importunate
Widow these emphases are transposed. The sterner teaching
is in the bold center of the picture (prayer's persistence must
be like the entreaty of a widow-woman before a cruel judge),
while the genial assurance is the bright background.

Consider, then, that recurrent theme in the message of Jesus
—His argument from our little to God's great, from our bad
to God's good. Repeatedly He made His appeal to the fineness
of human motive: " 'Which man of you' would not do this?
Surely God will do as much, and more!" That appeal is basic
in the Christian conception of God. Jesus was not a scholastic
carefully framing philosophic definitions of the Godhead. He
was an artist painting on the glowing canvas of His parables
unforgettable pictures to quicken our dull spirits to a sense of
the Divine. There is a chapter of the New Testament [8] which
begins in prosy definition: "Now faith is the assurance of
things hoped for, a conviction of things not seen." Then, as
if in the realization that truth cannot be imprisoned in a ped-
ant's cage of labored words, the writer throws away his school-
man's stylus and returns to brush and canvas. He paints por-
traits and adventure in arresting line and color—"By faith
Abel." . . . "By faith Enoch." . . . "By faith Abraham"; and
soon the prosy definition flames with meaning! Jesus was an
artist. In the last resort a definition is a symbol, since words
are a symbol. Then why not choose the better symbol of picture or story? A definition is a prison, but a story (if it is told
as Jesus could tell it) is a sunrise.

We cannot communicate any conviction, least of all our conviction about God, except through the medium of symbols.
When we speak of God as "Law," we are choosing a legal system as our sign for Him. It is not a happy figure, for the
laws we know best are created and maintained by human mind
and purpose; it becomes convincing only when we think of *His*
living mind and purpose behind *His* laws. When we speak of

<hr>

8 Hebrews 11.

"the mechanism of the Universe" we are choosing a symbol more unworthy than "law"; for a machine is inert, and derives all its virtue from the inventiveness of man. This symbol becomes intelligible only when we postulate the inventiveness of God. Inevitably we think of God under the guise of *human* signs. Our care must be to choose our divinest human symbols. The savage mutilates himself with knives because His God is a savage; He is guided, not by reason and love, but by caprice; His sudden cruel whims must be mollified by blood. The Attilas of mankind dream of a God of battles, Who "wears riding-boots and a helmet"; and the bloody sack of cities is the dark issue of that hateful creed. The Humanism of Jesus began with the premise that it is psychologically impossible for a man to worship anything less than the best in himself. He construed the Divine in terms of the ideally human: "If *ye* then, being *evil*, know. . . ." Let the taunt of "anthropomorphism" be flung at such a faith, and the sufficient answer will be: "Of course it is anthropomorphic. Do you expect a human to fly beyond the bounds of his humanity? But, being *anthropo*morphic, it at least compares God with the best in human life, and not with a law or a machine. If it were *mechano*morphic or *nomo*morphic the gibe would be just." [9]

In the story of the Friend at Midnight, Jesus makes specific appeal to the ideally human as a proper symbol for our understanding of God. Behind that appeal He places the weight of His own authority: "*I* say unto you." [10] "The flat stones of the lakeshore" (He says in effect) "resemble our Jewish bread; but a true father would not deceive his son by offering him stones for bread. He would not give him a serpent knowing that it might easily be mistaken for a fish. He would not place a scorpion [11] in his hand in pretence of giving him an egg. He would not be cruel or treacherous with his own children. If ye, being evil, know how to give good gifts, *how much more* shall your heavenly Father . . ." The reluctance of the neigh-

9 A similar argument is brilliantly stated in Canon B. H. Streeter's "Reality," Chapter I, in the section entitled "The Power of Metaphor."
10 The "I say unto you" in v. 8 is not emphatic (*lego umin*); it makes appeal only to the reasonableness of the situation. But in v. 9 it is emphatic (*kai ego lego umin*); Jesus is adding the weight of His personal authority.
11 When its limbs are closed about it, a scorpion resembles an egg.

bor in the story is therefore not a picture of God's reluctance
so much as an incident designed to heighten a contrast.   An
earthly friend may need to be aroused from sleep, but "He
that keepeth Israel shall neither slumber nor sleep." [12]   An
earthly friend may be reluctant and grudging, but "He that
spared not his own Son . . . how shall he not also with him
freely give us all things?" [13]   By such an argument that epitaph
said to have been placed on the tombstone of an early Norse-
man buried in Scotland [14] is not blasphemous, but distinctly
fine:

> "Here lie I, Martin Elginbrodde:
> Hae mercy o' my soul, Lord God;
> As I wad do were I Lord God,
> And ye were Martin Elginbrodde."

The best in human life, purified, intensified, and magnified, is
essentially of the nature of God's life.   A vast universe of
Divine mystery abides, and into it we cannot penetrate.   He
far transcends our highest imagining.   Yet!—the drop of water
of our human goodness is of the same constitution as the ocean
of His goodness.   Our human light is broken, but it is of the
same nature as the Eternal Splendor.   Christianity is on impregnable ground when it says adoringly of Jesus: "He that
hath seen Thee hath seen the Father."

Yet this story has its shadow with its sun.   Jesus hints that
God, despite all tokens of His love, will not be moved except
by an importunate cry.   He will not answer save to a persistent
quest.   A man must come, even as the Friend at Midnight
came, in the sense of urgent need.   He must seek as unremit-
tingly; he must knock to the point of presumption and seeming
shamelessness.   This truth becomes dominant in the story of
the Unjust Judge.   Jesus spent long hours in prayer.   In the
nighttime He sought the lonely mountain side and there wrestled with God.   That power and peace came to Him through
such vigils is attested by the disciples' plea: "Lord, teach us
to pray."   It is probable that He spoke many parables of
prayer, for prayer was the atmosphere in which He walked.

12 Psalm 121: 3.
13 Romans 8: 32.
14 Quoted from George Macdonald by R. J. Campbell in his "The War and the
Soul."

But only two of these parables remain, and it is an immensely significant fact that both stress (the one with lighter, and the other with heavier emphasis) the need for patience and persistence. In the story of the Importunate Widow that teaching is in sharp focus: "And he spake a parable unto them" (says Luke) "to the end that men *must* pray [15] and not grow weary in praying." There is little reason to doubt that the gospelist has stated the purpose of the story.

It is clear that Jesus regarded prayer as the simple outpouring of human need. It may take many forms—thanksgiving, confession, adoration, or intercession; [16] but all these forms are but variants of the cry of human poverty. Thanksgiving is the cry of need—the acknowledgment that the cry has been heard, and the need supplied. Confession is the cry of need—rags and filthiness seeing a Throne and bewailing with piteous entreaties: "Woe is me! for mine eyes have seen the King." Adoration is the cry of need—awe-filled wonder and praise for the All-Fair, the All-Holy, the All-Loving Whose "greatness flows around our incompleteness." Intercession is the cry of need—love feeling the need of others and pleading for them! Prayer is not a mere form prescribed for those who would be religious, nor a magic shibboleth whose recital will bestow any blessing we may chance to covet. It is a movement of our spirits to God's Spirit, as inevitable as a tide swinging to the rhythm of the moon. It is the instinctive cry of human need. It will not come to God with ill-becoming or irreverent speech, but it will abhor the niceties of the stylist. At its most intense it will resemble the clamor of the Friend at Midnight, or the importunate plea of the Widow before the cruel Judge.

The implication of the stories is plain: Prayer must become a tireless beseeching, before God can richly reward it. Human experience will at times afflict us with the fear that heaven is empty or unfeeling, that the only answer to our prayers is the answer of an echo. God will *appear* at times as One Who must be aroused from slumber, and Who then gives only grudgingly of His abundance. He will appear as unheeding and cruel as a heartless judge. Thus Jesus confronts us with what

15 This is the emphatic meaning of the word.
16 See H. E. Fosdick's "The Meaning of Prayer," p. 123.

has been called "the indifference of God to anything less than
the best there is in man—the determination of Heaven not to
hear what we are not determined that Heaven shall hear." [17]

The history of religious experience affords ample proof that
great prayer is marked by importunity. Jacob wrestled with
his "angel" until he had wrested from him a new nature: "I
will not let thee go except thou bless me." [18] The followers of
Jesus tarried in supplication [19] before the Pentecostal fire descended on them. Paul besought the Lord thrice that He
would remove his "thorn in the flesh," before he at length
received, not the removal of his tribulation, but that "sufficient
grace" which made the burden seem light.[20] Did not Jesus
Himself pray until "His sweat became as it were great drops
of blood falling down upon the ground"? [21] The strong souls
of mankind have been under necessity of proving to God that
their prayer was the plea of their all-controlling desire.[22]

Jesus does not explain this seeming cruelty in the Divine
method. His words are an index to living rather than a rationale or a metaphysic. He believed and taught that only by
obedience can we enter into the secrets of the kingdom. Why
does the advance of Divine favor resemble our human march
—sudden progress after periods of apparent stagnation? Why
are the answers of God to our prayers like the works of human
genius—a flash of light following dark days of fruitless travail?
Why is His coming like the wheel of the seasons—a sudden
burst of green after winter's dreary months? Jesus gives no
reply save by implication and by scattered hints. We dimly

---

17 An illuminating sentence from a brief comment on this parable by Robert
Collyer in the "Expositor," First Series, Vol. VIII, p. 319.
18 Genesis 32: 26.
19 Bruce is correct in saying that both parables represent "delay experiences,"
but unconvincing in his contention that the first concerns individual sanctification,
and the second concerns the "public fortunes" of the kingdom. His assertion
about the "public" scope of the second parable is built on the flimsy ground that
the "judge" is a public servant! (See Bruce, op. cit., pp. 145, 148.) Trench makes
the better suggestion, op. cit., p. 330, that the first story concerns prayer for a
man's own self and the second a prayer for a man's neighbors. But it is not
necessary to draw these distinctions. Both stories seem to concern prayer in any
or all its forms. Trench, op. cit., pp. 331 seq., recounts the various allegorizings
to which the story of the Friend at Midnight has been subjected. His interest in
these allegorizings detracts from the value of his interpretation.
20 II Corinthians 12: 7.
21 Luke 22: 4.
22 H. E. Fosdick's "The Meaning of Prayer," Chapter VIII, forms (though without direct reference) a splendid commentary on the Parable of the Importunate
Widow.

discern that the delays of Heaven are for our sake. While we plead with importunity our patience is perfected, our humility deepened, our purposes clarified and purged of dross. While the door is closed we learn "to desire earnestly the best gifts." [23]

This truth shines clear, whatever else may remain uncertain: Our prayers must be freed of insincerity and the trivial spirit before heaven's bounty is unlocked. A plea for pardon cannot be perfunctory; it must beat with bruised hands before the door is opened! A prayer of intercession is not honored of God if its compassion is choked or thin; it must besiege God in the fullness of its love! There is no grace bestowed upon a cheap devotion. Equally in our prayers and in our conduct God hates the blasphemy of the get-rich-quick; we must earn our reward in honest toil of spirit and hand. Those who win the reward do not begrudge the toil. The haven has little joy for those who have not breasted stormy seas.

> "Prayer is the *soul's sincere desire,*
> Uttered or unexpressed—
> The motion of a hidden *fire*
> That kindles in the breast." [24]

"It is no affair of hasty words at the fag-end of a day, no form observed in deference to custom, no sop to conscience to ease us from the sense of religious obligations unfulfilled. Prayer is the central and determining force of a man's life." [25]

Such prayer will discover the "bow in the cloud." It will prove the truth of the argument from our "broken lights" to heaven's perfect day.[26] If a heartless judge will avenge a widow because of her importunity, will not the kind God avenge His own children? Such is the assurance given unto those who in the persistence of felt need knock at heaven's door. It is given on the authority of Jesus. It rests for sure support upon the integrity and compassion of His soul.

23 I Corinthians 12: 31.
24 James Montgomery, "What Is Prayer?"
25 H. E. Fosdick's "The Meaning of Prayer," p. 149.
26 However we may interpret the difficult verses in Luke 18: 6-8, this truth holds. Even if these verses were an addition by the early Church to be attributed to apocalyptic expectation (and that theory has not sure proof) they are true to the genius of His message, and they complete the parallel with the other story.

CHAPTER XVII

The Love of God (III)

THE GOD OF THE LOST (I)

THE PARABLE OF THE LOST SHEEP

"Now all the publicans and sinners were drawing near unto him to hear him. And both the Pharisees and the scribes murmured, saying, This man receiveth sinners, and eateth with them.

"And he spake unto them this parable, saying, What man of you, having a hundred sheep, and having lost one of them, doth not leave the ninety and nine in the wilderness, and go after that which is lost until he find it? And when he hath found it, he layeth it on his shoulders, rejoicing. And when he cometh home, he calleth together his friends and his neighbors, saying unto them, Rejoice with me, for I have found my sheep which was lost. I say unto you, that even so there shall be joy in heaven over one sinner that repenteth, more than over ninety and nine righteous persons, who need no repentance."

(Luke 15:1-7)

(Parallel passage: Matthew 18:12-14)

THE PARABLE OF THE LOST COIN

"Or what woman having ten pieces of silver, if she lose one piece, doth not light a lamp, and sweep the house, and seek diligently until she find it? And when she hath found it, she calleth together her friends and neighbors, saying, Rejoice with me, for I have found the piece which I had lost. Even so, I say unto you, there is joy in the presence of the angels of God over one sinner that repenteth."

(Luke 15:8-10)

THE GOD OF THE LOST (I)

The Parable of the Lost Sheep
The Parable of the Lost Coin

The grouping of the three parables of the Lost Sheep, the
Lost Coin, and the Lost Son is as deliberate and masterly as
the collection of the "kingdom" parables in the thirteenth chapter of Matthew's gospel. In the latter instance the connect-
ing idea is "the kingdom of heaven," in this the leitmotif is
sounded in the word "lost." "Lost" recurs like a bell to warn
and plead. Each of the three stories presents the theme in a
new key and with a different development, but in none is it
overlayed. The parables are a true trinity.

But the first two are also twin parables. As in the case of
the "Mustard Seed" and the "Leaven" one is pastoral in setting and the other domestic. Not only are the two strikingly
alike but there is a line dividing them [1] from the Parable of the
Lost Son. In the twin parables Jesus defends Himself against
the charge of association with "publicans and sinners," whereas
in the story of the Prodigal and the Elder Brother He carries
the issue to His critics. Again, in the twin parables God is
represented as actively seeking the lost, whereas in the third the
Lost Son is shown undertaking the return journey for himself
and welcomed by his Father's compassion and joy. This chapter considers the twin parables.

Jesus was being assailed for the company He kept. He welcomed "publicans and sinners" and He ate with them. [2] To the
ceremonial righteousness of His critics the latter offense was

1 The line of separation is shown also in the introductory words: "and he spake
unto them" introduces the first parable, while "or" is sufficient to lead into the
second. "And he said," repeated at the beginning of the third, indicates the
separation.
2 There can be little doubt that Luke has supplied the proper setting of these
parables. In Matthew the context (the receiving of little children) is suitable but
not nearly as convincing as the background which Luke provides. See Matthew
18 and Luke 15.

worse than the former, for the rabbinical law governing meals
was rigid.   Publicans were socially abhorrent and "sinners"
were regarded as morally beyond the pale.   The Pharisees made
it clear to the crowd thronging about Jesus that a man is known
by the company he keeps!   Yet there was no flash of anger in
His answer, but only a gentle reasonableness.   "What man of
you [3] losing even a sheep would not seek it?   Or what woman
losing even a coin would not search through the house for it?
You say these 'sinners' are lost.   Surely a lost man is more
precious and demands a more urgent seeking than a lost sheep
or a lost coin, and his recovery gives a fuller joy.   God sent me
to seek lost people."   It is so gentle, so incontrovertible a
defence. . . .

The Parable of the Lost Sheep

Jesus regarded a shepherd's toil with feelings deeper than
admiration.   As often as He thought of the faithful vigil, tender
care, and sacrificing heroism of those who kept their flocks
on Judean hills His nature kindled.   They were men worthy
to receive the Angels' Song!   The imagery of shepherd life is
recurrent in His teaching.[4]   "Good Shepherd" was a title He
justly claimed, and was one of His best names for God.

Who—or what—is God like?   We try to slay the question
but ever and again it revives.   During most of our waking
hours God is no more than an Abstract Noun.   But sometimes, as we look on "the wide composure of the sky" or the
radiance of a child, He becomes a Presence though vague.
Occasionally, in some flaming hour—in the impact of death,
the thrill of human love, the throes of conscience, or the pleading of prayer—He becomes the living Fact of facts.   "What
is God like?"—in no life can that question be finally dismissed:

> "Just when we're safest, there's a sunset-touch,
> A fancy from a flower-bell, some one's death,
> A chorus-ending from Euripides,—
> And that's enough for fifty hopes and fears
> As old and new at once as Nature's self,
> To rap and knock and enter in our soul,

---

[3] This appeal to ordinary instinct was a favorite appeal with Jesus.   See Luke
11: 5; 14: 5, 28, and many other examples.
[4] John 10: 1-18; Mark 6: 34, and Matthew 25: 32 will come to mind.

Take hands and dance there, a fantastic ring,
Round the ancient idol, on his base again,—
The grand Perhaps!" [5]

The church-spires which pierce our sky-line are the outward symbol of spires raised wistfully in the city of Man-Soul: "What is God like?"

Jesus answered the question. The world's instinctive faith is that He answered it from veritable experience. His friendship with God was not intermittent. God was never an Abstract Noun to Him, but always the Fact of facts. So He journeyed through the narrow valley of our earth answering our deepest question. He drew word-pictures of God that we might understand. Thus He said, "God is the Good Shepherd."

On the human plane the story is poignant. Not without stirring of heart can we hear of a shepherd seeking a lost sheep, despising distance and darkness in the search. But on the divine plane (humanity the flock and God the Shepherd) the story is like a daybreak. The Presence sometimes felt and sometimes feared, the Power Who rolls the planets on their course and draws the line of death across our human days —Who is He? "Our dearest faith, our ghastliest doubt"— what is He like? He is like a shepherd! He led us into this pasture of mortal life. He knows the folly by which we wander, drawn by this pleasant tuft and that lush watercourse, until the night is on us and the mountains rise like walls of rock. He seeks us through pain and peril. He will lead us at the last through the Valley of the Shadow, His lifted rod our guide!

"He is the Drover of the soul; He leads the flock of men
All wistful on that weary track and brings them back again.
The dreaming few, the slaving crew, the motley caste of life—
The wastrel and artificer, the harlot and the wife. . . ."

"Yet not unled, but shepherded by one they may not see—
The one who walked with starry feet the western road by me!" [6]

Human life is so frequently loveless that it is not easy for mankind to think of God as a Shepherd. We can believe in

5 Robert Browning, "Bishop Bloughram's Apology."
6 Evelyn Underhill, "Uxbridge Road." ("Immanence," E. P. Dutton and Co.)

His power—those flames of fire incredibly vast leaping forth from æonian suns into a gulf of space incredibly deep are tokens of power. We can believe in His holiness—the moral law written on tablets of conscience speaks of an eternal Right. We can believe in His beauty—the fringe of the sunset is His garment's hem. Jesus taught us to believe also in His love—His courage of love which bestowed our freedom, His pain of love which seeks us when freedom has become our ruin!

The message of the story—this avowal of God's love—is concentrated in three of its words:

"LOST." Jesus seldom called people "sinners"; He called them "lost." [7] Sometimes they are lost like sheep, not from viciousness or deliberate choice but from weak will and heedlessness. Sometimes they are lost like coins, not from their own guilt but from another's fault or the mischances of life. Sometimes they are lost like the prodigal through calculated self-will. The word breathes pity more than condemnation, and it reveals God's loneliness!

It is a universal word. The Pharisees never classed themselves as lost. They were quick to fling the title "sinner" at other men. But their barren self-righteousness seen in the white light of the spirit of Jesus brands them as more hopelessly lost than those whom they deemed outside the pale. Jesus has destroyed for all time the pretensions of the "unco guid." Who the "ninety and nine" may be we do not know. Possibly they are the "angels" of whom the story later speaks. As for human nature, it is "lost" [8]—not in the sense of being irreparably damned (these parables were given to contradict the horror of any such creed) but in the sense of being away from the fold of true blessedness, away from the currency of true service, away from the home of God's presence. Like sheep, men follow the zest of the moment—this transitory thrill of pleasure, that passing enrichment—until they reach darkness and the brink of the precipice! "Lost" is the final description of a civilization which has not given peace. . . .

[7] Matthew 10:6; 15:24; 18:11, and John 17:12, beside the references in Luke 15.

[8] Matthew's account uses the word "astray" instead of "lost." There are other interesting differences: Matthew says, "If so be that he find it" and Luke "until he find it." Luke adds significant details such as "he puts it on his shoulders" and "he gathers his friends and neighbors."

"Seeking." Jesus tells us that human experience, if we would interpret it aright, is God's quest of us. The upstarting of duty, the torment of our sins, the dim unrest which is the undertone of all our joys—these we usually call "moods," but Jesus calls them the echoing footfall of the seeking Shepherd and the call of His voice. He bids us believe that our hopes fulfilled and our hopes blasted, the gleam of noble character in past or present, and above all, that "Staff" set up on Calvary for the world's comfort—the whole range of human experience—is a Divine pursuit. If we ask "What does life mean?", Jesus answers: "It means God seeking, seeking, because you are precious to Him."

There are those who in the name of modern science pour scorn on the Christian doctrine of the preciousness of the individual. "Did God come to this molehill of a planet and die for men?"—so the sneer runs! It leaves us with a picture of a universe composed of vast wheels. Humanity is the little dust which the wheels raise for a moment into the light of mortal days. Sometime we shall learn that preciousness is not determined by physical size, and then we shall know the folly of the sneer. That was a wise Scot who refused to be "astronomically intimidated." A true father owning a mountain (even a mountain of gold) would part with the mountain sooner than part with his child. Furthermore the sneer can be confronted with facts. Conscience is a fact—and not less a fact if science should prove that it has risen to its high estate by lowly paths. Human love is a fact. Prayer, the deep which answers to the Deep, is a fact. Jesus is a fact. The soul asserts that in all these facts God draws near. Such experience of God is valid as any finding of the senses. Love is not less real because it cannot be poured into a test-tube. . . .

The human flock is all God's flock. We do not acknowledge one another's company. Modern self-righteousness says "moron" instead of "sinner," but we are nevertheless one flock, and every sheep is precious to the Shepherd. Therefore He is ever seeking.

"Until." There are ninety and nine safely in the fold, but love is not satisfied by a favorable percentage between those safe and those lost. Souls are not digits. It is not tactful to say to a father when one child has gone: "Oh, well, you need not worry. You have others left." God seeks *one* life. When He has found it He does not upbraid, nor drive it home. He carries it on His shoulder. He rejoices more over the recovery of the one lost than in those who have not strayed.

Millennium doctrine is of value in that it keeps alive the mood of instancy in the Christian faith, but it is a dark perversion in its portrayal of the character of God. Will God save good people in a mass, gathering them into His garner, and consign the bad people in a mass to unquenchable fire? Will He make perfect His world by sweeping out of it all who are imperfect? The doctrine is a flat contradiction of these parables. Jesus said with reiteration that all the forces of a benignant heaven are released for one lost spirit. If God forgets any, He forgets the good—if good there are! If He remembers any, He remembers those whom men despise. The only obstacle is our foolish self-will. The faith abides

> "That nothing walks with aimless feet;
> That not one life shall be destroyed,
> Or cast as rubbish to the void. . . ." [9]

For God—Godlike in patient love—will seek the lost "until He find it."

The Parable of the Lost Coin

Jesus may have seen the "woman" of this story during His Nazareth years. Perhaps the "coin" was a large fraction of her scanty savings or the last coin needed to complete the sum carefully accumulated for the payment of a temple tax.[10] Perhaps it was one piece of a circlet of coins which she wore about her head.[11] In any event it was precious. She lit her candle —for her humble cottage received light only through the low door—and searched diligently. Dust rose from the reeds spread thick on the floor and the little house was filled with commotion. No nook or corner was left unvisited until at last a gleam of silver rewarded her toil. At once she gathered

9 Tennyson, "In Memoriam" (Canto LIV).
10 Bruce makes this suggestion (*op. cit.*, p. 275).
11 Plummer ("I.C.C.," *in loc.*) precludes this interpretation, but Grieve (Peake's Commentary), Burton (Expositor's Bible) and others hold it admissible. There is nothing in the Greek "drachma," so it would seem, to forbid it.

around her the women [12] of the village and told the exciting incident—doubtless with elaborations. A simple story!—but Jesus prints it across the face of the earth and heaven: "Likewise there is joy in the presence of the angels of God. . . ."

Again there is the word "lost," and the suggestion is that people are sometimes lost like a coin which slips from the hand. The fault is a fault of the hand, not of the coin. We cannot dogmatically say that Jesus had the fact in mind, but fact it is that many of the "publicans and sinners" lived in gloom not from choice but rather from cruel circumstances or the lapse of other men. What of little children crippled by congenital disease or torn by unruly temper? Lost, not from blame of theirs but through hereditary taint! Oliver Twist was taught to steal in such tender years that theft was as much his second nature as walking. He was lost through another's guilt! Wrong committed often rests in heavier consequence on the innocent than on the wrongdoer. When a father is sentenced to jail, the stigma branded on his children is more tragic than his imprisonment.

Sometimes it seems as if the insensate harshness of life causes the "loss" of character. A wandering microbe destroys health and hope. A wandering hurricane destroys a city and with the city many a human dream. A wandering temptation catches the spirit off guard. There are times when our human lot appears a meaningless clash of blind forces. We are cast aside in their unfeeling play. The human coin rolls into a dark corner. . . .

Again the story asserts the value of one life lost. Our modern civilization is strangely contradictory in regard to the "lost." On the one hand, it builds schools for the "underprivileged" child, engages in costly research for the sake of those smitten by incurable disease, and experiments with prison reform by which to reclaim the criminal. In these endeavors it is "come to seek and to save that which is lost." On the other hand, it permits and by crass "statescraft" invites the scourge of war, degrades a man to a number on a metal disc,

12 Trench suggests that the "woman" may symbolize the Church or Divine Wisdom, and that the story with a "nice observance of proprieties" makes Wisdom (a female personification) call her female friends together. (*Op. cit.*, pp. 385, 389.) It is an allegorizing which we may gladly ignore.

and drives him in his thousands in mass formation into a bloody maw. Likewise it herds men and women in factories, crushes them by mechanical and monotonous toil, buys them in the "labor market" and starves or feeds them according to "supply and demand." Our civilization is sometimes civil, sometimes uncivil, and always weirdly inconsistent. But the gospel of Jesus is committed, once and forever, to the value of the individual. By His cross He has bound all into a world-wide brotherhood and set on each the seal of preciousness. Men are no longer flung to wild beasts in the Coliseum to make a public holiday, and Jesus will "overturn, overturn" until people no longer sit long hours before a factory belt which is timed to their "highest working capacity." Jesus concentrates on the unit—the unit of the individual and the unit of a friendly human order. "There is joy in heaven over *one* sinner"—the fortunes of the lowest and least are followed with impassioned interest in the presence of God. Jesus called Himself "Son of man," and thus claimed kinship with every life shadowed or bright, known or obscure.

His mind is slowly conquering the earth. When a drunken sot is rushed from the gutter to the hospital, there to be healed by gentle skill and ministered unto from the public funds, we acknowledge the mind of Christ. His word about the "lost" constrains us, or at least an instinct tells us (an instinct which He quickens and interprets) that the life of a sot has intrinsic worth. So long as any glimmer of conscience is there, or any movement of love, it has bonds with the Eternal—for conscience and love witness to their own eternity. . . .

The story makes clear the intensity and thoroughness of the Divine search: "The spirit of man is the candle of the Lord." He lights the candle and searches the house. In one Life the candle burned with so bright a glow that the whole earth became radiant:

> "And so the Word hath breath, and wrought
> With human hands the creed of creeds
> In loveliness of perfect deeds. . . ." [13]

[13] Tennyson, "In Memoriam" (Canto XXXVI).

The search is not without dust! God often disturbs the
wonted floor of life. Happily, the prayer for "normalcy" is
as vain as it is unworthy. Consider the history of mankind
—what dust-clouds of controversy, what shaking of kingdoms,
what wars and rumors of wars, what overturnings of fixed
habit! Consider the cottage of individual life—swept by joy
and then by sorrow, by fortune and misfortune, by holy aspira-
tion and by agony of remorse! The little house is often in dis-
order! We wonder why. We talk of "good luck" and "bad
luck," or (if the affairs of a larger world are in question) of
tyrannies and bolshevisms, the uprising of races, and the ambitions of classes. Are these but names for the Divine search?
Is He seeking us through the sweeping of change—His human
coins besmirched but with the royal image uneffaced? He
searches "diligently"!

The parable concludes with an amazing picture of heaven's
joy. We do not easily think of God as joyous, and consequently our theologies are stilted and barren. We often think
of Him as impassive. The ocean of His being is neither torn
by storms nor shimmers in sunlight; it is constantly grey. An
impassive God, nevertheless, is not Godlike. A man rich in
play of feeling is worthier the name. Our mortal spirit suffering and rejoicing is more divine in aspect than an Unconscious
Force. Jesus speaks of the joy of God. We do not know
what Jesus meant by "angels." Our earth-born life is more
radiant than the pre-natal world, and, if analogy can be trusted,
life hereafter will make this life seem a drab imprisonment.
God has there His shining servants even as here He has His
messengers of duller wing. . . .

There is a river whose waters rise with the tides of the sea.
Miles inland muddy banks are filled, grounded boats are floated.
Occasionally the inrush takes the form of a wave. The people
on that river call the wave "the Ægir." The boys cry on its
approach: "The Ægir, the Ægir!" It is a name of noble origin
in Icelandic myths, the name of the Giant of the Calm Sea,
and it has remained in the language of that river as the sigil of
the early Norse invaders. Tennyson, who lived in the same
western country, caught the picture of that calm tide:

"But such a tide as moving seems asleep,
  Too full for sound or foam,
When that which drew from out the boundless deep
  Turns again home." [14]

The joy of heaven is like an ægir. It floods every inlet. It redeems muddy flats. It floats all the vessels of delight. It moves like a quiet wave through angelic worlds and thrills into worlds beyond. "There shall be joy in the presence of the angels of God. . . ."

And why? Because a "lost" coin has been found, because there is a character-gain revealed in some soul. If two men should come to us, the first saying, "A rich uncle has left me a million dollars" and the other saying, "By much struggle I have learned that what I own makes me neither rich nor poor, but rather what I am and what I give"—it is to be feared that our congratulation would be quicker and more sincere to the first man than to the second! Meanwhile heaven watches the issues of *character* with intense concern, and as souls grow more tender and truthful the tides of joy overflow. God is plunged in loss when any soul is "lost," diligent in search that the "lost" may be found, and glad with exceeding joy in the day of recovery. It is a gospel of hope which will yet transform the earth!

[14] Tennyson, "Crossing the Bar."

The Love of God (IV)

THE GOD OF THE LOST (II)

THE PARABLE OF THE PRODIGAL SON

"And he said, A certain man had two sons: and the younger of them said to his father, Father, give me the portion of thy substance that falleth to me. And he divided unto them his living. And not many days after, the younger son gathered all together and took his journey into a far country; and there he wasted his substance with riotous living. And when he had spent all, there arose a mighty famine in that country; and he began to be in want. And he went and joined himself to one of the citizens of that country; and he sent him into his fields to feed swine. And he would fain have filled his belly with the husks that the swine did eat: and no man gave unto him. But when he came to himself he said, How many hired servants of my father's have bread enough and to spare, and I perish here with hunger! I will arise and go to my father, and will say unto him, Father, I have sinned against heaven, and in thy sight: I am no more worthy to be called thy son: make me as one of thy hired servants. And he arose, and came to his father. But while he was yet afar off, his father saw him, and was moved with compassion, and ran and fell on his neck, and kissed him. And the son said unto him, Father, I have sinned against heaven, and in thy sight: I am no more worthy to be called thy son. But the father said to his servants, Bring forth quickly the best robe, and put it on him and put a ring on his hand, and shoes on his feet: and bring the fatted calf, and kill it, and let us eat, and make merry: For this my son was dead, and is alive again; he was lost, and is found. And they began to be merry."

(*Luke* 15: 11-24)

THE PARABLE OF THE ELDER BROTHER

"Now his elder son was in the field: and as he came and drew nigh to the house, he heard music and dancing. And he called to him one of the servants, and inquired what these things might be. And he said unto him, Thy brother is come; and thy father hath killed the fatted calf, because he hath received him safe and sound. But he was angry, and would not go in: and his father came out, and entreated him. But he answered and said to his father, Lo, these many years do I serve thee, and I never transgressed a commandment of thine; and yet thou never gavest me a kid, that I might make merry with my friends: but when this thy son came, who hath devoured thy living with harlots, thou killedst for him the fatted calf. And he said unto him, Son, thou art ever with me, and all that is mine is thine. But it was meet to make merry and be glad: for this thy brother was dead, and is alive again; and was lost, and is found."

(*Luke* 15: 25-32)

THE GOD OF THE LOST (II)

The Parable of the Prodigal Son
The Parable of the Elder Brother

"The most divinely tender and most humanly touching story ever told on our earth," [1] says George Murray. The appraisal is not extravagant. To judge this parable with our words is futile and sacrilegious—like the attempt to measure the sunrise with the span of our fingers. For it is more than words; it is fashioned from the love which endured Calvary.

No story more instantly touches the nerve of actual life. Let it be read, without any comment or explanation, and it conquers us. Its vivid strokes have caught human history. The boy who has churned his life into a fleshly mess is condemned by it, and saved. The mystic likewise sees in it an epitome of human experience, our return from the far country of visible things to the Father Invisible, the "Dweller in the Innermost." Mark its sure portrayal.

The Parable of the Prodigal Son

There is, first, the assertion of self-will: "Give me the portion of thy substance that falleth to me." Home was irksome; its freedom carried restraints. The boy craved a freedom without restraints. The tediousness of his dull brother and the loving rule of his father fretted him. Life beckoned. There were entrancing worlds beyond the disciplines of home. Illusory worlds!—the primeval lie of liberty without law! His father made no attempt to hold him. How could he? Home would not be home to a boy of alien will. He made no immediate attempt to find him when he "took his journey." The

---

1 George Murray, *op. cit.*, 163.

boy must first find himself. So he divided unto each son his
rightful share.

Aversion of desire soon became apostasy of conduct. "Not
many days after"—the resolve was quickly carried into effect.
"He gathered all together"—called in all loans, sold all the
lands, turned all the jewels into money—and went his carefree
way. He chose a "far country"—as far as possible from the
old hated restraints. Now he could *live* in unfettered joy!

So the primeval lie became the deed. Why not express ourselves? Why be held in the intolerable bonds of ancient shibboleths mumbled over us by our fathers, mumbled over them
by their fathers? Why obey these stale conventions, when the
red blood is dancing in our veins? The primeval lie! The
delusion that we can destroy laws by denying them! A man
can demonstrate his freedom by jumping from a twentieth-
floor window. But the law of gravitation is not thereby destroyed; the man is destroyed. Physical freedom is always
within limits: "Which of you by being anxious can add one
cubit to his stature?" [2] Mental freedom is always within
limits; a proposition cannot at once be true and untrue. Moral
freedom is always within limits; there is a moral law. We may
deny it; but wisdom was not born with us. The hard won
sanctities of the race are not utterly invalid. The moral findings of long experience are not a vast and foolish blunder.
There is a law! For those who can see and hear, the Mt.
Sinai of our human nature is not less awesome than the desert
Mount; it has its clouds of divine mystery, its thunder voice,
its lightening splendors, its inviolable decrees.

Apostasy of conduct became spendthrift folly: "He wasted
his substance." At first there was the zest of self-mastery, the
abandon of being free. He was whirled along through happy
days and sparkling nights. But daily he was "scattering" the
substance which not many weeks ago he had "gathered."
Living to gratify the moment's whim is a scattering business.
It wastes talent which cannot grow except we "scorn delights
and live laborious days." [3] It disintegrates the will. It throws

2 Matthew 6: 27.
3 John Milton, "Lycidas."

the imagination into fever and chaos. It breaks the body. It leads by a *descensus avernus* into wretched bondage.

Spendthrift folly became destitution. "There arose a mighty famine." The outer famine came to mock the inner woe; for nature's moods seem often to accord with the peace or violence of man's desires.[4] "He began to be in want." His once-radiant spirit was as bedraggled now as his once-radiant clothes. The ancient laws mumbled foolishly from age to age became avenging angels. But he will stick to his poor bargain! The page being blotted, he will blot it more! "So he went and joined himself to a citizen of that country." "Went and pinned himself"—so the phrase runs. In the finality of need he thrust his abject servitude on a Gentile master who sent him to feed swine. *"Sent* him"—where is now his boasted freedom? Now he is *driven,* and driven to feed swine—a task whose utter shame only a Jew could feel. He tried to feed on the husks of the carob-tree; but, though he filled himself, he did not feed. Swine's food is not for men. "And no man gave unto him." The companions of his revelry all forsook him. Having sucked him dry, they threw him away bitter pith and rind. Even had they remained loyal they could not have restored the vitality which they had drained.

So the primeval lie came home to roost. The man who lives to do as he likes becomes the slave of his likes. Playing miser to his body, coveting the titillations of the flesh, he finds at last that his body masters him and "sends" him "to feed swine." The man who in boasted independence will brook no lordship is whipped along ignominiously by every vagrant mood, and driven by an unrelenting memory. . . .

"But when he came to himself." That is as divine a word as any from the lips of Jesus. Alien from God, we are alien from our veritable selves. It is not a mere manner of speaking

---

[4] A classic instance is in Shakespeare's "Macbeth." Lennox thus describes the night on which Banquo was slain, though as yet Lennox knew not of the murder:

> "The night has been unruly: where we lay,
> Our chimneys were blown down; and, as they say,
> Lamentings heard i' the air; strange screams of death,
> . . . the obscure bird
> Clamour'd the livelong night: some say, the earth
> Was feverish and did shake."

which prompts us to say of the irritable or ungenerous mood
of a friend, "He is not *himself* to-day." Irritability is unnatural. When the far country has constrained a man in un-
destined bondage, there is a stirring in his soul—a movement
as inexorable as the stars, as splendid as God is splendid—
whereby he comes to himself. The man at odds with the
austere vision is not the real man. Self-will is not our true
self. The far-country can never be our homeland.

Jesus did not make light of sin. He painted its tragic consequence with terrible fidelity. But He could not believe that sin
is the act of genuine humanity. "When he came to himself"—
such is His final and invincible optimism. Ultimately graft in
politics will cease—for it is not consonant with human nature.
Ultimately selfishness will wither—for it is parasitical. Ultimately theft and war will be done away—for they outrage the
constitution of our spirit. Ultimately the race will come to
itself! A man can have no nobler comrade than his truest self :
"the light which lighteth every man coming into the world." [5]

A recent commentator has pronounced fictitious the repentance of the prodigal. "Those who make this an example of true
repentance," he writes, "read something into the story that
Jesus never put there. It is simply the desire of a hungry man
for something to eat. True, he thought up a nice little speech
about his unworthiness and sinning against heaven, because he
imagined that would be necessary in order to win his father's
favor." [6] But surely such an interpretation is the slashing of a
sincere and lovely canvas. We may grant that the motive of the
prodigal was not unmixed. An utterly unblemished purpose is
not in human nature. In spite of our hastiness to question the
sincerity of others, when have we surprised ourselves in an
ambition absolutely clear? Our best intentions are streaked
with base alloy—but they are not all base! Body and soul are
marvellously compact together; and that which strikes the
body (as for instance, the famine of the far country) does not
leave the soul untouched. Education by violence may still
educate. The penitence of a sick bed has proved ere this a true
penitence. Let it be admitted that hunger drove the boy

5 John 1: 9.
6 G. H. Hubbard, *op. cit.,* p. 300.

home; the hunger motive, even so, was savingly entangled with memories of a father's love, and with shame for the turpitude which had flouted love.[7]

"Why feedest thou on husks so coarse and rude?
I could not be content with angel's food.

"Harsh tyrant's slave who made thee, once so free?
A father's rule too heavy seemed to me.

"What sordid rags float round thee on the breeze?
I laid immortal robes aside for these.

"What has thy forehead so to earthward brought?
To lift it higher than the stars I thought." [8]

He resolved to cast himself on his father's mercy. He would ask to be made as one of the hired servants. Stripes and chastisement were found, at the last, to be better than sin's bondage; life at home, on any terms, was more joyous than the far country.

The confession was as genuine as the penitence. Pharaoh confessed in the desolation of the plagues; but when the plagues passed he hardened his heart. Saul confessed under the prophet's accusation; but later returned to his headstrong course and perished on his own sword. Judas confessed, casting away the pestilential pieces of silver; but afterwards he hanged himself. The prodigal confessed without excuse or palliation. He pleaded no extenuating circumstance—though he might justly have done so as the story later reveals. He realized that to sin against his father was to sin against his nature's deepest law—"against heaven and in thy sight." His was the very nakedness of true confession.

But he never framed it fully in words. The speech of contrition, prepared and rehearsed as he had trudged home by that same road along which he had once fared forth so eagerly, was never completed. He was not allowed to say, "Make me as one of thy hired servants." For "while he was yet afar off his father saw him." He had watched for him daily. He recognized him even in his rags. He knew the

---

[7] Thus Dr. Plummer ("I.C.C.," Luke, p. 375), says categorically that the Prodigal's penitence was as real and decided as his fall.
[8] R. C. Trench, "Poems."

swing of his step, the lines of his body. Every feature had been treasured in memory, looked at, wept over many times during those weary years. Seeing him at last, the father ran with incoherent joy and kissed the boy again and again. "Bring forth the best robe"—all the marks of the far country must be covered! "A ring on his finger"—token of authority! "Shoes on his feet"—slaves went barefoot, but a son must be shod as befits the family honor! "For this my son was dead and is alive again." There was no word of sharp reproof, no making sure of a sufficient sense of guilt, no requirement of probation, no sentence to quarantine until the disease of sin should have been cured. There was only the fullness of a father's love!

Who, then, is the "prodigal" in this story? Anybody given over to gross fleshliness? Yes, and the whole race of men besides—a planet living for externals, and acting the primeval lie of "self-expression." Substance is of many kinds; it is the stuff of personality as well as stocks and bonds. Wasting is of many methods; it is the wasting of mind as well as of body. The far country is far in many directions; it is far in motives rather than in miles. Even in church a man may be an exile from his Father's house.

Who is the "father" in this story? He is the picture of God, the most winsome picture ever drawn on earth! This parable is the heart of the gospel. God is eager to forgive utterly, and to restore. For there is no forgiveness except utter forgiveness. To "forgive but not forget" is to refuse to forgive. And there is no forgiveness that does not restore:

> "For the love of God is broader
>   Than the measures of man's mind,
> And the Heart of the Eternal
>   Is most wonderfully kind." [9]

When our clever sciences have been forgotten, when all other stories pall, when the earth waxes old like a garment, this story will still be young. It will still have power to untangle our ravelled life. It will still win us to our hearts' true home.

[9] F. W. Faber, "Hymn."

The Parable of the Elder Brother

Who has not wished that the parable had ended in the welcome to the Prodigal?[10] "They began to be merry"—that is the fitting climax. The Elder Brother is a sudden discord, but without him the story would have been untrue to life. The year has its winter storms, the disciples' band its Judas, the compassion of Jesus for the outcast its dark cloud in the murmuring of the Pharisees: "This man feasteth with publicans and sinners." Jesus was compelled to relate the aftermath to the Prodigal's return so that Pharisees of that and every age might have a mirror whereby to see themselves and God.

The Elder Brother compels us to rearrange our list of cardinal sins. Jesus played similar havoc with the world's list of virtues. In certain items the ethic of Jesus may resemble the ethic which preceded Him, but in one main regard it was revolutionary: it made love the prime requisite and crowning grace of character. "And if I have the gift of prophecy . . . and all knowledge; and if I have all faith . . . and if I bestow all my goods to feed the poor . . . and have not love . . ."[11] Insight, knowledge, faith, philanthropy—the whole gamut of virtues—are nothing without love. There is similar upheaval in our list of sins. The "gross" sins, as seen in the shame of the Prodigal, have been reckoned the most culpable. For these misdeeds we drive women, and occasionally men, out of respectable society. (We even stigmatize their children as "illegitimate," though why children should be so branded passes understanding; for they alone are innocent. Some man or woman is guilty; society at large, in some measure, is guilty; but the child, thrust into life without knowledge or consent, cannot be guilty. The parents may be "illegitimate," but not the child.) Sins of the passions have darkly crowned the list; whereas jealousy, anger, pride and harsh judgment have hardly been counted sins. They are faults, rather; they are unfortunate defects of temper. Such is our appraisal of the cardinal

10 Pfleiderer (see "Century Bible," Luke, p. 236) argued that the parable did end at v. 24; but there is little reason to doubt that Luke has supplied the proper context for all three parables (*vide* Luke 15: 1, 2), and the context shows the necessity for the portrait of the Elder Brother.
11 I Corinthians 13: 2, 3.

wrongdoings. But Jesus said to the self-righteous Pharisees, "The publicans and the harlots go into heaven before you." [12] Jesus treated sins of passion with pity. Let it be said with emphasis that He never condoned such guilt or minimized it. But He met it with mercy, while He treated sins of temper with withering denunciation. The woman of shadowed reputation was forgiven—"Thy faith hath saved thee; go into peace," [13] but the hypocrite was called a "whited sepulcher." [14] The Prodigal was welcomed with kiss, and robe, and feasting, but the exclusive pride of the Jews was scorched with a wrath terrible to behold: "It shall be more tolerable for the land of Sodom and Gomorrah in the day of judgment. . . ." Perhaps our list of cardinal sins should be rearranged. Perhaps "faults" of temper may be as culpable in certain settings as transgressions of the flesh.

The Prodigal as Jesus has drawn him seems a more attractive figure than the Elder Brother. If one of these men had to be an only companion on a camping trip it is not certain that the majority of men of goodwill would choose the Elder Brother. The Prodigal would give an impression of unstable will, of unsound spiritual health; but he would be generous, enthusiastic, and companionable. It is to be feared that the Elder Brother, while eminently respectable, would be thin-lipped and churlish. Jesus does not suggest that we exonerate the Prodigal; but he does suggest that jealousy and a critical aloofness can be as poisonous as sins called "gross." Perhaps the Elder Brother was a main reason why the Prodigal left home. Perhaps Rudyard Kipling's version of the Prodigal is partly true:

> "My father glooms and advises me,
> My brother sulks and despises me,
> My mother catechises me,
> Till I want to go out and swear!" [15]

The Elder Brother is drawn sharply as in an etching. We see him returning from his toil on the farm. He heard unaccustomed sounds of dancing and demanded an explanation:

12 Matthew 21: 31.
13 Luke 7: 50.
14 Matthew 23: 27.
15 Kipling, "The Prodigal Son (Western Version)." ("Kim," Doubleday, Page & Co.)

THE GOD OF THE LOST 197

"What does all this racket mean?" A servant gave answer eagerly: "Thy brother is come; and thy father hath killed the fatted calf, because he hath received him safe and sound." "Oh, how glad I am!" (the answer might have run). "And how happy my father will be! What a load of anxiety off his mind! And that brother of mine (he was always wild, but everybody liked him), is he really safe and sound?" So the Elder Brother *might* have spoken! But, no! his face darkened. He would not go in. When his father came to plead with him, his anger broke into speech, every word more ungenial than the last: "Lo, these many years do I serve thee"—("serve": nothing very filial there!)—"and I never transgressed a commandment of thine"—(reasonably well satisfied with his own integrity!)—"and yet thou never gavest me a kid that I might make merry with my friends." (But the story has told us that he received his larger share of the estate when his brother went away. And if his idea of a "good time" is to be rid of his father, to carouse with his own cronies, how is he different from the Prodigal?)

The recital proceeded, becoming angrier and harsher in judgment: "But when this thy son was come"—(he did not say "my brother"; he said "this precious son of thine")—"which hath devoured thy living with harlots"—(there was no final proof of that degradation but he was not in any mood to give the benefit of a doubt)—"thou hast killed for *him*"—(black emphasis on "him")—"the fatted calf." This Elder Brother is a lovely spectacle! There he stood angry, petulant, uncharitable, jealous! Can we be sure that while the Prodigal was a sinner, the Elder Brother was a good man albeit with certain defects? Or would it be truer to say that there were two prodigals—one a prodigal in the far country, the other a prodigal at home; two prodigals—one alien from the father's love through sins of passions, the other through sins of temper; two prodigals—one eating the husks of fleshliness, the other eating the rancid food of a sour and sullen mind? Would that be truer? Is our list of cardinal sins in need of revision? Is it clear that in the accurate balances of heaven the sins of those who break the moral code always weigh heavily, and the sins of the respectable always light?

In the parable the Elder Brother is not impressive. In the parable we are ready to hurl stones at him. Out of the parable he is not anathematized. Out of the parable he is held in considerable regard. And, in strict fairness, a certain tribute must be paid him. He was steadily industrious; on the day of rejoicing he came in late from the field. He was conscientious, dependable, and consistent. He was faithful, even if he was not free. He was a just man after a fashion, even if he was not generous. There were no depths in his record, even if there were no heights. He was a man to give stability to the structure of society.

Then wherein was he wrong? He was *ungrateful!* "Son, thou art ever with me, and all that I have is thine"; but he was not thankful either for his father's comradeship, or for the daily bounty of his home. It never occurred to him that most of his good fortune was by gift and not by merit. His brother was now enjoying one feast of outstanding happiness and welcome, but *he* had sat daily at a table of peace. For his brother a spring of water had been struck suddenly from the rock of destitution, but for *him* a quiet river of water had ever flowed. God had saved *him* from that heat of blood which proved his brother's undoing. God had spared *him* the temptation which would have found the Achilles' heel of *his* "gross" weakness. He might have said of his younger brother and said with truth —but for ingratitude he did not say it—

> "O God, Thou knowest I'm as blind as he,
> As blind, as frantic, not so single, worse,
> Only Thy pity spared me from the curse.
>
> "Thy pity, and Thy mercy, God, did save,
> Thy bounteous gifts, not any grace of mine,
> From all the pitfalls leading to the grave,
> From all the death-feasts with the husks and swine." [16]

The respectable, whose names will never form a scandalous headline, rarely pause to give thanks for a clear heredity and the favoring circumstance.

He was *self-righteous.* "Lo, these many years do I serve thee"—dwelling on his faithfulness until he convinced himself

---

16 John Masefield, "The Widow in the Bye Street." ("Collected Poems," The Macmillan Company, 1921.)

that he was much abused and very ill-rewarded. "Neither transgressed I at any time thy commandment"—an extravagant claim! There is scant room for improvement in any man who is assured of his own virtue. Verily, he has received his reward! [17] Further achievement is possible only in one so conscious of his failings, that he says of the far distant goal: "Not that I have already obtained or am already made perfect, but—I press on." [18] But complacency is not the worst ill that self-righteousness is heir to: there is a more baleful consequence, and therein we see the darkest transgression of the Elder Brother.

He was *loveless*. Home is the place where we lay aside the mask which a hard world compels us to wear. Home is the abode of mutual confidence, the free outpouring of our inmost mind, where joys are doubled by comradeship and pains are halved by sympathy. But the Elder Brother, though always at home, was never at home. He was too convinced of his own merit, too critical of others, too fond of hugging his own supposed hardships, ever to comprehend his father's grief for the lost, ever to comprehend the self-inflicted wreck and torture suffered by his younger brother. Jesus said that if any one "offended" and caused another to stumble, "it were well for him if a millstone were hanged about his neck and he were thrown into the sea." [19] Better not to have been born than to quench the flow of sympathy! Better not to live than not to love!

This ingratitude, this hard self-righteousness, this lovelessness we call a "defect." It is, forsooth, only a strain in the marble. People can harbor these faults, and still be "good" people; but the prodigal is utterly taboo.

Consider the havoc caused by the Prodigal who stayed at home. He spoiled his own life—what a hidden loathsome realm was disclosed by his brother's sudden return, a noisome world beneath his respectable industry. He shut himself off from God's life—how could he pray when held captive by such evil moods? He cast a shadow on his father's life. And

17 Matthew 6: 5.
18 Philippians 3: 12.
19 Luke 17: 2.

as for the Prodigal, what must have been his effect on him? "If this is home," we can hear the younger brother saying, "then I like the far country better."

> "I never was very refined, you see?
> (And it weighs on my brother's mind, you see)
> But there's no reproach among swine, d'you see,
> For being a bit of a swine.
> So I'm off with wallet and staff to eat
> The bread that is three parts chaff to wheat
> But glory be!—there's a laugh to it,
> Which isn't the case when we dine." [20]

Many a man has been driven back to the far country by the lovelessness of the elder brother. "If that is what Christianity means! If that unyielding exclusiveness, that loveless respectability, is what Church makes of a man . . . !" When religion is linked with class pride, or with a capitalistic régime which regards other men as "hands," religion then is almost worse than the blasphemy of the far country. Judged by the havoc of their consequences, there is little to choose between the sin of the younger brother and the sin of the older.

But the story has mercy for both sons. It is a gospel to beckon both the prodigal afar off and the prodigal at home. The father did not reason with his elder son. To argue with him would have confirmed him in stubbornness. He pleaded his love. "Son," he called him; "child"—"boy," the name by which he had called him when he was a little lad running about the farm! "Boy, thou art ever with me, and all that I have is thine. We are one in companionship. We are one in possessions. We must be one in redemptive joy. It was meet that we should make merry, for this thy brother"—("thy brother"—how gentle the reminder!)—"was dead and is alive again, was lost and is found."

Jesus has full right to tell the Parable of the Other Son. Was He not an "Elder Brother" who left home, and went into the far country "to seek and to save that which was lost, and to give his life a ransom for many"? [21] He trusted only to holy love—and that love can save both the prodigals.

20 Rudyard Kipling, "The Prodigal Son (Western Version)." ("Kim," Double-day, Page & Co.)
21 Luke 19: 10, Matthew 20: 28.

But, meanwhile, let it be clear (lest imagined righteousness should be quick to condemn the "far country") that the Prodigal Son was at home with his father as this story ends; but the Elder Son was outside. No one shut him out. He shut himself out. He would not go in. He was barred from heaven by his lovelessness.

PARABLES OF THE PASSION WEEK

THE KINGDOM OF GOD
AS A JUDGMENT

CHAPTER XIX

THE TEST OF DEEDS

THE PARABLE OF THE TWO SONS

"But what think ye? A man had two sons; and he came to the first, and said, Son, go work to-day in the vineyard. And he answered and said, I will not: but afterward he repented himself, and went. And he came to the second, and said likewise. And he answered and said, I go, sir: and went not. Which of the two did the will of his father? They say, The first. Jesus saith unto them, Verily I say unto you, that the publicans and the harlots go into the kingdom of God before you. For John came unto you in the way of righteousness, and ye believed him not; but the publicans and the harlots believed him: and ye, when ye saw it, did not even repent yourselves afterward, that ye might believe him."

(Matthew 21: 28-32)

THE TEST OF DEEDS

The Parable of the Two Sons

This story is direct and simple. There is no cloudy word. It names explicitly those for whom its teaching is intended: "The publicans and harlots go into the kingdom of God before *you*,"—"you" being the Pharisees and their followers. If we should ask who are modern representatives of the Pharisees, we might be driven to answer, "Some good church people." The Pharisees were scrupulous about Temple observances, and they were ardent patriots.

The parable is equally explicit in its teaching. The "man" who "had two sons" is God. It is timely to remark on the childlike, not childish, clarity of the message of Jesus about God. Our modern vogue is to refer to the Deity under titles misty and mystifying. God is the "Omnipresent Urge," the "Absolute Essence," and the "Stream of Tendency." The foggier the title, the more it pleases us. But Jesus said, "After this manner pray ye: Our Father . . ." [1] That Name meant nothing crudely anthropomorphic. It did not counsel less of reverence and awe. It did not attempt to sweep away that vast realm of mystery which attaches to any worthy concept of the Divine. But it did imply a Spirit Who "beareth witness with our spirit," [2] and Who loves us with so deep a love that the best human affection can only faintly intimate it. Jesus advanced no philosophical definition of the Godhead. Rather he drew word pictures: "God is like a Gardener . . . like a Shepherd . . . like a Father . . ." When religion parts company with the simplicity of Jesus it gropes in darkness.

God, then, has two sons. He bids them work in his vine-

[1] Matthew 6: 9.
[2] Romans 8: 16.

yard.[3] The Pharisee answers, "I go, sir." He does not omit
the "sir"; he is punctilious and polite; he is alert in seeming
obedience—"You can depend on me, sir." The tax gatherer
(hated Jewish collector of the Roman conqueror's taxes, bat-
tening on the misery of his compatriots) and the harlot (scum
and outcast of society) reply: "I will not." The answer has
no "sir." It is curt, boorish, and deliberately insolent. But
the Pharisee does not go; [4] while the outcast, feeling some stab
of conscience, finally obeys. Thus the simple story. Then
comes the simple question: "Which of the two *did* the will of
his father?" There is a world of emphasis on that word "did."
Could any parable be more direct? The thought is translucent.
The etching is firm. There is no wavering or uncertain line.

The story is as impartial as it is clear: "For John came unto
you in the way of righteousness." It is as if Jesus said, "I do
not judge you by your obedience to me, but by your response
to John. He taught you, and what he taught was good.[5]
There were no startling innovations in his message. He required such fastings and ablutions as you approve. He was
guilty of no Sabbath desecrations such as you charge against
me. You shall stand at the bar of *his* message. By your
churchly attitude you say to God who has spoken to you
through John, 'I go, sir'; yet you do not go." Sometimes we
wish that we might meet Jesus in the flesh. That, we imagine,
would be of all experiences the most radiant. Perhaps it would
be also the most ruthlessly penetrating! The only mercy would
be that the unsparing truth of Jesus is its own kindness. If He
should say to us, "I will not ask you how much of God's command you ought to have heard. Let the question concern only
that command which you have heard. I make no issue of your
response to Me, but only of your response to that voice which
you yourselves have felt to be right. Have you obeyed?"—how
would it seem to meet Jesus in the flesh?

3 Arnot, *op. cit.,* p. 223, suggests that the farm in this story is a small family
holding, whereas in the Parable of the Laborers and the Hours it was the large
holding of a magnate.

4 Bruce, *op. cit.,* pp. 442, 443, remarks that the charge of insincerity could have
been laid against the Pharisees without the introduction of the character of the
second son. But it is evident that the story is enhanced in value by the sharp
contrast of characters, and is thus made to cut both ways—one way in condemnation and the other in redemption.

5 This seems to be the meaning of the phrase "in the way of righteousness."

Once more, the parable is swept by an almost terrible urgency.[6] The language is abrupt. The condemnation burns. "Publicans and harlots go into the kingdom of God before *you.*" The phrase "publicans and harlots" was proverbial as applied to all beyond the pale. It is said that there is an analogous phrase current in Korea—"pigstickers and harlots." [7] For Jesus thus to speak was, at least in the eyes of the Pharisees, to sin against good taste. But to saddle the words on them; to say, "These people, bad as you believe them to be, will enter the kingdom before you—you, the pillars of the Judean Church," was insult's crown of insult. Such language could not have escaped His lips except under the impulse of a terrible urgency. He spoke thus because the destiny of man hung on His teaching. He knew what insincerity could do— this pretense of honoring God and then failing utterly in the test of deeds. He knew what it *would* do on Golgotha before the week had passed! He knew that it breeds a verminous realm until character becomes rotten at the core. If we had His eyes, we likewise would fear insincerity more than we fear shame or death; nor would we wonder at this crashing of doom in His words.

The thrust of the teaching is sharp: "Which of the two *did* the will of his father?" The ritual of worship without some serious attempt at worthy living is a painted lie. Floating incense without deeds as fragrant as incense is a reek and a disgust.

"Wherewith shall I come before Jehovah, and bow myself before the high God?" they asked of an old prophet. "With burnt-offerings?"

"No," he answered, *"you cannot ceremonialize your way into God's favor."*

"With thousands of rams?"

"No, you cannot bribe the Eternal."

"With ten thousands of oil?"

"No, you cannot ease yourself into the Divine presence."

"Then I will give my first-born for my transgressions, the fruit of my body for the sin of my soul."

6 Compare Chapter V of this book where the same urgency is noted concerning the same theme; namely, the duty of deeds.
7 Bruce, *op. cit.,* p. 445.

"No!" thundered the old prophet, *"you cannot seduce God even with shed blood! He hath showed thee, O man, what is good; and what doth Jehovah require of thee, but to do justly, and to love kindness, and to walk humbly with thy God?"* [8]

So much depends on what we do. One man says, "I go"; but goes not. Another says, "I go not"; but later goes. The curt denial in words is not to be approved.[9] Insolence is not virtue, even though it afterwards repent. It is no grace for a man to say, "I do not pretend to be religious"; nor does such a confession justify him. Avowed badness is not made goodness by being avowed. But a curt denial in words, even without the subsequent repentance, is better than the eagerness of false piety. The denial has at least the merit of being honest.

We may say with our *reason,* "I go," religion having commended itself to our intellect; and it is no requirement of Christian faith that reason should be stultified. "Come now and let us reason together, saith Jehovah." [10] Yet reason in itself is not enough. Under Jesus the mind not only *may* test all that purports to be true, but *must* test it. That self-mesmerism which cries "I believe, I believe," until it flogs intelligence from honorable doubt into dishonorable acquiescence, is not even remotely Christian. "Ye shall know the truth, and the truth shall make you free." [11] But reason degenerates into windy speculation unless it acts. There is no ground for the customary assumption that a man's philosophy can be true even when his deeds are vicious. The mind cannot be imprisoned in a hermetically sealed chamber, immune from the poison in the will. The ultimate question remains: "Which of the two *did* the will of his father?" [12]

We may say with our *emotions,* "I go," religion having commended itself to our instinctive feeling; and it is no requirement of Christian faith that a true emotion should fail of its reward. Under Jesus there may be hours when sentience will

8 This famous passage, Micah 6: 6-8, is best interpreted as a "controversy" (see Micah 6: 2) between the people and the prophet, as has been attempted above.

9 Hubbard, *op. cit.,* pp. 388 ff., and Arnot, *op. cit.,* p. 288, have wisely emphasized this point. The latter says with characteristic pungency ". . . but it is a fatal mistake to assume that, provided you are not a hypocrite, you will be welcomed into heaven with all your vices on your back."

10 Isaiah 1: 18.

11 John 8: 32.

12 For elaboration of this thought, see Chapter V of this book.

become a white and living flame. The disciple ought to have
his luminous hours:

> . . . "and then
> Stream'd thro' my cell a cold and silver beam,
> And down the long beam stole the Holy Grail,
> Rose-red with beatings in it, as if alive,
> Till all the white walls of my cell were dyed
> With rosy colors leaping on the wall;
> And then the music faded, and the Grail
> Past, and the beam decay'd, and from the walls
> The rosy quiverings died into the night." [13]

There is place in true religion for such seasons of vision. But
Jesus warns us that the emotion which says, "I go," and is
not straightway translated into deeds is an insincerity even
worse than curt denial. Straightway!—for the command is:
"Go work *to-day*." The commands of Jesus are instinct with
immediacy. He is not content to receive the promise of to-
morrow's goodness: "We must work . . . while it is day: the
night cometh, when no man can work." [14] The Epistles have
caught this instancy in the message of Jesus: "*To-day* if ye
shall hear his voice harden not your hearts." [15] Behold, now
is the acceptable time; behold, now is the day of salvation." [16]

We may say with *ritual-worship,* "I go"; and Christian faith
lays no veto upon worship, but exalts it. There is so much
worship which finds no issue in conduct that it is easy to exclaim
in false antithesis, "Not ritual, but deeds!" But Jesus never
spoke thus. Worship and conduct to Him were indissolubly
joined. We have the evidence of His example, as well as
certain precious words of His, to justify the belief that worship
genuinely espoused is the highest exercise of which life is
capable. He spent long hours, sometimes half the night, in the
adoration and agony of prayer. The inference is plain; without prayer worthy living is well-nigh impossible. Yet Jesus
avows that deeds which irreverently deny God, but afterwards
repent to do His bidding, will gain heaven; while worship which
makes vows only to break them will fall under the curse!

"Son, go work to-day." We understand the divine require-

---

13 Tennyson, "The Holy Grail" ("The Idylls of the King").
14 John 9: 4.
15 Hebrews 4: 7.
16 II Corinthians 6: 2.

ment. Though the whole counsel of God is not revealed (such omniscience we cannot even glimpse), we know enough for the daily task. There is in the book of Leviticus a commandment, "Thou shalt not curse the deaf, nor put a stumblingblock before the blind." [17] The deaf cannot hear the curse, nor the blind see the obstacle; they are robbed of defense. Or the precept can be given wider scope, thus: "Thou shalt not slander the absent, nor plot against their peace." The book of Leviticus can teach us that to canvass cruelly the motives of the absent or the defenseless is unworthy. We are to live in decent charity. We understand what is required. But do we *obey?*

The dictates of Jesus are like beams of light. We may quarrel about His rightful name—we do so quarrel—but there is no quarrel about the life He lived. We look on Him, and doubt vanishes as to the life *we* should live. We hear the high call of God in Him: "Son, go *pray* to-day." But the hard world shuts us in, and we do not pray. Meanwhile some outcast of the earth, who has cursed God to His face, repents in dust and ashes; and, in a prayer we would hardly call a prayer, throws himself on the Divine mercy and is justified.

Thus the voice of Jesus strikes upon the chaos of modern religion like a clear bell. He shames our crude evangelism which vitiates its zeal with ignorance, vulgarity, and mercenary motive. He shames the current popularizing of religion, the truckling to the curious, the dangling of a bait to catch a crowd. He shames our orthodoxy with its petty dogmas, its imagining that the mystery of God and the ultimate verity of the Cross can be squeezed within a few poor words of man's invention. He shames our liberalism with its light rejection of the hard-won truths of generations, and its fond imagining that a new thing is therefore a true thing. He shames our psychologizing of religion with its pretense of sounding the depths of the soul by giving strange names to the levels of consciousness. Across this modern Babel, this chaos and distraction, the voice of Jesus rings like a bell. Into this fetid brawl He comes like a cool wind driven across the stars. This is His message: Do what you know to be right, and ampler truth will dawn upon

17 Leviticus 19: 14.

you as you walk.   Carry your reason into sanctified energy.
Fulfill your emotion in transfigured conduct.   Let worship and
neighborliness be the divine alternation of your life.   Thus you
will gain the kingdom as you help others gain it.   Thus you
will prove your sonship in the test of deeds.

CHAPTER XX

THE REJECTED OVERTURES OF GOD

THE PARABLE OF THE CRUEL VINEDRESSERS

"Hear another parable: There was a man that was a householder, who planted a vineyard, and set a hedge about it, and digged a winepress in it, and built a tower, and let it out to husbandmen, and went into another country. And when the season of the fruits drew near, he sent his servants to the husbandmen, to receive his fruits. And the husbandmen took his servants, and beat one, and killed another, and stoned another. Again, he sent other servants more than the first: and they did unto them in like manner. But afterward he sent unto them his son, saying, They will reverence my son. But the husbandmen, when they saw the son, said among themselves, This is the heir; come, let us kill him, and take his inheritance. And they took him, and cast him forth out of the vineyard, and killed him. When therefore the lord of the vineyard shall come, what will he do unto those husbandmen? They say unto him, He will miserably destroy those miserable men, and will let out the vineyard unto other husbandmen, who shall render him the fruits of their seasons."   (*Matthew* 21 : 33-41)

(Parallel passages: Mark 12 : 1-9; *Luke* 20 : 9-16)

THE PARABLE OF THE REJECTED CORNERSTONE

"Jesus saith unto them, Did ye never read in the scriptures,
     The stone which the builders rejected,
     The same was made the head of the corner;
     This was from the Lord,
     And it is marvellous in our eyes?
Therefore say I unto you, The kingdom of God shall be taken away from you, and shall be given to a nation bringing forth the fruits thereof. And he that falleth on this stone shall be broken to pieces: but on whomsoever it shall fall, it will scatter him as dust. And when the chief priests and the Pharisees heard his parables, they perceived that he spake of them."   (*Matthew* 21 : 42-45)

(Parallel passages: Mark 12 : 10, 11; *Luke* 20 : 17, 18)

CHAPTER XX

THE REJECTED OVERTURES OF GOD

The Parable of the Cruel Vinedressers
The Parable of the Rejected Cornerstone

Shakespeare could recompose an ancient tale so that under his magic it glowed with unsuspected colors, and laid on the mind undreamed-of compulsions. So, in higher manner, with Jesus. Often had Israel been likened to a vineyard.[1] The simile had become almost prosaic. But under the touch of Jesus, it was reborn a concerto with ravishing melodies, movements to melt the spirit, and finally a crash of doom. See how this old story,[2] grown too familiar, is changed "unto something rich and strange."

First, it sounds the gamut of *human privilege*. The vineyard was "planted"; it was not a wilderness; it was a well-cultivated plot on a very fruitful hill. It was "hedged about" to protect it from wild beasts. It had its "winepress" for the harvesting of fruit; its "tower" whence the approach of marauding foes could be seen, and where the vinedressers could find shelter. Every gift had been lavished, every preparation made, that it might "bring forth abundantly." The reference is clearly to Israel. Abraham, the father of his people, had left Ur of the Chaldees, because it was a city of evil breath. From that moment the Hebrews were a chosen people destined to bequeath to mankind the consciousness of a Holy God, as the

1 The classic instance is Isaiah 5: 1-7. Others are Deuteronomy 32: 32, Psalm 80: 8-16, Isaiah 27: 2-7, Jeremiah 2: 21, Hosea 10: 1.
2 This parable is clearly of a strongly allegorical character. Its authenticity has been questioned (a) on that ground, (b) because it reflects a historical situation later than that of the time of the telling of the story, and assumes Christ's death, and (c) because it claims Messiahship with a frankness inconsistent with the usually guarded claims of Jesus. In rebuttal it may be urged *seriatum* (a) that some of the parables have a strongly allegorical cast, as, for example, the Parable of the Soils, (b) if the parable were of a later date it would probably suggest the manner of the death of Jesus and make reference to His *resurrection*, (c) the Messianic claims of Jesus became more open as he approached that death of which he seemed to have clear premonition. (See Peake's Commentary, p. 695, and Professor Burkitt's comment in the "Century Bible," volume on Mark, p. 325.)

Greeks were later destined to bequeath the sense of beauty, and the Romans the strength of governmental law. All endeavors converged on Israel that she might fulfill her appointed task. Moses came to lead her toward a land "flowing with milk and honey," and to lay upon her great decrees— tablets of stone reflecting the eternal verities written on the fleshly tablets of the heart. Israel had been "planted." She had been taught the worship of the one God while other nations were still immersed in polytheistic barbarism; she had been blessed in singers whose psalms have since become the world's confessional and hymnary; she had been "hedged about" by prophetic warnings, harrowed by persecutions, and fertilized by countless mercies.

The story strikes the note of *human freedom*. The vinedressers in this story were under no restraint. They were left in sole possession. They could live as freemen. The only condition of their leasehold was that they should pay in fruit produced. Such is our freedom. It is not an unlimited freedom (the garden has its bounds), but it is within limits a real freedom. We are not free to choose our heredity, but we are free to make the best or worst of it; not free to choose our native talent, but free to double the talent or to bury it; not free to select the vineyard, but free within the vineyard's capacity to hold it to ransom for its harvest (even though with bruised hands), or to surrender it to a chaos of weeds. Such a freedom is attested by valid evidence. We know it by what Dr. Henry Van Dyke [3] has called "our judgments of regret" and "our judgments of condemnation." Why should we regret any action if it is merely automatic? Yet we do regret. Why should we condemn any action, as, for instance, the action of a man brutishly whipping a child, if both he and the child are predetermined to the event by an inexorable chain of circumstance? Yet we do condemn. Freedom is its own evidence. On that score no apology need be made. Human love is its own evidence, and when love knows itself to be love not a million experimental crucibles nor all the findings of modern psychology can add to or subtract from its conviction. If we cannot

[3] Henry C. Van Dyke, "Joy and Power," Chapter II.

trust our innate knowledge of freedom—a real freedom, though within limits—we cannot trust either the sight of our eyes or the hearing of our ears, much less the instinctive faith of the scientist that the universe is cosmos and not chaos.

Having sounded the theme of privilege, the parable next reveals an equal *responsibility*. There was a rightful demand for the fruit of the garden. The plot of Israel was given, not for pleasuring, but that there might come to birth a race washed white. The veil of allegory is translucent; we can see beyond cavil that it is the fruit of character which God expects. The teaching of Jesus was constantly concerned with human worth. When the disciples prattled of earthly gain, He swung the discussion back to sanity: "What doth it profit a man to gain the whole world, and forfeit his life?" [4] When men of fine promise were squandering their powers on a fishing boat, He called them to the human crusade: "Come ye after me, and I will make you fishers of men." [5] If the question of harvest prospects excited them, He recalled them to the foremost garnering: "Lift up your eyes! The fields—the human fields—are white already unto harvest." [6] The demand of God is that this little plot of earth shall produce an industry that blooms like a garden, homes that are like ripened grain, souls ever "wearing the white flower of the blameless life." [7] That obligation was laid on Israel, and it is laid on every land. To deny the obligation were futile: who among us can command his conscience? The moral imperative moves before our human pilgrimage, condemning or approving, speaking ever in regal tones. It were as foolish to deny responsibility as to deny freedom. Thus the parable reveals both privilege and obligation, and, with these, Jesus' overwhelming sense of foreordaining by God. God planted the garden of Israel. God hedged it. God sent his messengers unto it. The succession of the prophets was not happenstance. Human history is not fortuitous; it issues from the purpose of the Eternal. Great men are not an accident, nor the "national product of their heredity and environment"; a Will sends them! God is not a prisoner within His own

4 See Mark 8: 36.
5 Matthew 4: 19.
6 John 4: 35.
7 Alfred Tennyson, in the "Dedication" to "The Idylls of the King."

laws, devoid of initiative, impotent as an idol; He is God indeed. "He can create and He destroy." [8]

Another major movement, in this new world symphony based on an old world song, is *the witness of Jesus to Himself*. God (Jesus says) sent unto them "other *servants*"; then, "last of all, He sent unto them His *son*." [9] The gospel of Mark draws the distinction with an even sharper line: "He had yet one, a beloved son: He sent him last unto them." The claim is the more impressive because it is unforced, being woven into the texture of the story without explanation or discussion. This Galilean Peasant retelling one of the old Jewish stories declares in effect: "Elijah, Zechariah, Jeremiah, Isaiah and John the Baptist were prophets and more than prophets. They were servants of the Most High. They were sent forth from God to do His bidding. When one by one they had been harshly used, God sent His 'son.'"

If the Fourth Gospel—the proclaiming of the Logos made flesh—is to be dismissed as *mere* interpretation (and few thoughtful minds will so dismiss it), such testimonies as this parable have still to be met. The unique self-consciousness of Jesus is even more significant when revealed by indirection than when it is explicit: "Blessed are they that have been persecuted for righteousness' sake"—"Blessed are ye when men shall . . . persecute you . . . for my sake," [10] as though He and righteousness were in some deep sense identical. This self-witness seems to be woven into the fabric of His teaching. He constantly hinted a relationship between God and Himself, which transcends the relationship between God and us, and *we* feel that His communion with God was a mystery of light beyond our fathoming. Elijah, Isaiah, John the Baptist were "servants." "Last of all He sent His son!" Jesus thus refuses (though the refusal, in the paradox of His nature, is without

8 From the hymn, "Before Jehovah's Awful Throne" (Isaac Watts).
9 George Murray, *op. cit.*, p. 301, denies the force of this distinction. He says: "but treated strictly as a parable, and not originally as allegory, it would be uncritical to think that the son in the story was meant to be interpreted as a heavenly figure." But what if the story *is* of an allegorical cast? And what if its reference (by force of long usage) is to the history of Israel? The "servants" are the succession of Israel's prophets, and "son," as contradistinct from "servants," implies a difference. This contention receives added weight from the context of the parable. Each of the first three gospels makes the story a commentary by Jesus on His discussion with the Pharisees concerning His authority.
10 Matthew 5: 10, 11.

any loss of humility) to be catalogued with the greatest of mankind. Never has the earth seen such sovereignty in the midst of such incomparable lowliness. "The claim is amazing!" we cry. Then we check ourselves before a greater wonder, namely, a life which in every act and accent, every attitude and word honors the claim, enshrining it in flesh and blood.

This self-witness of Jesus was endorsed by those who walked and talked with Him. True it is that the custom of that age made almost inevitable the deification of so radiant a personality. True that the Romans, for instance, deified their glorious leaders. But this also is true: the Romans, having elevated their "great ones" to the pedestal of deity, did not make any of them an "only" god, nor did they make any persistent claim for their gods' unblemished souls. Their multitude of deities had faults as well as virtues, weaknesses as well as powers. The deification of Jesus was of a different order. Certain Jews, trained in a rigidly monotheistic faith, and taught from their earliest years to say, "the Lord thy God is one God," [11] found themselves acknowledging with glad compulsion an unwonted "grace and truth" in Jesus. They beheld Him,

> "How He walked here, the shadow of Him love,
> The speech of Him soft music, and His step
> A benediction."

Confronted by His poise and proportion, by the courage of His Face set like a flint, by the heartbreaking compassion of His Cross, by His felt Presence, vitalizing and empowering when others were calling Him dead,—they went groping for words new enough and vast enough to portray Him: "The Logos became flesh and tented among us." [12] He was "Man"; He was "Teacher"; He was "Prophet." But these were titles which, when applied to Him, were so feeble as to be almost futile. They were as feeble as a handbreadth laid against the immensity of the sky,—so pitiably inadequate as to be almost false. Thus His followers were constrained to discover new resources of language for His sake: "We have seen his glory—glory such as an only son enjoys from his father—seen it to be

11 Deuteronomy 6: 4.
12 John 1: 14.

full of grace and reality." [13]   This peculiar impact of Jesus
upon the mind of man continues down the years.   A modern
critic who throws all orthodoxies to the winds, and who
writes for "modern men" (whose only approach to Jesus, he
avows, is after the flesh), remarks strangely: "We have to
know Him after the flesh.   There is for us no other way.   But
to know Him after the flesh is to know Him after the spirit:
for we shall find that He was, in very truth, the ineffable
Word made Flesh."   He declares further that modern men
through the effort to make the earthly life of Jesus real to
themselves "find their souls possessed by love and veneration."
Finally he confesses instinctive adoration for the soul of Jesus:
"We shall look like men, on the man Jesus.   He will stand our
scrutiny.   Keep we our heads as high as we can, they shall be
bowed at the last." [14]

The conviction deepens that the supremacy of Jesus needs
no better evidence than this perennial witness of the human
spirit to Him.   Our orthodoxies may crumble—poor and un-
necessary supports to prop up His sovereignty—but man's agelong "acknowledgement of God in Christ" remains.   "He sent
unto them his servants.   Last of all he sent unto them his
son." [15]

There is a third dominant movement in this old story made
new: *the persistent and sacrificial love of God.*   It is reported
that Dwight L. Moody once said that until he became a father
he had much to remark about the love of Jesus, but that afterward the burden of his preaching was oftener the love of God. [16]
God is the real subject of this story.   He planted the garden
and bountifully endowed it.   He rightfully required the garden's yield at the hands of the vinedressers.   He sent servant
after servant with such unwearied persistence that we marvel
at His forbearance and the withholding of the merited chastisement.   He finally sent His "son."

Frequently we speak about the almightiness of God, yet here
we see Him beaten in the person of one servant, killed in the

13 John 1: 14 (Moffatt's Translation).
14 J. Middleton Murray, "Jesus—Man of Genius," p. xiii and p. 372.
15 It is worth mentioning that the adjective "beloved" as used in Mark's account
seems to be, in part of its connotation, synonymous with "only."
16 See Dr. J. D. Jones' sermon on this parable in "The Gospel of Grace"

person of another, and stoned to death in the person of a third. Almighty? A God of power? Yes!—for we cannot measure Divine power until we know the Divine purpose. Niagara Falls has titanic strength to sweep a man to destruction, or to turn giant wheels; but it has no power to forgive sins, or to teach a little child to pray. Power is estimated aright only in the light of purpose. If God's purpose is a garden of redeemed humanity, the true almightiness is an almightiness of holy love. Such an almightiness this story reveals: "He had yet one, a beloved son: he sent him last unto them, saying, They will reverence my son." It was love's final and uttermost entreaty.

The true picture is not that of Jesus receiving in His body the darts which an angry God has hurled at us, but rather that of God in Jesus receiving all the "slings and arrows of outrageous fortune" which rebellious humankind has hurled at Him. Behind the cross of Golgotha there is a cosmic Cross flinging its vast shadows. Behind the spear piercing the side of Jesus there is a spear piercing a "Lamb slain from the foundation of the world." In no parable told by Jesus, not even in the story of the Prodigal, is the love of God in its persistence and its sacrifice more poignantly revealed.

Thus from a Jewish folk-song Jesus draws new and mighty harmonies—the music of human privilege and obligation, the music of His own sonship, the melting music of God's love. Now hear the climax of this symphony—on a tragic note of human failure. The vinedressers were guilty of an ascending series of horrors.[17] Elijah was driven by Israel into the wilderness; Isaiah, if tradition be true, was sawn asunder; Zechariah was stoned to death near the altar;[18] John the Baptist was beheaded. The bitterness of ancient persecution flowed with such undiminished venom through the veins of the Pharisees to whom Jesus spoke, that He charged them with all the persecu-

17 Luke's account speaks of three servants, the first of whom was beaten, the second painfully used, the third wounded and cast forth, and finally of the coming of the son who was killed. Matthew and Mark speak of several servants who were killed before the arrival of the heir. This latter account is truer to the historical facts. The Synoptic problem is interestingly raised by a comparison of the three versions. Luke alone has "God forbid. But he looked upon them and said . . ." In Matthew's version, the listeners answer the question, "What will he do unto those husbandmen?" There are other significant divergences.

18 II Chronicles 24: 21.

tions of the years, and required of them "the blood of all the prophets which was shed from the foundation of the world." [19] Soon they would kill Him. He describes that dark event as though it were already consummated.

Why did they so requite the mercy of God? Not because there was no record to teach them, for all history cried aloud, "This is the way." Not because they lacked the power to discriminate between good and ill; for they confessed, "This is the heir," and then straightway forswore their noblest conviction. Self-will was their curse. They resolved that the garden of life should be theirs—theirs for gain, theirs for fame, and not God's for worthy manhood. "Let us keep the inheritance."

It may be urged that we to-day are not guilty of such outrage. We do not stone the prophets in one generation, and in the next elect them to the calendar of saints. But are we sure? The Gettysburg Speech at the time of its delivery was overshadowed by another oration, of ninety minutes' length, given on the same occasion. Such comments as were made on the Gettysburg Speech were for the most part adverse. "A silly little speech," said one newspaper. He used "soldiers' graves as a stump for political oratory," charged another; while the *Springfield Register* (the newspaper in Lincoln's home town) bluntly declared: "When he uttered the words he knew he was falsifying history and enunciating an exploded political humbug." [20] This concerning the Gettysburg Speech! And why? Because Lincoln dared to suggest that the black man has human rights. In short, the old cry was raised, "Let us keep the inheritance." If some new Lincoln were to say to us, "Behold the appalling monotony, and the threatening uncertainty of employment under our boasted industrialism. In a planet which could yield enough and to spare, need these things be? Must life be thus bruised? Where are the human fruits?" —would we listen to him? It is dangerous for a prophet to touch the nerve of our money or our comfort. . . .

The story ends in a crashing of doom. As if the setting of the original parable supplied no colors dark enough with which

19 Luke 11: 50.
20 See the "Life of Abraham Lincoln," by William E. Barton, Vol. II, p. 220. The epilogue of George Bernard Shaw's "Saint Joan" is an incisive comment on our habit of garlanding dead prophets' tombs and slaying the living messenger.

to paint the coming condemnation, Jesus deliberately changes the figure. He harks back to the imagery of one of the Hallel psalms: "Did ye never read in the scriptures, The stone which the builders rejected the same was made the head of the corner?" [21] That living stone, even when passive, would be a stone of stumbling to any man neglecting it. Again, ceasing to be passive, hurtling through life in the momentum of holy wrath, it would crush its victims and scatter them as chaff.[22] The garden would be taken away from its recreant tenants and given into worthier hands: "The kingdom of God shall be taken away from you, and shall be given unto a nation bringing forth the fruits thereof." [23] God cannot falsify His own nature and deliver His garden to become a wilderness of weeds. Or (if we like the language better) selfishness is its own curse, just as love is its own reward—and opportunity has its end. "These things have I spoken unto you . . . that ye should go and bear fruit and that your fruit should abide." [24]

21 Psalm 118: 22. It is instructive to notice that the rabbis regarded this psalm as Messianic.
22 Dr. W. C. Allen ("I.C.C.," Matthew, pp. 232, 233) believes that this verse (Matthew 21: 44, Luke 20: 18) is an early gloss. The verse is evidently constructed from Daniel 2: 45 and Isaiah 8: 14.
23 Note that Matthew in this verse (v. 43) uses "the kingdom of God" instead of his familiar "kingdom of heaven." For the significance of this change, see Peake's Commentary, p. 718. The word "nation" in this verse need not necessarily exclude a worthy core or remnant of the Jewish nation.
24 John 15: 11, 16.

CHAPTER XXI

MAKING LIGHT OF THE KINGDOM

THE PARABLE OF THE GREAT FEAST

"And when one of them that sat at meat with him heard these things, he said unto him, Blessed is he that shall eat bread in the kingdom of God. But he said unto him, A certain man made a great supper; and he bade many: and he sent forth his servant at supper time to say to them that were bidden, Come; for all things are now ready. And they all with one consent began to make excuse. The first said unto him, I have bought a field, and I must needs go out and see it; I pray thee have me excused. And another said, I have bought five yoke of oxen, and I go to prove them, I pray thee have me excused. And another said, I have married a wife, and therefore I cannot come. And the servant came, and told his lord these things. Then the master of the house being angry said to his servant, Go out quickly into the streets and lanes of the city, and bring in hither the poor and maimed and blind and lame. And the servant said, Lord, what thou didst command is done, and yet there is room. And the lord said unto the servant, Go out into the highways and hedges, and constrain them to come in, that my house may be filled. For I say unto you, that none of those men that were bidden shall taste of my supper."

(*Luke* 14: 15-24)

(*Parallel passage: Matthew* 22: 1-10, being The Parable of the Banquet of the King's Son.)

THE PARABLE OF THE WEDDING ROBE

"But when the king came in to behold the guests, he saw there a man who had not on a wedding-garment: and he saith unto him, Friend, how camest thou in hither not having a wedding-garment? And he was speechless. Then the king said to the servants, Bind him hand and foot, and cast him out into the outer darkness; there shall be the weeping and the gnashing of teeth. For many are called, but few chosen."

(*Matthew* 22: 11-14)

MAKING LIGHT OF THE KINGDOM

The Parable of the Great Feast
The Parable of the Wedding Banquet of the King's Son
The Parable of the Wedding Robe

St. Luke quotes the story of the Great Feast as part of the table-talk of Jesus at the house of Simon the Pharisee. Jesus had commended humility [1] (not a noticeable virtue in the Pharisees at the board!) and then had aggravated heresy in the suggestion that rich men desiring to entertain at dinner should not limit their invitations to the socially acceptable but should beckon "the poor, the maimed, the lame, the blind." With subtle humor He added reasons: "Lest haply they (thy rich neighbors) also bid thee again"—(perish the thought! When would any Pharisee issue invitations with such a possibility in mind?). But with the outcasts of society (He said) the generosity would be safe from rebuttal, "because they have not wherewith to recompense thee."

We may imagine that the atmosphere was strained, the topic of conversation distinctly awkward. But some ready-tongued Pharisee saved the day. "Blessed is he that shall eat bread in the kingdom of God!" [2] he exclaimed. The ejaculation sounded well—even though it meant nothing. It had a pious ring and the added merit of commanding every one's assent and thus of restoring the broken rapport of the gathering. *"But* He

---

1 Luke 14: 7-14. See Chapter VIII of this book.
2 Dr. Adeney ("Century Bible," Luke, p. 225), with his characteristically irenic spirit, maintains that this remark was "wistful" and sincere. Arnot, *op. cit.,* p. 387, agrees that he "was well-meaning, but dim and confused in his conceptions." Other commentators (Dods, Plummer, Bruce, Hubbard) describe him as "self-complacent," "a pious old humbug," etc. There is no need to accuse him of deliberate and premeditated insincerity, but the setting presupposes the likelihood of Pharisaic "piosity," and the emphatic "But" which introduces the reply of Jesus indicates that Jesus took issue with the mood of the remark and insisted on swinging the conversation back to reality. On the question of the proper context of this parable, see footnote to p. 224.

said to him . . ." and the bubble of unreality was instantly pricked as Jesus related another story resistless in its simple truth.

St. Matthew assigns a similar parable (or is it a recension of the same original story?) [3] to a different context. He locates it with a group of parables spoken against the scribes and Pharisees during the Passion week. It is stronger in language and sterner in tone than the Lucan rendering, but in theme it is the same.

The Parable of the Great Feast
The Parable of the Wedding Banquet

A rich man planned a feast and invited his friends. In Matthew's account the "certain man" becomes a "king," and the "feast" is the wedding-banquet of the king's son—an occasion which, to the oriental delight in festive celebrations, would be the acme of delight. Thus Jesus again makes joy a dominant note in the kingdom-music.[4] John the Baptist would not have used a feast as a symbol of the overture of God to men. The kingdom to him was an advancing doom. But "the Son of man came eating and drinking." [5] Has the world ever fully understood the gladsome mood of Jesus? His "good news" may expose the disciple to the fires of shame confessed to God and man, but the fires are refining fires and their suffering is

---

[3] A difficult question to which there is no final answer. Matthew's version shows clear traces of admixture. Vv. 6, 7 reflect the fall of Jerusalem and were probably written after that event. They break the literary and even the didactic integrity of the parable. Harnack suggested that these two verses are akin to certain verses in Luke's parable of the Pounds (see footnote, p. 242 of this book), and Grieve (Peake's Commentary, in loc.) and Allen ("I.C.C.," in loc.) agree that they should be omitted. But, even when this omission has been made, Matthew's parable and Luke's show little similarity in wording, even though they are undoubtedly similar in theme. If they are "doublets from one original," the redactors must have worked with different versions of the original.

Thus interpreters are divided into two main classes: (a) those who hold that the two parables are similar in theme but different in original occasion—"the same theme handled twice by the same artist, but in different languages and for diverse purposes" (Bruce, op. cit., p. 461) and (b) those who hold that the two parables were originally one story. Among (a) may be listed Trench, Arnot, Monro Gibson (in Expositor's Bible), Maclaren, Dods, and Plummer ("I.C.C."). Among (b) Calvin himself finds a place and with him Grieve, Allen ("I.C.C."), Box ("Century Bible") and Murray. Most of those who identify the two parables believe that Luke's version is nearer to the original in substance and Matthew's in context. There is no sufficient data for a final opinion. This book suspects that the two stories were originally identical but is content to base its exposition on the undoubted fact that they are similar in teaching. For the relationship of the Story of the Wedding Robe to the other story, see footnote on p. 228 of this book.

[4] See Chapters I, V and XXII of this book.

[5] Matthew 11: 19.

not worthy to be compared with the deep joy bestowed. The
kingdom-music sweeps through all the cadences of unrestrained
delight. Forgiveness is to the uttermost (such is its song!)
and righteousness is not an outer yoke grievous to be borne
but an inner fountain welling up unto eternal life! Thus God
makes His dwelling-place with man. In His presence even
tribulation is but the tossing of the upper ocean: there is peace
in the depths. "Your joy no man taketh from you," [6] Jesus
said. He knew a joy not *in spite of* pain (as though He had
said, "Come what may, I am resolved to maintain My cheerfulness"), not *in respite of* pain (as though He had said,
"There are saving hours when the load is lifted"), not *in denial of* pain (as though He had said, "The day is really not
dark"), but *because of* pain! Cleaving to God's will in scorn
of bitter consequence and suffering vicariously in the grief of
the world was a joy so intense that pain itself became sacramental—the lower octave of a rapturous song!

Thus He spoke to men about the "great feast" of the kingdom. We have not understood Him. The picture seems folly.
We make Him inarticulate because our ears are dull. . . .

To this feast, when the table was spread, the host summoned
his invited neighbors. He sent a *vocator*, according to the
custom of the time, to remind them of the proffered joy:
"Come for all things are now ready." But with one accord
they made excuse.[7] One man had just bought a field and must
needs inspect his purchase. Presumably he had not bought a
field unseen, but property beckons men to glut their eyes upon
it and cry in the mazed voice of acquisition, "This is *mine,*
this is *mine.*" Another man had bought five yoke of oxen.
He was that very moment on his way [8] to test them. Presumably he had not been fooled into giving good money for
lame and blind oxen, but he was caught in the inexorable
claims of "big business" (were there not *five* teams?) and
business cannot always pause for the genial neighborliness of

6 John 16: 22.
7 These excuses seem to me to be a pivotal factor in the story. George Murray,
op. cit., p. 175 ff., and Bruce with lighter emphasis, *op. cit.,* p. 461 ff., have maintained that the story is one of "grace" rather than of "judgment." Its main purpose is (they think) to teach the welcome of the kingdom to the multitude. Such
undoubtedly is one of its truths, but the story seems to be aimed primarily at those
who made light of the invitation to the feast.
8 Such is the force of the Greek version.

life, much less for the sanctities. This man was obsessed with
business (like a child absorbed in toy trains) but like all obsessed people he was sure that he alone was "practical" and
sane. The third man explained that he had recently married
and could not come.[9] The other two "prayed" with some
courtesy "to be excused," but this man had no niceties: "I
cannot come." Wedded loyalty should be a gladsome and a
sacred plot,

> "Fringed pool,
> Ferned grot—
>   The veriest school
> Of peace, . . ." [10]

but it can be enclosed with such high walls as to shut out the
sight not only of other gardens more barren (and pleading
their need) but even of the sky. A home becomes a prison if
it has no windows opening on other homes and on the distant
hills and the stars.

Thus the neighbors excused themselves, though to refuse an
invitation so generous at the moment of summons was a dis-
courtesy hardly less than an affront.[11]

Matthew's account avows of the "king" that he sent "other
servants." [12] He indulged the first brashness only to meet repeated insult. Matthew also lays bare the root of the refusal:
"They made light of it, and went their ways." There is a
"making light" which is commendable. To laugh in the face
of one's own fear—that is the crown of heroism. When we
read of Charles II making apology on his deathbed for being
"a most unconscionable time dying" we feel that the historians
who would make him an unmitigated knave have done him less
than justice. But that "making light" of the kingdom which
comes of "making heavy" of farms and merchandise is the
mark of a despised birthright. "Nothing succeeds like suc-

<hr />

9 Deuteronomy 24: 5 gives the ancient law respecting men just married. They
were exempt from military service and from tribal responsibility for one year.
10 Thomas Edward Brown, "My Garden."
11 Canon Tristram observes (see "Century Bible," Luke, p. 225) that among the
Arabs such a declination of a second invitation was regarded as equivalent to a
declaration of war.
12 Bruce, op. cit., p. 469, following Trench, op. cit., p. 227, declares that the
second group of servants were the apostles, Jesus being the original "summoner."
This seems unwarranted allegorizing, and postulates a prescience on the part of
Jesus of a kind which He was slow to claim and which is not characteristic of His
teaching.

cess"? It would be truer (in any high sense of the word "succeed") to say that nothing fails like so-called success. It belittles and ignores the spiritual meaning of life. . . .

"Spiritual" is a term admittedly hard to define. The words with which we attempt to imprison it are nets spread to catch the wind. It "breaks through language and escapes." "The wind bloweth where it will, and thou . . . knowest not whence it cometh and whither it goeth: so is every one that is born of the Spirit." [13] But as a working definition this might serve: *The spiritual endures.* Houses do not endure; they crumble. Flesh does not endure; it rots. Stars do not endure; their fires grow cold. Sin does not endure; it commits suicide. But conscience endures (though it be but as a torture) speaking of an eternal Right. Human love endures speaking of an eternal Love. Ideals endure, the waving banners of our human pilgrimage, speaking of an eternal Perfection. Jesus endures, haunting and redeeming the longings of the race. The spiritual endures! Once the spiritual became flesh and blood, and summoned men to the feast with living voice; but "they made light of it and went their ways, one to his farm and another to his merchandise."

Yet the banquet-hall was filled. For this surprising story tells how the host sent his servant through the streets of the city to invite cripples, ne'er-do-wells, and drabs to the feast. When this motley crowd could not tax his boundless hospitality, he dispatched servants into the whole countryside with urgent pleas to the vagrants on the highroads and the waifs of the hedges: "Constrain [14] them to come in." Familiarity and a dull imagination have hidden from us the amazing sight of that strange banquet. Lame beggars jostled each other with their crutches! Blind beggars groped ravenously towards the bounteous tables! Dumb beggars mumbled horribly their inarticulate delight!

> "Walking lepers followed, rank on rank,
> Lurching bravoes from the ditches dank, . . .
> Vermin-eaten saints with mouldy breath,
> Unwashed legions from the ways of death—" [15]

13 John 3: 8.
14 That this word "constrain" (which means "strongly to persuade") should have been made the occasion for religious persecution is illustration of the extreme to which Biblical literalism and "religious" bigotry will go.
15 Vachel Lindsay, "General William Booth Enters Heaven." ("Collected Poems," The Macmillan Co.)

These became for the nonce members of high society! These
entered the enduring kingdom!

> "Drabs and vixens in a flash made whole!
> Gone was the weasel-head, the snout, the jowl;
> Sages and sibyls now, and athletes clean,
> Rulers of empires, and of forests green!" [15a]

Thus was the feast supplied with guests.

The thrust of the teaching is inescapable. If the religious
leaders of Israel proved recreant, a pristine response might be
found among that dim crowd whom the Pharisees deemed
"accursed." If the chosen people despised their election, the
hated "stranger" living in far fields beyond the city might
prove worthier of God's favor. If the "classes" forget the
name of Love, a Savior may be born among the "masses" as
of old. If occidental "efficiency" makes light of the spiritual,
the "effete" Orient may speak "words of eternal life." It
pleases God to open uncorrupted springs among His "poor and
maimed and blind and lame." There is an end of privilege to
those who construe privilege as vested interest rather than as
faith and love: "For I say unto you that none of these men
that were bidden shall taste of my supper." [16]

The Parable of the Wedding Robe

Matthew has hung as a pendant to the story of the Great
Feast another parable [17]—that of the Wedding Robe. Commentators have soberly suggested that the chequered assembly
at the Great Feast were "not instantly hurried into the great

---

[15a] Vachel Lindsay, "General William Booth Enters Heaven." ("Collected
Poems," The Macmillan Co.)

[16] These words (Luke 14: 24) seem to have been spoken by Jesus as a comment
on the story. The emphatic "you" suggests as much; though Bruce, *op. cit.*, p.
338, maintains that they are the words of the "host" and therefore part of the
parable.

[17] It is quite generally agreed that this was originally a separate story. Trench
argues against Strauss for the integrity of Matthew 22: 1-14, but even Arnot admits
that the Wedding Robe is another (though connected) parable, and Bruce (*op. cit.*,
p. 464) also, though he thinks the two stories were originally joined by Jesus.
Murray (*in loc.*), Box "Century Bible" (*in loc.*), and Grieve (Peake's Commentary) are clear-cut in the opinion that this is another and distinct story. The
casual reader can supply the introductory sentence which is all that is necessary to
give it wholeness. Hubbard takes Matthew's account for granted. His work seems
to me to be marred in this and some other instances by his failure to allow for
the great contribution which critical and exegetical study can make to the interpretation of the parables.

hall" [18] but that opportunity was given them to array themselves in appropriate garments provided by the host. It is better to assume that the story is distinct and separate, though like the story of the Great Feast in its background.

The wedding-banquet of a king's son was prepared with lavish hospitality. The guests were assembled in resplendent robes. They were awaiting the state entrance of the king. He came; the festive hour was crowned! But no sooner had he come than his eye fell on a man dressed as if he had come direct from his "farm" or his "merchandise"—a man without sense of propriety, neglectful of even elementary courtesies, guilty of unpardonable rudeness. His companions appear not to have noticed his uncouthness. It went unchallenged until the king came! But the king was kind. He was ready to believe there was good reason for the seeming temerity: "Friend, how camest thou in hither not having a wedding-garment?" [19] But no good reason could be offered: "And he was speechless."

He might have said in ancient words: "Woe is me! for I am undone; . . . for mine eyes have seen the king." [20] Only in the white light of a royal presence could he know the blackness of his offence. Other men had made light of the kingdom —and stayed away; but he had made light of it—and come! They were at least avowed in their despising of the spiritual— they went to their possessions. But this man accepted the overtures of grace, attended the feast—with a spirit still alien and worldly! In appearance he was serving God; in reality he was serving mammon. He was going through all the motions of religion, while secretly his discipleship was with the world.

The grace of God (Jesus would have us know) is joy unspeakable—but not for the jaunty, the heedless, or the hypocritical. It demands its preparation. A man must strip away the robe of sophistication, and come clothed in childlike trust: "Except ye turn, and become as little children ye cannot enter.

18 Thus Storr. See Arnot, *op. cit.*, p. 272.
19 There is some argument for the suggestion that at such a banquet the king himself would provide the necessary wedding-robes. Trench (*op. cit.*, pp. 235, 236) and Dods (*op. cit.*, p. 195) offer interesting illustrations to confirm the suggestion. It adds force to the parable because it scores in deeper colors the negligence of the erring guest, but it is not essential to the story.
20 Isaiah 6: 5.

. . ." [21] He must lay aside the garment of his sin, and come clothed in penitence: "Except ye repent, ye shall all likewise perish." [22] He must doff his old earthy loyalties for the new robe of righteousness.[23]

Insincerity is robbed of all disguise when the king enters. It has no haven save the poor haven of "outer darkness." It is cast forth from the brightness and warmth of the banquet-hall where Jesus plights His troth with those who would sincerely love Him. It is flung into the narrow street which has no light!

[21] Matthew 18: 3.
[22] Luke 13: 3.
[23] This parable has not escaped the allegorizers. Olshausen suggests that the man without a wedding-garment is Judas (!) and there has been a Protestant-Catholic controversy about the significance of the "robe," Catholic expositors maintaining that it symbolizes "charity" and Protestants that it stands for "faith." There is no need thus to circumscribe the meaning.

CHAPTER XXII

PREPAREDNESS AND EMERGENCY

THE PARABLE OF THE WISE AND FOOLISH BRIDESMAIDS

"Then shall the kingdom of heaven be likened unto ten virgins, who took their lamps, and went forth to meet the bridegroom. And five of them were foolish, and five were wise. For the foolish, when they took their lamps, took no oil with them: but the wise took oil in their vessels with their lamps. Now while the bridegroom tarried, they all slumbered and slept. But at midnight there is a cry, Behold, the bridegroom! Come ye forth to meet him. Then all those virgins arose, and trimmed their lamps. And the foolish said unto the wise, Give us of your oil; for our lamps are going out. But the wise answered, saying, Peradventure there will not be enough for us and you: go ye rather to them that sell, and buy for yourselves. And while they went away to buy, the bridegroom came; and they that were ready went in with him to the marriage feast: and the door was shut. Afterward came also the other virgins, saying, Lord, Lord, open to us. But he answered and said, Verily I say unto you, I know you not. Watch therefore, for ye know not the day nor the hour."

(*Matthew* 25: 1-13)

CHAPTER XXII

PREPAREDNESS AND EMERGENCY

The Parable of the Wise and Foolish Bridesmaids

There were mystery plays based upon this parable as early as the fourteenth century—a testimony to its poetry and dramatic power. The spirit of Jesus was constrained by the tenderness and tragedy of human lot. He wove life into stories which by their perfection of truth and form are unforgettable. We must interpret this parable for what it is—a poignant, pleading tale—and forget that commentators have tormented themselves and it in their attempt to allegorize and theologize its details.[1]

Ten bridesmaids go forth to meet the bridegroom and escort him to the home of his bride.[2] Oriental weddings are celebrated by night. Each bridesmaid carries a staff at whose top is a brazen bowl filled with rag and oil for a lamp.[3] The torches sway to their steps and send fantastic waves of light across the dark. The bridegroom's journey being delayed they fix their lamps in the ground and wait. Soon they nod drowsily; then they fall asleep.[4] But at midnight the sudden cry is raised: "The bridegroom cometh!" Eagerly their lamps are tended. But five bridesmaids cannot arouse their flickering lights. They have forgotten their extra oil. "Give us of your oil for our lamps are going out." "Nay," the others answer, "for there may not be enough for you and for us. Go to

1 Calvin (quoted by Dods, *op. cit.*, p. 205) protests against these extravagances of exegetical method.
2 We need not vex ourselves unduly with the question whether they actually journeyed forth along the highway to meet the bridegroom, or went to the home of the bride there to await him, or went to meet both bride and groom to escort them to their new home. Bruce, *op. cit.*, p. 501, argues at length for the second of these suggested courses and Plummer ("I.C.C." on Luke) agrees with him. Bruce seems to suggest (unconvincingly, as it appears to us) that decision on this point will affect the meaning of the story. Why should it?
3 So Lightfoot.
4 Dods, *op. cit.*, p. 205, has an interesting account of a similar wedding in modern India.

233

them that sell and buy for yourselves." Later, their negligence
redeemed, they reach the marriage chamber. Now their lamps
burn bright. Now they can hear the banquet-joy, the happy
laughter, the strain of harps. But the door is shut!

Another poet, humble follower of his Poet-Lord, has caught
the poignancy and pleading of that closed door:

> "Late, late, so late! and dark the night and chill!
> Late, late, so late! but we can enter still.
> Too late, too late! ye cannot enter now.
>
> "No light had we: for this we do repent;
> And learning this, the bridegroom will relent.
> Too late, too late! ye cannot enter now.
>
> "No light: so late! and dark and chill the night!
> O let us in that we may find the light!
> Too late, too late! ye cannot enter now.
>
> "Have we not heard the bridegroom is so sweet?
> O let us in, tho' late, to kiss his feet!
> No, no, too late! ye cannot enter now." [5]

The story says again that the kingdom of heaven is like a
wedding.[6] Jesus came to woo and win mankind to his own joy.
Luke assigns the parable to the last week of His earthly life.
That striking context is not disproved by the gladsomeness of
the figure, for we have assurance elsewhere that the valedictory
of Jesus to His disciples was the gift of gladness: "These
things have I spoken unto you that My joy may be in you, and
that your joy may be made full." [7] This joy came of self-
renouncement in God's name for man's sake!

In one aspect, Christian discipleship is the carrying of a
cross; in another, the cross itself is the purchase price of peace.
The world's way also has a double semblance; but, whereas the
Christian's cross is set in joy, the world's pleasure is set in bitterness. There is no crown of thorns so cruel as a bartered
sanctity. There is no torture like the gratuitous torture of a
conscience turning to rend itself. There is no spear driven into
the side with sharper thrust than the spear of shame. But a
life laid down is joy beyond telling. Greater *joy* hath no man

---

[5] The little novice's song in Tennyson's "Guinevere" from "The Idylls of the
King."
[6] See Chapter I, p. 4.
[7] John 15: 11.

than this "that a man lay down his life for his friend." The kingdom of God is like a wedding feast.

The coming of the kingdom is to be greeted expectantly in lives alert for its advent. "Watch, therefore, for ye know not the day nor the hour." Mark the nature of true watchfulness. To be alert does not mean to be feverishly anxious. All the bridesmaids slept, and neither the wise nor the foolish were indicted for their drowsiness. They could not always be at strained attention. The wise fisher-wife, her husband out at sea, will not haunt the end of the dock and peer night and day across the waves for sign of a returning sail. She will rather care for her cottage and mother her children, glancing now and then through the open door for promise of the homing ships. It is not in human nature to be sleeplessly vigilant, with the torturing question ever on our lips: "Is He coming?" Watchfulness is rather a set of the soul; it is the undertone of expectancy sounding through the daily faithfulness.

Is the "coming" prophesied in this story Jesus' "Second Coming"? We do not know. Interpretation must not be confined within the limits of that doctrine. It may hold within those limits; it *certainly* holds beyond them. The early Church awaited the speedy return of Jesus in the flesh. Undeniably the Epistles are filled with predictions of His imminent rearrival: but the hopes were not fulfilled. That fact is a determinative fact in any present-day discussion of the Second Coming.[8] Such a discussion has here no main relevance, except as it affects interpretation. The story cannot solely or chiefly refer to Jesus' return in flesh, for these three good reasons: First, there is a widespread opinion among competent

---

8 It is axiomatic in scientific method that facts shall test theory. The fact that Jesus has not returned leaves us with this dilemma: Jesus was mistaken as to the date, fact or manner of His return, or the disciples were mistaken in their interpretation of His prophecies. Most of us would expurge the first term of that dilemma. The second term remains, and beckons us to a new examination of the teaching of Jesus. That teaching has apparently conflicting elements. There are statements which, *prima facie,* support the hope of His physical return. There are other statements which, *prima facie,* discourage any such hope and bid us look rather for a spiritual coming. Thus these questions become pivotal: How much has the teaching of Jesus been colored in the hands of redactors by the eschatological hopes then current in Palestine? Which doctrine of the "Second Coming" (spiritual, physical, post-millennial, pre-millennial) is most in accord with His total message and with His conception of human need and human welfare? These questions are beyond the scope of this book, but we venture here the modest opinion that a considered reply to them will not encourage any dogmatic assertion of Christ's physical return.

and reverent scholars that some of Jesus' teaching has been colored by the apocalyptic hopes of the redactors and their times.[9] Second, the plea for spiritual preparedness was dominant in His message. It sounds, for instance, in such germparables as The Householder and The Thief, The Porter, The Watchful Servants, and The Closed Door.[10] Not all of these occur in an apocalyptic context, and we may assume that the plea, "Watch, therefore," was an integral element in His entreaty. Third, if the reference of this story is solely or chiefly to the "Second Coming" it has mocked discipleship for upwards of two thousand years, enjoining alertness for an event which has not happened. We must seek a vital, rather than a doctrinal, application of its truth.

Then do the words, "The bridegroom cometh" herald the approach of death? Say some commentators in effect: "We are to live righteous lives that we may be ready to die righteous deaths." Verily; but the changeful, challenging days of mortal life must surely have their own purpose. They cannot be merely the slave of a dying moment or of a heaven out of sight. Dying will probably be a simpler test than we anticipate. Not often does the dark angel's arrival strike terror. The nerves are then mercifully slack, and the spirit eager for release. Is there not a story of a man who, blindfolded, was suspended a few inches from the ground and told that he was hanging over a chasm? The rope was cut and he expected to fall through sickening space to a violent doom. Instead he lit gently on his feet. The test of actual dying may not be more severe! A true preparedness for death will honor this clear fact: the only way to heaven is through heaven. In May, 1780, the famous Dark Day descended on New England. Men felt the Judgment Hour had come, and senators rushed from the Senate Chamber to the meeting-house to pray, or would have rushed had not one Senator Davenport prevailed over them:

"Bring in the lights: let us be found
Doing our duty's common round.

9 Thus Montefiore (see Peake's Commentary, p. 271) thinks this parable "grew up to explain the delay in the coming of the kingdom," and George Murray (op. cit., p. 211) refers to the strong emotions of that age about the Second Coming and believes this parable was "turned to account for the benefit of the apostolic age."
10 Matthew 24: 43; Luke 12: 39, 13: 25; Mark 13: 34.

Bring in the candles: keep to the task:
What more can Judgment Angels ask?"[11]

This parable is laid upon life—life now and life hereafter.

What, then, *is* "the coming"? It is the *divine unexpectedness* of our experience. The kingdom comes like a thief in the night!—like a flood!—like a returning master!—like a bridegroom long-delayed but suddenly appearing![12] Jesus rang the changes on similes—now terrible, now glad—to teach us the ordained alternation of experience by which periods of routine are punctuated by crises of calamity or joy. The command, "Watch, therefore," rings out bidding us prepare during eventenored months for the midnight of sudden testing. Temptation comes "like a thief in the night," giving us no chance to choose a favored battle-ground, compelling us to stand to the challenge and fight. Sorrow sweeps down like a flood and blots out all the familiar landmarks. Joy and opportunity surprise us as with a cry: "The Bridegroom cometh." The danger of the commonplace is that by force of habit it may unfit us for heaven's hour of surprise. Thus the emergency of gladness or grief finds us off-guard and unprepared. The latch is not lifted for God's "angel unawares." Watch, therefore!

We are to be ready not only for the worst but for the best;[13] not only for the thief in the night but for the wedding-joy. To prepare for the worst is proverbial wisdom; to prepare for the best, an unwonted grace. In August, 1914, many countries were equipped for war, but in November, 1918, no country was equipped for peace—as a botched and impossible Peace Treaty abundantly proved. Nations and men provide for advents of terror but are all unready for the advent of God. There is a character in a recent novel[14] who was strong in limb, gifted in intellect, with quickness of sympathy and a subtle charm. But a wanton imagination had made him a philanderer. Fleshliness was so much his thought that when he met the woman whom he loved and who gave him in return love's utter confidence, he

---

[11] Edwin Markham's "A Judgment Hour" ("Gates of Paradise," Doubleday, Page and Company), which describes the incident.
[12] Matthew 24: 38, 43.
[13] See a chapter entitled "Preparation for the Best," in Dr. John Kelman's "Ephemera Æternitatis."
[14] A. Hamilton Gibbs' "Soundings."

could not keep even her image free from smirch. An unclean
fancy left him no escape; it was "like a recurring decimal." He
was prepared for "a thief in the night" but not for the rapture
of a perfect love. How intense the pain when some fetter of
our own forging mocks the bugles of heaven! Resources for
"a rainy day,"—but what of resources for the splendid day of
Divine beckoning?

Sometimes life moves on monotonous wheels. Habit claims
us:

> "To-morrow and to-morrow and to-morrow,
> Creeps in this petty pace from day to day." [15]

We work, eat, write letters, sleep. There is no hint of the
coming of a king; no movement in the gray hills to betray the
spiritual hosts. Then suddenly the cry is raised, "The Bridegroom cometh!" and the humdrum hours flash with eternal
meanings! Then we are challenged like Galahad to the quest
of the Grail. Then we know if the slow weeks of the "common
task" have been so lived as to gird us for the high emprize.
"No man," it has been said, "has more religion than he can
command in an emergency." That we should sleep at nightfall
after the eager day needs no forgiveness, but that in the eager
day we should have bought no oil to replenish our lamps against
the midnight cry is negligence which only heaven's forgiveness
can mend.

If a man lack that inner resource, others cannot transfer to
him their grace. The reply of the wise virgins to the extremity
of their comrades sounds unpardonably selfish and smug: "Peradventure there will not be enough for us and you. Go ye
rather to them that sell and buy for yourselves." But interpreted in terms of experience the answer is not smug; it is
inevitable. Imagine a flippant woman caught in the flood of
unexpected sorrow. Her response to sanctifying motives has
been only in fitful moods. Imagine a friend who has tended
inborn faith until it burns with steady flame. Can the flippant
soul borrow her friend's faith in that dark emergency? Is
character instantly transferable? Nay, she must go where
strength is sold at the price of sacrificial pain! When tempta-

---

[15] Shakespeare, "Macbeth."

tion comes as a thief in the night there can be no loaning of moral fiber. When the trumpets of God sound reveille, a shabby conscience cannot be exchanged forthwith for a memory void of offence.

Any manner of prior life seems sufficient for the routine day, but not for the hour of the midnight cry. A merely perfunctory faith will not then avail. Then the reinforcements gathered in the quiet season turn the tide of battle. Then the oil bought at a price and husbanded against the joyous emergency trims the spirit's lamp to greet the king. To read the Bible until its immemorial insights become the texture of thought, to pray until prayer is the day's rule and rapture, to look on Jesus until His image is stamped on the retina of our eyes and we see all things through Him—this does not proclaim itself essential in life's *ordinary,* but in life's *unexpected* it is the difference between wisdom's light and folly's groping.

"And the door was shut." There is an end to opportunity. The "tide in the affairs of men" does not remain at flood; it ebbs. There may be another tide, but *that* tide has gone. We plead with time to pause in her flight, but time is adamant to every plea and hurries on. Our vigilance or negligence are scored deep in a living book. Neither our piety nor wit "can cancel half a line," nor all our tears "wash out a word of it." It is not in human skill to reach back and recapture the hour when the king came—and found us sleeping. We fain would live that hour again, but we cannot. "The door is shut." Therefore do men and women become like Bewick Finzer:

> "Familiar as an old mistake,
> And futile as regret." [16]

But in the mercy of God the king comes often on His way. To-morrow He may come radiant as dawn. At midnight He may come in sudden gladness. But only our vigil and our care in these dull, present hours, will enable us to greet Him with hearts aflame!

"Watch, therefore, for ye know not the day nor the hour."

[16] Edwin Arlington Robinson, "Bewick Finzer" ("Collected Poems," The Macmillan Co.).

CHAPTER XXIII

OPPORTUNITY, FIDELITY, AND REWARD

THE PARABLE OF THE TALENTS

"For it is as when a man, going into another country, called his own servants, and delivered unto them his goods. And unto one he gave five talents, to another two, to another one; to each according to his several ability; and he went on his journey. Straightway he that received the five talents went and traded with them, and made other five talents. In like manner he also that received the two gained other two. But he that received the one went away and digged in the earth, and hid his lord's money. Now after a long time the lord of those servants cometh, and maketh a reckoning with them. And he that received the five talents came and brought other five talents, saying, Lord, thou deliveredst unto me five talents: lo, I have gained other five talents. His lord said unto him, Well done, good and faithful servant: thou hast been faithful over a few things, I will set thee over many things; enter thou into the joy of thy lord. And he also that received the two talents came and said, Lord, thou deliveredst unto me two talents: lo, I have gained other two talents. His lord said unto him, Well done, good and faithful servant: thou hast been faithful over a few things, I will set thee over many things; enter thou into the joy of thy lord. And he also that had received the one talent came and said, Lord, I knew thee that thou art a hard man, reaping where thou didst not sow, and gathering where thou didst not scatter; and I was afraid and went away and hid thy talent in the earth: lo, thou hast thine own. But his lord answered and said unto him, Thou wicked and slothful servant, thou knewest that I reap where I sowed not, and gather where I did not scatter; thou oughtest therefore to have put my money to the bankers, and at my coming I should have received back mine own with interest. Take ye away therefore the talent from him, and give it unto him that hath ten talents. For unto every one that hath shall be given, and he shall have abundance: but from him that hath not, even that which he hath shall be taken away. And cast ye out the unprofitable servant into the outer darkness: there shall be the weeping and the gnashing of teeth."

(Matthew 25 : 14-30)

(Parallel passage: Luke 19 : 11-27, being The Parable of the Pounds)

OPPORTUNITY, FIDELITY, AND REWARD

The Parable of the Talents
The Parable of the Pounds

Jesus daringly predicted that though heaven and earth might dissolve His words would still live.[1] He believed His message to be indestructible; and history as it unfolds is His vindication. His dicta originally spoken to few, "not many wise, not many mighty," [2] are now pondered by the race. Each succeeding generation brings its tribute to His authority.

This parable of the Talents is evidence. Great men have felt in it the spear-thrust of truth. Carlyle thundered it as a Sinai-law of life: ". . . this is the question of questions: What talent is born in you? How do you employ that?" [3] Dr. Johnson prayed—a gentle modesty indwelling his strength— "that when I shall render up at the last day an account of the talent committed to me, I may receive pardon for the sake of Jesus Christ." [3] Macaulay remarked that this parable has given to the language a new adjective, "talented." [3] Robert Louis Stevenson, addressing the Samoan chiefs at the opening of that road which from love for him they had built to the door of his Samoan house, reminded them that the true champion of Samoa was not the man of barbarous customs who made a constant havoc of war but "the man who makes good roads . . . and is a profitable servant before the Lord, using and improving that great talent that has been given him in trust." Instances of the convincing power of the parable might be multiplied. With good warrant did Jesus once prophesy: "My words shall not pass away."

In His day provincial rulers would journey to Rome at the

1 Matthew 24: 35.
2 I Corinthians 1: 26.
3 Quoted in the "Expositor's Dictionary of Texts," pp. 948 ff.

accession of a new emperor to crave continuance of their rights.[4] Sometimes the subjects of the subordinate monarch would make counter plea that their ruler be deposed. Herod, the Great, thus sought the favor first of Mark Antony and later of Augustus. Archelaus, Herod's son, prayed Augustus to grant him the paternal sovereignty and he was made Ethnarch of Judea despite the protest of a deputation of fifty representative Jews. The servants left in charge of affairs during the absence of their king on such an errand needed all the faithfulness they could muster.[5] Such faithfulness found ample test in the hostility of the populace. If their lord should be deposed loyalty to him might cost them their lives. But if they were unfaithful and their lord returned—well, rulers of that time were none too lenient with unfaithful servants! Augustus gave the kingdom back to Herod because Herod was intelligent and energetic, but he yet said of him that he would feel safer as Herod's pig than as his son! It is on such a "page of contemporary history" that Luke has grafted the story of the talents. Or perhaps we should say that Jesus Himself originally gave that setting to His parable.[6]

4 See the chapter on "The Talents" in the book, "The Pilgrim," by Dr. T. R. Glover. This is easily the most stimulating study of the parable which I have read, and I hasten to acknowledge gratefully my indebtedness.

5 The Lucan version in its context (Luke 19: 11) hints an eschatological reference in the words "into a far country." Dr. Plummer ("I.C.C.," ad loc.), seems to accept this as the main reference of the parable. Dr. Bruce agrees with earlier commentators that the story has a "veiled reference to the present and future fortunes of Jesus." But Loisy has denied any reference to the Parousia, and George Murray (op. cit., p. 2-5) believes the eschatological coloring was supplied by the redactors. This is not the place to discuss doctrines of the "Second Coming." Suffice it to say that Jesus did not return in the flesh as the early Church hoped and believed. Despite the failure of that hope the parable has its abiding truth, which this chapter seeks to propound.

6 The vexed problem of the relationship between the parables of the Talents and of the Pounds cannot be evaded. Many scholars believe that both sprang originally from a common source, and most of these hold also that Matthew's form is closer to the original. Dr. W. C. Allen ("I.C.C.," on Matthew), Dr. A. J. Grieve (Peake's Commentary), Dr. Marcus Dods (op. cit.), and George Murray (op cit.) identify the two parables at least as to their source, and Dr. W. F. Adeney (Century Commentary on Luke) and Dr. A. Plummer ("I.C.C." on Luke) admit strong likenesses. The teaching of the two stories is similar, though prima facie not identical. The general viewpoint of these commentators harks back to Unger, Bleek, Ewald, Meyer, and Strauss. The latter (in "Leben Jesu") pointed out that the Lucan version is inconsistent in its reference first to "servants" and then to "citizens," and in recording actions appropriate now to a "king" and now to a "trader" or "householder." He further suggested that Luke 19: 12, 14, 15, 27, with slight alterations and arranged in sequence, form the nucleus of another parable of "The Rebellious Citizens."

The views of opposing commentators may be summarized as follows: G. H. Hubbard (op. cit.) following Alexander Maclaren ("Expositions") and J. Monro Gibson ("Expositor's Bible") maintains that the two parables present not an identical or a different teaching but "diverse aspects of a kindred truth." In effect these

There were three servants. One received five talents with which to trade. He followed the market closely, knew the prospects of the crops, anticipated the arrival of caravans from Damascus, marked the movement of troops, and on the information thus gleaned he invested his five talents so shrewdly that he realized a profit of one hundred percent on his transactions. Another servant was entrusted with two talents. He was, we may suppose, a blunt and honest man with none of the finesse and mental quickness of his more talented neighbor. He plodded away at his task. If his money was invested in farming, he drove his oxen hard. If a vineyard was his to tend, he pruned or tied or gathered diligently, working from sunrise to sundown. So by the sheer fidelity of toil he made his two talents yield four. The third servant was of a different stripe. He hid his one talent in the ground. The action, as judged by the standards of that day, was not lazy. To hide money in the ground was the traditional way of saving money. Commentators have dwelt at length on the "apology" [7] which this third servant offered for his negligence. But his explanation was not an apology. He had read his lord's character with discernment. He knew him to be of the Herod type, "reaping where thou didst not sow." He was afraid, and—"lo, thou

scholars accept the parables at their face value. Their interest is almost exclusively that of expositors rather than exegetes. G. H. Hubbard says explicitly (*op. cit.*, p. xviii), "we must cast aside . . . the microscopical analysis of grammar and lexicon, the massive enginery of scientific and historical study"—a demand with which we can sympathize so long as we remember that sound interpretation rests ultimately on exegetical fact. Trench and Arnot earlier held the traditional view. (Trench, *op. cit.*, p. 270 ff., and Arnot, *op. cit.*, p. 521 footnote.) They contend that the two parables were spoken under different circumstances, and that Luke's seeming inconsistency is due to the fact that Jesus was addressing two groups of hearers —His own disciples corresponding to "servants" and the multitude corresponding to the hostile "citizens." A. B. Bruce (*op. cit.*), agrees and further pleads that the smallness of the entrusted sum as coming from a king—("one talent" in the Lucan account)—is understandable since Jesus was a poverty-stricken king! Such argument is not convincing. It is built on the unproved assumption that Jesus regarded Himself as filling the main rôle in the parable, and it requires our belief that Jesus in telling a story alternated almost sentence by sentence in addressing two different groups of hearers—a hazardous and unlikely feat in homiletics! We are inclined to believe that Luke (quite permissibly and even brilliantly) grafted Matthew's parable onto a "king and citizens" setting, or that Jesus originally gave the story that setting and that Matthew's version, at least so far as the substance of the teaching is concerned, is the original.

7 G. H. Hubbard, among others, makes much of the third servant's "apology" (*op. cit.*, p. 184). Marcus Dods (*op. cit.*, p. 225) stresses the man's "wrong view of God." But the man probably considered himself virtuous in safeguarding the entrusted talent, and it is likely that he was not much mistaken in his estimate of his lord's character. That character is not to be pressed in our thoughts as closely related to a conception of God. It has only an *ad hominem* significance; it is a natural feature of the historical setting of the story.

hast thine own." He made no excuse, for he did not consider himself guilty of any neglect. He had kept his talent with most scrupulous care. Too scrupulous care! That was his crime! He would have proved himself more of a man had he planned and risked and lost!

Such was the story. It drew daringly on Judean politics for its background. If to-day it stabs wide awake our unexamined lives we may well believe that when first it was told it struck home with a point of truth exceeding sharp.

"Unto one he gave five talents, to another two, to another one; to each according to his several ability"—a clear and sober statement of the inequality of human endowment. The findings of the intelligence testers are not new: they were succinctly expressed long ago in this story. We are thrust onto this swinging ball called "earth" without our knowledge or consent. We are not consulted as to our equipment of body and spirit. On reaching years of maturity we begin to realize (with some heartburning, perhaps) that certain gifts and graces are ours within measure and that certain others have been denied us. Shakespeare has five talents in literature, Michelangelo five in art, Savonarola five in preaching, and Edison five in invention. These are the bright particular stars in the human firmament. The vast majority have two talents. They are the useful hosts of mediocrity. Then there are those who seem limited and handicapped—the one-talent people. "All men are created equal" in the sense that God intends that every man shall have an equal chance to prove himself, but the historic statement when taken at its face value is not defensible. For we are unequal in native gift—one man a Shakespeare and another always a hack-writer. We are unequal in opportunity—one man moving in that "fierce light which beats upon a throne," and another living out his lonely days as a trapper in far woods. We are unequal in advantages—one born in poverty and another given an education as a matter of course. All men are created unequal. . . .

But, lest God should be made a "respecter of persons," certain counter-balancing truths have been scored into the parable.[8]

8 I cannot feel that the teaching of the two parables (the Pounds and the Talents) is very different. In the parable of the Pounds each man receives one talent.

The five-talent man is evidently expected to produce five talents more if he would satisfy his lord. The two-talent man has discharged his duty if he can produce but two. The one-talent man does not fail of his lord's "well-done" if he can show one other talent for his labor. The one-talent man is not required to realize five talents on his scanty capital, neither can the five-talent man escape the curse if he presents one, or two, or four. A talent is evidently like any other coin: it has two sides. On one side is written "endowment," and on the other "responsibility." To the measure in which a man is gifted, to that same measure is he accountable. Fatuously we covet our neighbor's one hundred talents—as if we could have his talents without his obligation! With every load of jewels there is delivered a load of care. Our gifts are not detachable from their commensurate burden.

Again, it must be noted, lest Heaven be charged with a gross favoritism, that the story represents every man as having some talent. No one is left empty-handed. Every one is in some regard "talented," and a talent is no small sum! Who knows but that in the economy of God a man with one talent may not quicken the earth more than his neighbor with five? Such a truth is more than hinted, but meanwhile this is explicitly stated:

> "To each man is given a day and his work for the day;
> And once, and no more, he is given to travel this way." [9]

There is a deeper fact to quiet forever any charge that heaven is unfair. The reward of the five-talent man was his lord's commendation: "Well done, good and faithful servant: thou hast been faithful over a few things, I will make thee ruler over many. Enter thou into the joy of thy lord." The kingdom of ten cities or five was not the essence of the recompense; the true satisfaction was the master's approval. The

---

Endowment is equal. But granted that the talent in question may be "the word of the Kingdom," as various commentators have suggested, the fact of human inequality cannot be overruled. I am inclined to think that the man who made five talents from his one was not less faithful than his neighbor who made ten talents (as G. H. Hubbard has suggested) but simply less gifted. He received only five cities for his sovereignty as compared with his neighbor's ten because he was less capable, not because he was less dear in the esteem of his lord. (See Luke 19: 16-19.)

9 Edwin Markham, "The Day and the Work" ("Gates of Paradise," The Macmillan Co.).

cities were small amends compared with the king's acknowledgment of kingliness in them! It is significant therefore that the commendation of the two-talent man is in identical language with that spoken to his more gifted brother.[10] Not a word is changed, not an accent of the voice is different. Thus we are introduced to a new system of measurements. There is a widow-woman in the portrait gallery of the Gospels who cast a farthing into the Temple treasury and of whom Jesus said that she gave "more than they all together." [11] By what reckoning did Jesus arrive at such an estimate? Judging her gift by monetary value she gave less than anybody. Judging it by love-value she gave more than the total gifts of all the other worshippers. So in computing success Jesus has His own revolutionary standards. The question is not, "How many talents have you earned?" but rather, "How many, compared with the number entrusted to you?" The demand is not, "What treasure?" but rather, "What faithfulness?" Surely the judgments of heaven are without a flaw! There is no penalty for poverty of endowment, and no acclaim for excess of gifts. Instead there is a scrutiny which searches life not for fame but for enterprise of fidelity, not for genius but for goodness: "Well done, *good* and *faithful* servant."

An impressive incident is told about the death of David Livingstone.[12] When he was buried in Westminster Abbey many eyes were fixed on the Negro who stood at the head of the casket. This was the Zanzibar servant who had brought his master's body from the African swamp, asking as his only recompense that he might attend it on its sad journey across the sea. In the matter of talents two men could hardly have lived in greater contrast. Livingstone was passing rich in talents—in medical skill, in charm of nature, in vision of a

10 It must be acknowledged that in the Lucan account the words of commendation in the respective cases do differ. This is the justification (and about the only justification, so far as we can see) for the view advanced by G. H. Hubbard and others that the second servant is represented in the Lucan story as being a man of only passable integrity and industry. It is too flimsy a basis (especially in the light of our recent knowledge of the synoptic problem) on which to build a distinction when so many signs point to similarity.

11 Mark 12: 41, Luke 21: 2. The meaning of "more than they all" seems by the original to be as here represented.

12 As related in Luke S. Walmsley's, "Fighters and Martyrs for the Freedom of Faith," pp. 508, 509.

friendly world washed white. The negro slave had but one talent—his mind dense, his color a curse (since white people will hate a man for the color of his skin), his only gift to look up and follow like a faithful dog. But the two—how unequal in grace!—were one in courage of faithfulness, and therefore brothers in the approval of their common Lord.

But the main rôle of the parable is acted by the man with one talent. The story is told for his sake. His portrait is drawn with elaborate care. His two fellow servants are sketched in strong lines as becomes their clear-cut character, but this man is painted with sharp detail; and as the story advances, he occupies the bold center of the picture. He is not a bad man. He is not drunken nor wasteful. He is not lacking in a sense of responsibility, or he would have squandered his talent. He is something of a judge of character, for he has described an oriental ruler to the life—though his expectation that such a ruler would tolerate his safety-tactics shows that his judgment of character was not carried to a conclusion. What was wrong with him? He lacked imagination (the kind of imagination that a man may cultivate) and he failed in courage!

He did not see that his talent was needed. The ruler is depicted by Jesus as caught in overpowering wrath because one talent was not used. Fourteen talents in all had already been proffered, but his anger knew no bounds because one talent had been allowed to rust. The anger of the story is not hollow melodrama; it proclaims the verity that every talent is needed in the divine economy. In the Sancta Sophia men of many talents were needed to conceive and fashion the vast span of arch and dome. Only fingers rarely skilled and minds rarely beautiful could have set the porphyry and mosaic. But hands equally faithful (though less subtle) were required to dig the foundation and lay the masonry. When every man's gift is *necessary* to the rearing of the temple, and the artist depends upon the delver, the distinction between "great" talents and "small" becomes somewhat stupid and illusory. The failure of the one-talent man leaves as bad a blotch as if the ten-talent man had been treacherous. It is the one vote which will ulti-

mately redeem politics, and the single voice which will ultimately make a world's insistence on peace. . . .

> "There is waiting a work where only your hands can avail;
> And so if you falter, a chord in the music will fail." [13]

This man lacked imagination to see that every talent is precious. He depreciated his gift. One of the many surprises
of the message of Jesus is His constant insistence on the worth
of what others call "obscure" service. He spoke of the crucial
importance of a "cup of cold water" [14] given in love. He declared that not "one jot" of the law should pass away.[15] He
insisted that to feed the hungry or to visit the prisoner, was
a deed of cosmic and eternal significance.[16] He gave warning
repeatedly that it is not in human wisdom to know when a deed
is "great" or "small"; that hidden fragrances of the spirit may
give a "small" action the smell of a sweet savor to the end of
time. The widow-woman casting her mite into the treasury
and the unknown Simeon carrying a Cross have glorified the
race immeasurably more than the pride of Herod and the wisdom of Gamaliel. But the one-talent man, succumbing to the
one-talent temptation, was blind to everything except life's
surface.

His worst fault, however, was that he lacked the courage of
adventure. This is the crux of the story. He shrank from
risk, though he could have known that nothing is gained without risk. The universe is amazingly fruitful for talents. In a
few years five can become ten. It multiplies talents as a harvest multiplies seed. On the other hand, the universe is amazingly *fatal* for talents. If neglected, if unrisked, they vanish.
Hiding them in the ground will not save them; they rot!
Power used with discretion and adventure is increased power;
power left stagnant is seized with paralysis. "Take the talent
from him and give it to him that hath ten." It is not a threat,
but rather a sober statement of living law. Feed a capacity
for music or for sympathy, and it will grow with an ever-

---

13 "The Day and the Work," Edwin Markham. ("Gates of Paradise," The Macmillan Company.)
14 Matthew 10: 42.
15 Matthew 5: 18.
16 Matthew 25: 40.

deeper root. Neglect it, and it will disappear like a wraith. "Take away the talent from him!" Employ the instinct for prayer (for it is an instinct and is proved only as it is obeyed) and soon the skies will be filled with spiritual hosts. Bury the instinct and soon those selfsame skies will be as inert as slag!

> "Heaven does with us as we with torches do;
> Not light them for ourselves: for if our virtues
> Did not go forth of us, 'twere all alike
> As if we had them not. Spirits are not finely touched
> But to fine issues." [17]

The end of the man who will not risk his virtues is torment of conscience, "weeping and gnashing of teeth," and the poor comfort of "outer darkness." [18]

This truth we think we recognize. On the page of Scripture we acknowledge it. But in the affairs of the world it is still despised. We wage a war that engulfs half the planet in woe, and we emerge with, "Let's get back to normalcy" (hateful word!) as our only wisdom! "Let us keep our world as it is," we cry. Let us bury our talent and hold it intact. Nothing must be risked. Let us get back to the customary exploitation of the earth's natural resources, the customary inflow of profit on investment, the customary mechanical, killing drabness of the industrial order! "Normalcy" built Pompeii with its fashionable chariots, its prize fights in the guise of gladiatorial combats, its benefactors and its proletariat, its contrasts of poverty and wealth. [19] "Normalcy" built the commercial prosperity of Ostia. It had its trades-union officials (or those who corresponded to them) who doubtless met with employers' representatives to discuss wages and the expulsion of blacklegs. It had its election announcements, its caucuses, its keynote speeches that did not ring true, its party pledges as stable as air. "Normalcy" was there, and "normalcy" was deservedly destroyed beneath volcanic lava. "Normalcy" is the buried talent.

17 Shakespeare, "Measure for Measure."
18 Bruce, *op. cit.*, p. 207, quotes Calvin to the effect that feasts were commonly held at night, and that "outer darkness" means a thrusting forth into a night black by contrast with the bright joy of the bridal chamber. It is exquisite imagery neither to be whittled down into a trivial doom, nor to be burdened with a doctrine of eternal damnation.
19 See an interesting chapter on "The Ages of Faith and the Ages of Reason," in R. J. Campbell's "The War and the Soul."

And we have thought that Jesus was commending merely an industrious and routine virtue! As if He who risked the sublime venture of a Cross could ever bless a staid stagnation! Still we shrink from "dangerous experiments" in industry. Still we content ourselves with an army-and-navy diplomacy. Still we are true to our "traditional policy." Still we bury our talent in the fond hope that it will last, and shrink from the risk in which alone it can live.

But we may be educated, perchance, by violence. Successive "weepings and gnashings of teeth" may finally convince us of the crime and folly—and cowardice—of a buried talent. Then we shall turn to His strong courage Whose words shall not pass. His counsel will still be law when heaven and earth have dissolved like a mist.

CHAPTER XXIV

THE JUDGMENT OF THE KINGDOM

THE PARABLE OF THE LAST JUDGMENT

"But when the Son of man shall come in his glory, and all the angels with him, then shall he sit on the throne of his glory: and before him shall be gathered all the nations: and he shall separate them one from another, as the shepherd separateth the sheep from the goats; and he shall set the sheep on his right hand, but the goats on the left. Then shall the King say unto them on his right hand, Come, ye blessed of my Father, inherit the kingdom prepared for you from the foundation of the world: for I was hungry, and ye gave me to eat; I was thirsty, and ye gave me drink; I was a stranger, and ye took me in; naked, and ye clothed me; I was sick, and ye visited me; I was in prison, and ye came unto me. Then shall the righteous answer him, saying, Lord, when saw we thee hungry, and fed thee? or athirst, and gave thee drink? And when saw we thee a stranger, and took thee in? or naked, and clothed thee? And when saw we thee sick, or in prison, and came unto thee? And the King shall answer and say unto them, Verily I say unto you, Inasmuch as ye did it unto one of these my brethren, even these least, ye did it unto me. Then shall he say also unto them on the left hand, Depart from me, ye cursed, into the eternal fire which is prepared for the devil and his angels: for I was hungry, and ye did not give me to eat; I was thirsty, and ye gave me no drink; I was a stranger, and ye took me not in; naked, and ye clothed me not; sick, and in prison, and ye visited me not. Then shall they also answer, saying, Lord, when saw we thee hungry, or athirst, or a stranger, or naked, or sick, or in prison, and did not minister unto thee? Then shall he answer them, saying, Verily I say unto you, Inasmuch as ye did it not unto one of these least, ye did it not unto me. And these shall go away into eternal punishment: but the righteous into eternal life."

(Matthew 25: 31-46)

CHAPTER XXIV

THE JUDGMENT OF THE KINGDOM

The Parable of the Last Judgment

There is the story [1] of a boy who heard of a hillside from whose rocks, seen from a distance, a massive shield had been carved—as though some giant had left it lying there amid sloping meadows. The shield, he was told, was a place of vision and resolve; and he went to seek it. But no sooner had he crossed the valley than, looking back, he saw the shield clearly patterned on his own hillside. One of its quarters was the garden where he had daily played. So we trek towards purple mountains trusting to find there the "words of eternal life." Meanwhile the "eternal words" are in these simple stories told by Jesus in which we have lived since we were born.

But familiarity robs us of the sense of wonder—a gift we can ill afford to lose. If a tree shot instantly into full foliage we would cry, "Miracle!"; yet the growth of leaves in ten days is not less mysterious than would be their growth in ten seconds. We are *accustomed* to slow growth—and custom breeds contempt. The words of Jesus are not less marvellous when embodied in an ancient writing than they would be blown through golden trumpets from the skies. But in a familiar Book they have become ordinary, and the task and despair of the interpreter is to speak with some new accent, some uncorrupted insight which will recover the lost radiance.

Is this parable an actual utterance of Jesus? We are told that He was sitting with His disciples on the Mount of Olives looking down upon Jerusalem. [2] He should have been looking into an abyss, for in a few hours He would die the death of the Cross. But He saw no picture of the shameful end. Instead there unfolded before Him as He gazed the pageant of

1 G. K. Chesterton suggests it in the Introduction to his "The Everlasting Man."
2 Matthew 24: 3.

253

a great assize—a pageant of such mingled pathos and majesty, of such convicting truth, that it is stencilled on the world's thought in lines of amazement and awe.

"When the Son of man [3] shall come in His glory"—

(*His* "glory"?—this Artisan of Nazareth on Whom Rome would soon place a callous heel to crush Him as a man crushes a moth?)—

"and all the angels with Him, then shall He sit on the throne of His glory"—

(*"all* the angels?"—*"His* throne?"—when all He asked on earth was a manger for His birth and a gallows for His death?)—

"and before Him shall be gathered all nations"—

(earth's teeming millions, of every kindred, tribe and tongue, coming to the throne of the lowly Galilean!)—

"and he shall separate them from one another, as the shepherd separateth the sheep from the goats."

Did this weary Man on the Mount of Olives Himself speak these wild words? It is probable. There was in Him a Divine arrogance encompassed by unparalleled humility. It finds expression too frequent and too clear to be denied. To attribute these sayings to the twelve disciples or to the adoration of the early Church raises as many questions as it solves. Why should the followers of Jesus exalt Him to a judgment-throne above "all nations"? Granted that the language may be that of apocalyptic hope, why should the hope find embodiment in a Carpenter from Galilee? "Let us not therefore judge one another," they said; "for we shall all stand before the judg-

[3] The meaning of the title "Son of man" as used by Jesus is a subject of much debate. Most scholars believe that it argues a Messianic consciousness in Jesus. Certainly its original meaning in the Book of Enoch is Messianic. But to Jesus the title "Messiah" had a far higher and purer significance than it received in average Jewish hope. The acknowledgement of the early disciples that He was the Christ sprang from their instinctive recognition of the Divine in Him. Their feeling for Him was akin to nothing else in human feeling except their feeling for God. How the ideal of Jesus transmuted the old ideal of a "Messiah" is nowhere better illustrated than in the teaching of this parable.

ment-seat of Christ." [4] Why did they say it? For that matter, why do we to-day instinctively bring modern practice to
the touchstone of His life? We would not dream of singling
out some mechanic in the Catskills as the criterion of current
motives and manners. Then why choose an Artizan who lived
in Galilee years ago and make Him our Judge? It is very surprising! It is almost as if His prophecy were coming true. . . .

The parabolic element [5] in this utterance must not be ignored.
Images forthshadowing the judgment are not to be converted
into historical events.[6] Nevertheless the images are not to be
minimized; for they do reveal the tests by which, according to
Jesus, judgment here and hereafter must proceed.

"As a shepherd separateth the sheep from the goats" [7]—as
easily, with the same unerring certainty! Syrian sheep were
usually white and Syrian goats were usually black. When the
combined flock came home at night the division could be made
without mistake, even in the gathering dusk. With the same
sureness will the separation proceed among mankind. There
is no need for pleading and counter-pleading, and the marshal-
ling of evidence is superfluous; for some souls are seen to be
white and others black.

But such a judgment (our immediate protest runs!) is a
parody of facts. Human character is not usually found in
black or white. It moves constantly to and fro through innumerable shades of grey. Joaquin Miller reflects about the
poet Byron, whom some would hurry to pronounce black:

> "In men whom men condemn as ill
> I find so much of goodness still,
> In men whom men pronounce divine
> I find so much of sin and blot,
> I do not dare to draw a line
> Between the two, where God has not." [8]

---

4 Romans 14: 10, 13.
5 It would seem that there is no more than a nucleus of parable in what we have
called "The Parable of the Last Judgment," but that nucleus is sufficiently definite
to justify the title. The sudden transition from "Son of man" (v. 31) to "King"
(v. 34) may hint the composite character of the scriptural passage. The original
parable may have been pastoral in setting and adapted later to the "Parousia" expectation. (See "Peake's Commentary," in loc.) Dr. Allen ("I.C.C.," in loc.),
suggests that this whole "splendid" section reads like a Christian homily.
6 See p. 139 of this book.
7 See Ezekiel 34: 17.
8 From Joaquin Miller's "Byron." ("Complete Poetical Works," Harr Wagner
Publishing Company.)

The reflection approves itself. Yet Jesus dared to "draw a line." Often He asserted sharp contrasts in human disposition. Some build on the rock (He said) and others on the sand; some are "wheat" and others "tares"; some walk the narrow way to life and others the broad way to destruction. But is there among us any virtue of a whiteness unblemished and any perfidy of a blackness unrelieved? Dare we draw the line? No. Nevertheless Jesus made it clear that character in its main intention, in the "set" of its motives, is either right or wrong. Some faces are turned to the light, be that light distant or near, and others towards darkness. Some souls serve God; in spite of many lapses they still own the sway of conscience and compassion. Other souls serve idols; in spite of many compunctions they still own the sway of idols—the money-idol with a brazen face, the pleasure-idol wearing a fool's mask, the fashion-idol decked in silks, the fleshliness-idol with lecherous eyes. Some are on the right hand of the throne, and others on the left; the warp of their spirits allocates them.[9]

Then what is the dividing line that Jesus drew? Clearly it cuts across our customary lines of distinction. We are not judged *now* by nationality: the color of a man's skin does not *now* make him black or white.[10] We are not judged *now* by social prestige or by any accident of earthly rank. Lines of creed seem *now* to be transversed, and the ritual observance of religion is not mentioned. But unaffected kindness is mentioned!—

> "Inasmuch as ye did it unto one of these my brethren, even these least, ye did it unto me."

9 Plato, "De Republica," pp. x, 13, records the experience of a man whose soul temporarily left his body, and who, being thus permitted to see the judgment, came to a place where there were two chasms in the earth and two openings in the heavens opposite to them. Between these sat the judges of the dead. They commanded the just to go to the right hand up through the heavens, and the unjust downwards to penalty. Both the just and the unjust bore on them marks of the deeds done in the flesh. Similarly Virgil locates the Elysian Fields on the right of the palace of Dis and the gloom of Tartarus on the left. ("Æneid" *vi*.)

10 The phrase "all nations" in this parable has been the occasion of much controversy. It frequently means the Gentile world as distinguished from the Jewish, and consequently the suggestion has often been advanced that Jesus is here stating a test of character applicable to the Gentiles who have not heard of Him, and not applicable to Jews from whom a higher enlightenment is expected by reason of their higher privilege. The suggestion is not necessary. Wise judgment will, of course, ignore no fact of opportunity or hindrance; but basically there cannot be a different criterion in one part of the world than holds in another. It is better to take the phrase "all nations" in its comprehensive meaning. How the criterion established by Jesus relates itself to the revelation of truth in His person this chapter attempts to show.

This test of kindness was not new in His teaching: "For whosoever shall give you a cup of cold water to drink, because ye are Christ's, verily I say unto you, he shall in no wise lose his reward." [11]   Again He said, "Whosoever shall receive one of such little children in my name, receiveth me." [12]   But in this parable all qualifying phrases are omitted.   The test is plainly stated: Whoever keeps the wellspring of kindness uncongealed is worthy of eternal life.   The inference is that this essential kindness is acceptable in the judgment even though it may lack the badge of Christian discipleship.   The idiom of this kindness is made equally plain: it feeds the poor, is hospitable to the stranger, clothes the naked, visits the sick, and shares the loneliness of the prisoner.[13]   These are not grandiose achievements.   The world allows them no meed of fame; they have no accompaniment of trumpets.   Yet it would appear that Jesus regards them as

> ". . . that best portion of a good man's life:
> His little, nameless, unremembered acts
> Of kindness and love." [14]

They inherit a kingdom prepared from the foundation of the world!

Yet this criterion is not to be interpreted in any shallow confidence.   Jesus does not mean that an occasional philanthropy is a sufficient substitute for a living faith.   If a man writes a check for charity, salving his uncomfortable scruples as he makes the gift, is he therefore justified whatever may be the pattern of his daily conduct?   Are moral distinctions to be confounded, and duty turned into a sentimentalism?   Such questions need no answer.   Character is judged not by its fitful bad or its fitful good, but in its wholeness and by its controlling motives.   Of what avail is a man's charitable sop flung to a beggar, if that man's prevailing purposes are so unsound that his influence spreads like an evil breath?   The inwardness of

11 Mark 9: 41.   Notice the qualifying phrase—"because ye are Christ's."   The corresponding chapter in Matthew (10: 42) has a different qualifying phrase: "And whosoever shall give to drink unto one of these little ones a cup of cold water only, *in the name of a disciple*, verily I say unto you he shall in nowise lose his reward."
12 Mark 9: 37.
13 The best rabbinical thought placed such kindnesses above mere almsgiving Compare Isaiah 58: 7.
14 William Wordsworth, "Lines Composed Above Tintern Abbey, 1798."

kindness has yet to be learned. Why do we forget that Jesus said: "The good man *out of the treasure of his heart* bringeth forth that which is good"? [15] And why do we ignore that other penetrating word: "Give for alms those things which are *within*"? [16] Jesus Who insisted that murder and adultery are ultimately sins of the hidden desire, and not alone of the deed, will never approve a merely superficial kindness. Kindness is unworthy the name unless it is written in the "inward parts." The true almsgiving is the unconscious outgoing of a noble spirit.

Such almsgiving will not live independently of Jesus. In Him the nature of veritable kindness became flesh. He did not create the hope of immortality, but He brought that dim and buried hope to life and light. He did not originate the "golden rule," but He gave it final meaning so that it becomes almost unintelligible without Him. Similarly, He did not bestow the motive of love, but He quickened it and made it regnant. There is in truth a "light which lighteth every man coming into the world," [17] but those who have seen Him through eyes unveiled by dogma or prejudice confess gladly that only in His light can they see light. It has come to pass that we cannot throw a penny to a beggar without having in the back of our minds His words: "Inasmuch as ye have done it unto one of the least of these . . ." Behind every cross that we may choose to carry another Cross is lifted in healing and incentive. At the last He made no demand that kindness should be done "in His name." The modes and forms of recognition were not dear to Him; He thought not of Himself. Therefore the true almsgivings for which He pleaded have become the "Gesta Christi"!

There are surprising verdicts in that judgment; strange reversals of human estimates; dramatic overturnings and revealings. Even the just are taken aback: "Lord, when saw we *thee* hungry, and fed thee?" Their simple kindness had not been done with any sidelong glance for man's approval. It had been unconscious of merit in itself. Moreover it had been unaware

15 Luke 6: 45.
16 Luke 11: 41.
17 John 1: 9.

of the complete self-identification of Jesus with human need:
"When saw we *thee* hungry?" The *com-passion* of Jesus is
the earth's spiritual miracle. If some Zaccheus had made havoc
of his life, Jesus felt Himself involved in Zaccheus' fall: "I
must abide at thy house." [18] If a woman was held in the grip
of an inner demon Jesus felt Himself socially accountable:
"*Ought* not this woman to have been loosed?" [19] If a church
had lost its prophetic vision, Jesus felt Himself chargeable with
that church's failure: "I *must* preach the good tidings of the
kingdom of God." [20] The unutterable need of the family of
God laid imperious claim on Him: "The Son of man must suffer . . . and be killed." [21] So He asked with a love which
leaves us defenceless, "Behooved it not the Christ to have suffered these things?" [22] So He asks to-day as He sees the
shame of our streets, our obsession with things, and the dim
benighted multitudes in other lands: "*Ought* not the Son of
man to suffer? With the world as it is, there is nothing to do
but accept a Cross. I could have done no other, could I?"
O Brother-Heart of Jesus!—the honor of the human name was
His to keep! The stain of the human sin was His to cleanse!
The fullness of human joy was His to seek, and to purchase
by His blood! That "feeling with" our human need proclaims
Him Messiah, and ordains that kindness done to any comrade
of earth is kindness done to Him. "Inasmuch as ye have
done it . . ." [23]

The unjust were even more surprised by their condemnation
than the righteous by their recompense of joy. Wherein had
they been unjust? No positive crime had been laid to their
account. They were not charged with theft, adultery or murder. They had kept respectability inviolate. "When saw we
thee hungry?" Had they known that royalty was incognito in
the beggar at their gate and in the stranger whom they left
shelterless they would have been instant with every courtesy.

18 Luke 19: 5.
19 Luke 13: 16.
20 Luke 4: 43.
21 Luke 9: 22.
22 Luke 24: 26.
23 Many medieval legends set forth the identity of Jesus with the "least" by telling how the saints saw Him in those whom they pitied and helped. Such stories
are told of St. Augustine, St. Martin and others. John Greenleaf Whittier's "Saint
Gregory's Guest" is one of many poems composed on this theme.

Of course they would! It was to their gain to cultivate the good graces of royalty! Therein was their crime: they had done all things with an inward-turning eye, and had despised the brotherhood. Jesus plainly tells us that when they quenched the fountain of love they quenched the fountain of life. There was no need that sentence should be pronounced against them. They passed dark judgment on themselves. By their self-chosen path and by their own momentum they went into "eternal punishment." [24]

Genuine love is life, and lovelessness is its own curse; such is God's decree from the foundation of the world! With this dictum of Jesus we may fittingly close this simple study of His parables. For this is the central impact of His teaching, the one insistent plea of His life and death, the truth with which His continuing presence haunts our earth. When a young scribe inquired the secret of life, He asked him: "What is the commandment?" The scribe thereupon recited with assurance, "Thou shalt love the Lord thy God with all thy heart . . . and thy neighbor as thyself." The answer of the Master was final: "This do and thou shalt live." [25] To love God (God seen in the mystery and faithfulness of earth and sky, God heard in the deep undertone of the music of humanity, God become incarnate in Jesus) and to love our neighbor (especially the neighbor who by reason of life's merited or unmerited tragedy most needs our love)—is to live! There is no other life here or hereafter. To slay that motive of love is to die. A man who has extinguished the glow of genuine sympathy may still have appearance of life, but the reality of life has gone. He has a "name to live and is dead." [26] He is going horridly through the antics and gestures of life; like those men and women of Dante's imagining whose bodies walked and talked in the City of Florence but whose souls were already incarcerated in the

[24] "Punishment" is not the strongest Greek term that could have been employed. It usually signifies "chastisement," and has some of the meaning of "remedial penalty." Similarly "endless" is indefinite. It sometimes means "everlasting," but not always; and the core of its meaning is probably qualitative rather than quantitative. But when this careful discrimination of meaning has been made, it must be remembered that Jesus used not the Greek but the more uncertain Aramaic. While we cannot affirm that the words forbid all hope for the future, neither can we affirm that they encourage hope. The prospect is dark and the end is not yet! Such is the conclusion which the phrase allows.

[25] An abbreviation of Luke 10: 25-28.

[26] Revelation 3: 1.

nether world. We may call such a man "a live wire," but he is only a jerky bundle of galvanised flesh. Having lost his love for God and man, he has lost life. "This my son was dead." [27] No funeral procession had wound its sad way to an open grave—but he was dead to love! What *we* call "death" is merely an accident of the body; real death is otherwise—and far more profound.

Such was His teaching Who "spake as never man spake." [28] We are here for a few years on a little swinging ball which we call—for the sake of courtesy and to bolster up our courage —an "earth." We are on a balloon excursion for the space of mortality. We can trample on our fellow-passengers, if we wish. We can crowd them from the best seats, despise them because their clothes are poorer than ours, and generally seek our own comfort—or we can prove ourselves friends remembering Him Who said, "I have called you friends." [29] Those who live as friends seem to breathe already the air of that land toward which we are hurrying. With deep confidence they say: "We know that we have passed out of death into life because we love. . . ." [30] When they are told that such kindness may bring them poverty, sadness, and harsh fortune, and that One Whose Name means Savior languished on a bitter Cross for His reward; when they are told that passengers who grab and scramble are counted "successful," they smile as with an inner certainty of joy unspeakable. What do they gain, these "friends" of the mortal journey? Nothing—except Life!

THE WORDS THAT I HAVE SPOKEN UNTO YOU
ARE SPIRIT AND ARE LIFE.

I CAME THAT THEY MAY HAVE LIFE, AND MAY
HAVE IT ABUNDANTLY.

27 Luke 15: 24.
28 John 7: 46.
29 John 15: 15.
30 I John 3: 14.

INDEX OF SCRIPTURE REFERENCES

OLD TESTAMENT

	PAGE
Genesis 2:9	17
" 4:24	99
" 18:22-23	109
" 32:26	174
" 37:35	140
" 39:5-6	119
Exodus 16:19-20	56
" 32:30-32	109
" 38:24	100
Leviticus 19:14	210
" 19:18	xiv, 149
" 23:27	3
Deuteronomy 6:4	217
" 6:5	149
" 14:22	89
" 21:17	129
" 24:5	226
" 24:6	127
" 32:32	213
I Samuel 9:19	95
II Samuel 12:1-6	xiii
" " 6:22	111
II Kings 14:9	xvi
II Chronicles 24:21	219
" " 25:6	100
Job 3:16-19	140
" 3:21	28
" 14:14	140
" 22:9	168
" 27:17-22	133
" 33:29	99

	PAGE
Psalms 19:9	165
" 39:6	133
" 40:3	6
" 46:10	23
" 49:6	133
" 78:2	xx
" 80:8-16	213
" 118:22	221
" 119:83	8
" 121:3	172
Proverbs 2:4	28
" 25:6-7	84
Ecclesiastes 2:18-23	133
" 9:10	140
Isaiah 1:18	208
" 1:23	168
" 5:1-7	xiv, 213
" 6:5	90, 229
" 6:9-10	xx
" 8:14	221
" 11:3-4	95
" 13:21	74
" 27:2-7	213
" 30:21	55
" 32:2	27
" 33:17	125
" 34:14	74
" 38:12	124
" 54:4-10	4
" 58:7	257
" 62:2	6
" 65:1	30
Jeremiah 2:21	213
Lamentations 3:26	17

263

		PAGE			PAGE
Ezekiel	17:22	20	Joel	2:28-32	128
"	18:31	6			
"	31:3-9	20	Amos	2:6	99
"	34:17	255			
Daniel	2:45	221	Micah	6:2	208
"	4:10	20	"	6:6-8	37, 208
Hosea	2:19	4			
"	10:1	213	Malachi	3:5	168

NEW TESTAMENT

		PAGE			PAGE
Matthew	3:10	38	Matthew	10:41	164
"	4:15	106	"	10:42	248
"	4:19	215	"	11:16	xiv
"	5:3	15	"	11:16-19	50
"	5:10-11	216	"	11:19	224
"	5:17	9	"	11:21	41
"	5:18	248	"	11:23	151
"	5:21-22	80	"	12:19	23
"	5:33-34	36	"	12:43-45	72
"	5:34-35	111	"	13	28
"	6:2	163	"	13:3-9	40
"	6:5	163, 199	"	13:10-15	xx
"	6:9	205	"	13:18-23	40, 44
"	6:10	15	"	13:24-30	60
"	6:12	99	"	13:31-32	14
"	6:14-15	98	"	13:33	14
"	6:16	4, 163	"	13:34-35	xx
"	6:24	46	"	13:36-43	60, 61
"	6:27	190	"	13:44	26
"	6:33	15	"	13:45-46	26
"	7	xxvi	"	13:47-50	26
"	7:6	xxi	"	13:51-52	2
"	7:24-27	50	"	13:54	36
"	8:10	151	"	13:58	43
"	8:15	52	"	15:24	180
"	8:22	110	"	15:27	138
"	9:2	106	"	16:4	145
"	9:6	70	"	16:6	22
"	9:10	52	"	17:19-20	110
"	9:14-15	2	"	17:20	20
"	9:16	2	"	17:21	4
"	9:17	2	"	18:1-8	166
"	10:6	180	"	18:3	230
"	10:28	130	"	18:6-7	110
"	10:34	9	"	18:11	180

		PAGE
Matthew	18:12-14	176
"	18:13	69
"	18:21-35	92
"	18:35	99
"	19:23	159
"	19:24	87
"	19:27	160
"	19:30	159
"	20:1-16	158
"	20:4	161
"	20:28	200
"	21:18-21	108
"	21:28-32	204
"	21:31	196
"	21:33	56
"	21:33-41	212
"	21:42-45	212
"	21:44	221
"	22:1-4	228
"	22:1-10	222
"	22:11-14	222
"	22:34	150
"	23:6	87
"	23:23	89, 143
"	23:27	36, 196
"	23:29	56
"	24:3	253
"	24:35	241
"	24:38	237
"	24:43	236, 237
"	25:1-13	232
"	25:14-30	240
"	25:31-46	252
"	25:32	178
"	25:33	34
"	25:40	37, 248
"	26:6	52, 94
"	26:69	106
"	26:71	138
"	26:73	106
"	27:64	75
Mark	1:14	15
"	2:18-20	2
"	2:21	2
"	2:22	2
"	2:24-28	5

		PAGE
Mark	3:14	24
"	4:2-8	40
"	4:10-12	xx
"	4:13-20	40, 44
"	4:26-29	14
"	4:30-32	14
"	4:34	xiii
"	6:6	41
"	6:34	178
"	6:56	24
"	7:2-5	5
"	7:11	35
"	8:36	215
"	9:29	4
"	9:37	257
"	9:38	74
"	9:41	257
"	9:42	110
"	9:47	68
"	9:48	140
"	10:15	16
"	10:31	159
"	10:32	110
"	11:11-14	108
"	11:23	110
"	12:1-9	212
"	12:1-12	xiv
"	12:10-11	212
"	12:28	150
"	12:40-44	168
"	12:41	246
"	12:44	130
"	13:34	236
"	14:3	94
Luke	1:1-4	xxix
"	2:52	xxviii
"	4:17-21	6
"	4:25-27	151
"	4:43	259
"	5:33-35	2
"	5:36	2
"	5:37-39	2
"	5:39	10
"	6:20-25	137
"	6:38	163
"	6:45	258

		PAGE				PAGE
Luke	6:46	55	Luke	14:28	56,	178
"	6:46-49	50	"	14:31-33		72
"	7:2	128	"	15	xxvi,	177
"	7:9	128	"	15:1-2		195
"	7:31-35	50	"	15:1-7		176
"	7:48	94	"	15:4		69
"	7:40-49	92	"	15:8-10		176
"	7:50	196	"	15:11-24		188
"	8:2	75	"	15:12		130
"	8:4-8	40	"	15:24		261
"	8:9-10	xx	"	15:25-32		188
"	8:11-15	40, 44	"	16:1-9		116
"	8:43	130	"	16:8		118
"	9:22	259	"	16:8-9		123
"	9:57-58	45	"	16:9		133
"	10:7	53	"	16:11		124
"	10:25-28	260	"	16:13		128
"	10:25-37	148	"	16:19-31		136
"	11:5	178	"	16:31		44
"	11:8-9	171	"	17:1-10		110
"	11:5-13	166	"	17:2		199
"	11:19	74	"	17:4		99
"	11:24-26	72	"	17:6		20
"	11:41	258	"	17:7-10		104
"	11:50	220	"	17:20		23
"	12:3	68	"	17:21		15
"	12:13	163	"	18:1-8	118,	166
"	12:13-21	126	"	18:6-8		175
"	12:18	58	"	18:9-14		82
"	12:33	135	"	18:12		4
"	12:34	34	"	18:22		128
"	12:37	114	"	18:24		128
"	12:39	236	"	18:30		38
"	12:48	133	"	19:5		259
"	13:3	230	"	19:10		200
"	13:1-9	104	"	19:11		242
"	13:16	259	"	19:11-27		240
"	13:18-19	14	"	19:12, 14, 15, 27		242
"	13:20-21	14	"	19:16-19		245
"	13:23-24	67	"	20:9-16		212
"	13:25	236	"	20:17		56
"	14:5	178	"	20:17-18		212
"	14:7-11	82	"	20:18		221
"	14:7-14	223	"	21:2		246
"	14:15-24	222	"	21:4		130
"	14:24	228	"	22:4		174
"	14:25-30	72	"	22:18		15
"	14:26	110	"	22:25-26		7

		PAGE
Luke	23 : 31	133
"	24 : 26	259
John	1 : 9	192, 258
"	1 : 14	217, 218
"	1 : 19-23	52
"	1 : 29	53
"	1 : 39	24
"	1 : 43-50	30
"	2 : 19-21	56
"	3 : 3	16
"	3 : 8	227
"	3 : 29	4
"	4 : 14	4
"	4 : 20-21	151
"	4 : 32	129
"	4 : 35	215
"	6 : 63	xxix
"	7 : 17	58
"	7 : 46	261
"	7 : 52	106
"	8 : 32	208
"	9 : 2	106
"	9 : 2-3	74
"	9 : 3	106
"	9 : 4	209
"	9 : 40-41	35
"	10 : 1-18	178
"	12 : 3	94
"	12 : 24	19
"	12 : 39-40	xx
"	14 : 2	123
"	14 : 9	93
"	15 : 11	5, 221, 234
"	15 : 12	xiv
"	15 : 14	58
"	15 : 15	7
"	15 : 16	221
"	16 : 12	139
"	16 : 22	225
"	16 : 33	106
"	17 : 12	180
The Acts 4		151
" "	10 : 34-35	37
" "	16 : 20	3
Romans	1 : 20	xxi
"	5 : 13	35

		PAGE
Romans	6 : 2	96
"	8 : 16	205
"	8 : 24	16
"	8 : 32	172
"	10 : 20	30
"	11 : 8	xx
"	14 : 10	255
"	14 : 13	255
I Corinthians	1 : 26	241
" "	2 : 8	74
" "	2 : 9	139
" "	4 : 5	67
" "	5 : 7	22
" "	9 : 27	169
" "	12 : 31	175
" "	13 : 2-3	195
" "	13 : 11	52
II Corinthians	5 : 1	124
" "	5 : 17	7
" "	6 : 2	209
" "	12 : 2-4	58
" "	12 : 7	174
Galatians	5 : 9	22
Ephesians	2 : 2	74
"	5 : 16	33
"	6 : 6	77
"	6 : 12	74
Philippians	2 : 4	90
"	2 : 13	18
"	3 : 7	32
"	3 : 10	33
"	3 : 12	199
I Timothy	1 : 15	97
Hebrews	4 : 7	209
"	5 : 8	xxviii
"	11	170
"	11 : 8	xviii
"	12 : 2	5
I John	3 : 14	149, 261
Revelation	3 : 1	260
"	21 : 3	124

INDEX OF SUBJECTS

Abel, 170
Ægir, 185
Abraham, xvii, 42, 108, 109, 139, 141, 170, 213
Æsop, Fables of, xix
A fortiori, Christian argument, 169, 170
Allegory, simile as an abbreviated, xvi
  and parable, xvii, xxiv
  mistaken example of, 22
  parable in form of, 213, 215
Almsgiving, true, 257, 258
Amaziah, 100
Amos, 108
Andrew, 24
Antony, Mark, 242
Anthropomorphism, and conception of God, 171
Archelaus, 242
Aretas, 79
Ark of Covenant, 100
Arnot, xxvi, xxvii, 22, 62
Arthur, King, 73
Atonement, Day of, 3
Attilas, 171
Augustus, 242
Augustine, 32
Augustinians, 61

Bauer, xxvii
Beatitudes, 85
Bede, Adam, 55
Beethoven, xiv, 45
Bethlehem, 20
Bethsaida, 41
Bible, 121
Bigness, victimized by, 21

Brother, Elder, 195 seq.
Bruce, A. B., xxvii, 22
Burns, 76
Byron, 255

Caiaphas, 36, 69
Calvinism, xxv
Canterbury Tales, xix
Carlyle, 55, 89, 121, 241
Change, law of, 3
Charity, 153, 154
Charles the Second, 226
Chaucer, xix
Childlikeness, 51
Christianity, misconceived, 200
  professed, 58, 65
Church, at Geneva, xxv
  discipline, 63
  failure in, 64, 65
  and forgiveness, 98
  uprooting tares in, 67
Chrysostom, xxiii
Civilization, boasted, 85
  contradictoriness of modern, 183
Commandment, the new, xiv
Communism, 127, 128
Compassion, judgment demands, 257 ff.
  of Jesus, 258
  the Good Samaritan, 143, 144
Complacency, an effect of self-righteousness, 198, 199
Conscience, a fact, 181
  is wealth, 132
  Jesus a living, 36, 85
  torment of, 249
Conversion, 16
Copernicus, 86, 87, 109

Courage, one-talent man's lack of, 247, 248
Cynicism, a form of persecution, 46

Damascus, 20
Dante, 84
Darnel, 63
David, 108
Demons, 74, 75
Devil, xxv, 65, 75
Discipleship, Christian, 234
    conditions of, 79 ff., 112 ff.
    cost of, 73, 78, 79
    and duty, 113, 114
    and endurance, 112, 113
    and search for the truth, 122, 123
    and persecution, 46
    vow of, 45, 46
Dives, xviii, 138 ff., 143
Dods, Dr. Marcus, xxvii
Donatists, 61
Doré, 138
Dostoievsky, xxv
Dvorák, xv

Earth, heaven and, 21, 43
Edison, 244
Education by violence, 25, 192
Elijah, 216, 219
Eliot, George, 55
Emerson, 16
Emotion in religion, 57, 58
"Endless," meaning of, 260
Endowment, inequality of human, 244
Endurance, a challenge of discipleship, 112, 113
Ethics, history of, 57
Evil, 65, 66

Fable, and parable, xvi
Fasting, 2 ff., 36
Faithfulness, 246
Finzer, Bewick, 239

Foresight, 123 ff.
Forgiveness, and love, 96 ff.
    conditions of, 98 ff.
    duty of, 110
    God's utter, 194
France, 89
Freedom, human, 69, 214, 215

Galahad, 238
Galilee, 20, 29, 99, 106
Galsworthy, John, 80
Gamaliel, 248
Garibaldi, 73
Gautier, Theophile, 42
Gawain, 47
Gehenna, 140
Genesis, early stories of, xix
Gentile, 150
Gettysburg Speech, 220
Ghandi, Mahatma, 47
Gladstone, 99
God, a fact, 179
    a spirit discovered through the form, xxii
    abode of, according to ancient cosmology, 74
    authentic tidings of, xvi
    childlike clarity of Jesus' message about, 205
    anthropomorphic conception of, 171
    forgiveness of, xxii, 100 ff.
    from man to, 170
    judgments of, according to motive, 163
    judgments of, according to measure of opportunity, 164
    like a shepherd, xxii, 181
    mystery of, xxii
    persistent and sacrificial love of, 218
    the Father, 194
    the Great Taskmaster, 111, 112
    the search of, 181
    thorough in search, 184, 185
Good and evil, 67, 68
Goodwill among nations, 24

Gospel of growth, 16, 17
  of joy, 4
  redeeming hope of, 96
  social, 27, 93
Government and humility, 85
Greece, 108, 150
Greeks, 214
Growth, an enigma, 17
  of the kingdom, 20

Hades, 140
Hardy, Thomas, xviii
Hearing, responsibility of, 41 ff.,
  55
Heaven and earth, xxi
  a tent, 124, 125
  homelike, 124
  joy of, 185, 186
  of Dives and Lazarus, 139
  of obedient and loving life, xxii
  pictures of, 139
  rewards in, 164
Hebrews, xxviii, 213, 214
Hell, 69, 140, 141
Herod, 36, 78, 242, 243, 248
Heroes and Hero-worship, 55
Holmes, Oliver Wendell, 58
Holy Grail, 31, 33, 47
Hosea, 108
Hospitality in Orient, 94, 97
Humility, not cowardice, 85
  of the Publican, 89
  root in reverence and sense of
    need, 86
  root in sense of indebtedness,
    85, 86
  true, 84, 85

Idumea, 99
Imperialisms, national, 7
Individual, value of, 183, 184
Industrialism, 7
Insincerity, 229
Interpretation of the Parables,
  xxiii ff.
Isaiah, 108, 216, 219
Israel, 108, 213, 214, 228
Italy, 73

James, William, 58
Jeremiah, 108, 216
Jerusalem, 80, 106, 110
Jesus, the Teller of stories, xvii
Jew, the chosen, xviii
  and his neighbor, 150
Job, 106
Johnson, Dr., 241
John the Baptist, 4, 38, 52, 53, 108,
  216, 224
Josephus, 105
Joy, of kingdom, 16, 29, 30
  love is fullness of, 5
  through pain, 5, 32
Judaism, superseded by Jesus, 7
Judas, 193
Judea, 99, 106, 108
Judge, the Unjust, 168
Judgment, of the Kingdom, 34, 35,
  37, 38, 254
  standards of Divine, 163 ff.,
  256 ff.
Julian, Emperor, 117

Karamzov, the Brothers, xxv
Kindness, the test of, 256, 257
King Lear, 55
Kingdom of God, a silent agency,
  22, 23
  coming of, 237
  contagion of, 23, 24
  expansion of, 19, 20
  finding and entering the, 5, 30 ff.
  good news of, 5
  invisible and inward, 23
  its mystery of growth, 16, 17
  joy of, 30, 224, 225
  like a net, 34 ff.
  like a wedding feast, 234
  orderly development of, 19
  possession of poor in Spirit, 5
  revolutionary effect of, 160 ff.
  within mankind, 257
  wondrous adaptations of the, 18
  word of the, 42
  worth of the, 27 ff., 32 ff.
  vital force of, 17, 18

Kipling, Rudyard, 132, 196
Kismet, 159
Korban, 35

Lancelot, 47
Law, of change, 12
 of kingdom, 112
 of life is change, 11
 of retaliation, 79
 Levitical, xiv
 moral, 190
 Mosaic, 3
 rabbinical, 35, 36
 service of, 4
 universal, 36
Lawlessness, 9
Lazarus, the beggar, xviii, 137 ff.
Leaders, fault not always with, 43
Leaven, 22, 24, 27
Levite, 151
Life, eternal, 149
 what is eternal, 155
 words of, 44, 62
 like a wedding, 4
 love is, 260, 261
 reaches crisis of harvest, 68
 reality must be faced, 78
Lincoln, 220
Livingstone, David, 246
Louis XV, 88, 89
Love, and forgiveness, 96
 fullness of joy is, 5
 genuine, 257
 is life, 214, 260, 261
Lovelessness, 199, 200, 260
Lost, the, 180, 183
Lowell, Russell, 37, 43
Loyalties, conflict of, 80, 81
 the paramount, 80, 81
 shallow, 45, 46
Luke, xxix
Luther, 9, 62

Macbeth, 100
Macaulay, 241

Man, a certain rich, 129 ff.
 bereft of fellow feeling, 131
 lost intellectual joy, 132
 sick of soul, 132, 133
Marley, Jacob, 142
Mary, who loved much, 94 ff.
Masefield, John, 122
Masseo, Brother, 97
Materialism, 134, 135
Mayflower, the, 19
Merchant of Venice, xv
Messiah, 254
Metaphor, xvi
Michelangelo, 244
Miller, Joaquin, 255
Millet, 42, 109
Milton, John, 164
Mount Sinai, 36
Moses, 4, 42, 108, 109, 144, 214
Mozart, 87
Murray, George, xxvii, 189
Mustard seed, 19 ff.
Myth, xv
Myths of Plato, xv

Nathanael, 24, 30
Nature, impassivity of, 106, 107
Nazareth, xxv, 30, 63
Neighborliness, a God-given instinct, 155
 is religion, 155
 Jesus' definition of, 152 ff.
 renders personal service, 153
 renders thorough service, 154
 shows sympathy, 153
Neutrality, 73 ff.
New and the old, conflict of, xv, 3 ff.
Newton, Isaac, 86
Nicodemus, 24
Noah, xxv
Nonconformity, 62

Odyssey, of Homer, xix
Old and the New, conflict of, xv, 3 ff.
Old Testament, xvi, 4, 20

Palestine, xviii, 28, 29, 105, 137, 150

Parable, a story, xvii

Parable of New Wine and Old Wineskins, 3 *ff.*, 7 *ff.*

of Spontaneous Growth, 15, 16 *ff.*

of Treasures New and Old, 3 *ff.*, 9 *ff.*

of the Barren Figtree, 104 ff.

of the Bondservant, 110 *ff.*

of the Chief Seats, 82 *ff.*

of the Children at Play, 50 *ff.*

of the Children of the Bride-chamber, 3 *ff.*

of the Cruel Vinedressers, xiv, 212

of the Dragnet, 27, 34, 44

of the Elder Brother, 189, 195 *ff.*

of the Empty House, 72 *ff.*

of the Friend at Midnight, 166 *ff.*

of the Good Samaritan, 148 *ff.*

of the Great Feast, 4, 222 *ff.*

of the Hidden Treasure, 7, 8, 26 *ff.*

of the Importunate Widow, xix, 167 *ff.*

of the Laborers and the Hours, 158 *ff.*

of the Last Judgment, 252 *ff.*

of the Leaven, xxv, 15, 22 *ff.*, 167

of the Lost Coin, 176, 182 *ff.*

of the Lost Sheep, 176 *ff.*

of the Mustard Seed, 15, 19 ff., 167

of the New Patch and the Old Garment, 3, 5 *ff.*

of the Pearl of Great Price, 8, 26 *ff.*

of the Pharisee and the Publi-can, 82 *ff.*, 87 *ff.*

of the Pounds, 240 *ff.*

of the Prodigal Son, 188, 189 *ff.*, 219

of the Rash King's Warfare, 72, 77 *ff.*

Parable of the Rejected Corner Stone, 220, 221

of the Rich Fool, 126

of the Rich Man and the Beg-gar, 136

of the Soils, xvii, xx, xxiv, 18, 41 *ff.*, 55, 213

of the Talents, 240 *ff.*

of the Tares, 17, 35, 38, 44, 60 *ff.*

of the Two Debtors, 92 *ff.*

of the Two Sons, 204 *ff.*

of the Uncompleted Tower, 72, 77 *ff.*

of the Unjust Steward, xxiv, xxv, 28, 116 *ff.*

of the Unmerciful Servant, 92, 98 *ff.*

of the Wedding Banquet of the King's Son, 223 *ff.*

of the Wedding Robe, 228 *ff.*

of the Wise and Foolish Brides-maids, 4, 232

of the Wise and Foolish Build-ers, 50, 54 *ff.*

Parable, the word, xiii

Parable, what it is, xv *ff.*

Parables, interpretation of, xxiii *ff.*

modernity of, xxix

other, xiii *ff.*

rabbinical, xiv, xv

religion not theology, xxvi

the arrangement of, xxvi *ff.*

unchanging truth of, xxix

Paradise, 84, 156

Paris, 109

Patriot, 87

Paul, 32, 58, 74, 77, 97, 117

Pearls, 29

Pearls, Cleopatra's, 29

Perea, 99

Persecution, modern, 46

Persian Gulf, 29

Personality, forces in, 57

Peter, 24, 99

Pharisaisms, modern, 90, 91

Pharisee and Publican, 87 *ff.*

Pharisees, 53, 117, 178, 180, 205 *ff.*, 223

Pharisees, scribes and, 4, 224

Philanthropy, 153, 154

Philip, 24

Pilate, 36, 69, 78, 105, 106, 117

Pool of Siloam, 106, 110

Poor in Spirit possess the kingdom, 15

Popes, xxv

Possessions, 127, 130, 133

Prayer, outpouring of human need, 173

    sincerity of, 175

    tireless beseeching in, 173, 174

Privilege of Israel, 108, 213, 214

Prophets, 6, 37, 43, 44, 53, 144

Publican, the Pharisee and, 83 *ff.*

Religion, and neutrality, 74 *ff.*

    and ritual worship, 209

    chaos of modern, 210

    emotion in, 57, 58, 208, 209

    enemies of, 200

    of John's disciples, 4, 5

    of scribes and Pharisees, 4, 5

    reality in, 122

    reason in, 57, 208

    will in, 57, 58

Religious Experience, varieties of, 30

Renan, 79

Responsibility, price of endowment, 245

    price of privilege, 105 *ff.*, 215

Reverence, a root of humility, 86

Right and wrong, 35, 36

River of Lethe, 144

Rome, 45, 77, 108, 254

Rule, the golden, xv

Ruler, the Rich Young, 159, 160

Ruskin, 33, 58, 121

Sabbath, 5, 7

Saint Francis, 87, 97

Salvation by love, 98

    a gift and purchase, 32, 33

Samaria, Woman of, 24

Samaritan, the Good, 149 *ff.*, 151

Sanhedrin, 150

Satan, 65, 117

Saul, 193

Savonarola, 244

Scott, Captain, 109

Second Coming, 235, 236

Self-complacency, 106, 107

Selfishness, 141, 192

Self-righteousness, of Elder Brother, 198 *ff.*

    of Pharisee, 88 *ff.*

Self-will, 189, 192

Self-witness of Jesus, 216 *ff.*

Sermon on the Mount, 79

Serveto, Miguel, 62

Shakespeare, xv, 55, 191, 244

Shepherd, the Good, 69, 177 *ff.*

Sheol, 140

Sidon, 41

Simile, xvi

Simon the Pharisee, 83, 93, 223

Sin, Jesus and enigma of, 65 *ff.*

    Jesus and guilt of, 192

    sense of, and forgiveness, 96, 97

    and calamity, 106, 107

Sins, the cardinal, 195

Smith, George Adam, 128

Sodom, 109

Son of God, 216, 217

Son of Man, 254

Son, the Prodigal, 188 *ff.*

Sower, 42 *ff.*

Sower, the (Millet's), 42

Spiritual, the, xxii, 227

Standards, moral, 35

Steward, the Unjust, xxiv, 116 *ff.*

Stevenson, Robert Louis, xvii, 51, 241

Summum Bonum, the Kingdom is the, 29, 34

Symphony, the Fifth, 45

Symphony, the New World, xv, 216

Talents, 240 *ff.*

Teaching, the Rabbinical, xiv

Tennyson, 185
Theology, Parables and, xxv
    religion and, xxvi
Thistle and the Cedar, the, xvi
Thompson, Francis, 51
Thoreau, 109
Tithes, 89
Tower of Babel, 21
Treasure Island, 28
Trench, Archbishop, xxiii, xxiv,
    22, 62
Truth, the levels of, xxv, xxvi,
    xxix
Twain, Mark, 58
Twist, Oliver, 183
Tycho Brahe, xxvi
Tyre, 41

Universe, the pre-Copernican, xxvi
    its vastness as a barrier to
    faith, 181

Van Dyke, Henry, 214
Vergil, 84

War, the callousness of, 143, 144
Watts, George Frederick, 86
Watchfulness, true, 235
Wealth, deceitfulness of, 46, 47
    Jesus and, 127, 137 ff.
Wedding, Christian joy like a, 4, 5
    Jesus' ministry like a, 52
    Kingdom like a, 234
Wernle, xxiv
Whitman, Walt, 132
Wineskins, old and new, 7 ff.
Wisdom of God, 53, 54
Wordsworth, William, 164
World, presence of evil in, 64
    exchanging soul for, 133
    a neighborhood, 20
Worship, and deeds, 209
Wrong, right and, 35

Zaccheus, 259
Zeal, resourceful, 121
Zechariah, 216, 219